Alphabet Avenue

ALPHABET
AVENUE

Wordplay in the Fast Lane

► Dave Morice

CHICAGO
REVIEW
PRESS

Cataloging-in-Publication Data

Morice, Dave, 1946–
Alphabet avenue: wordplay in the fast lane / Dave Morice.
p. cm.
Includes bibliographical references (p.) and index.
ISBN 1-55652-304-1 (pbk.)
I. Word games. I. Title.
GV1507.W8M59 1996
793.73—dc20

96-29106
CIP

©1997 by Dave Morice
Foreword ©1997 by Richard Lederer
First edition
Published by Chicago Review Press, Incorporated
814 North Franklin Street
Chicago, Illinois 60610

ISBN 1-55652-304-1
Printed in the United States of America
5 4 3 2 1

To André Pujon

In seventeenth-century France, according to legend, André Pujon anagrammed his name into "Pendu à Rion" ("Hanged at Rion"). He had to substitute I for J to do this. To make the fateful anagram come true, he killed a man in Rion in order to be hanged for the crime in that city. And he was.

Greater love for wordplay no one hath.

ACKNOWLEDGMENTS

I WOULD LIKE TO thank all the writers whose material appears in one form or another in this book. In most cases, their names accompany their work.

I am grateful to several authors, including Ross Eckler, Willard Espy, Martin Gardner, Richard Lederer, O. V. Michaelsen, and Peter Newby, for allowing me to excerpt from their books, which are listed in the bibliography. Michaelsen's book is currently at press.

Other material in *Alphabet Avenue* originally appeared in the following magazines, newspapers, and books: *Word Ways, Alphabet Anthology, The Final E, Forwords, Games, Iowa City Magazine, The Iowa City Press-Citizen, Jnd-Song of the Golden Gradrti, Matchbook*, and *WordsWorth*.

Many of the palindromes and anagrams were first published in *The Enigma* and *The Eastern Enigma*, official publications of the National Puzzlers' League. For more information on the organization, write to The National Puzzlers' League, c/o Judith Bagai, Box 82289, Portland, OR 97282.

The name "Chuck Roast" in Chapter D comes from Tim Hildebrand's book *Rotwang*. The illustrations for the Alphabet Cube in Chapter K are by Milagros Quijada. Thanks to Joyce Holland for the typographical art that opens each chapter.

Special thanks to Richard Carlin, Ross and Faith Eckler, Richard and Simone Lederer, and Michele Soll, for reading the manuscript and suggesting ways to improve it. And to my son Danny for reviewing and critiquing the illustrations.

And much gratitude to Linda Matthews, my editor, for everything she has done to help make this book a reality.

Contents

```
                                            . . . . . . . . . . . . . . . . . . . . . .
              . . . . . . . . . . .          . . . . . . . . . . . . . . . . . . . . . . . .
           . . . . . . . . . . . . . . .        . . . . . . . . . . . . . . . . . .
         . . . . . . . . . . . . . . . . . . I  T . . . . . . .      . . . . . . .  A . . . . . . . . .
       . . . . . . . . . . E . . . . . . . I  T . . . . . . . . .      O  R  . . . .  A . . . . . . .
     . . . . . . . . . E . . . .      I  T . . . . . . . . . .      O  R        A        . . . . . . .
     . . . . . . E . . . .      I  T . . . . . . . . .      O  R        L  A  Y      . . .
     . . . . .      H  E        I  T                      O  R        L  A  Y
     . .            H  E        I  T              O          W  O  R  D  P  L  A  Y
                    H  E        C  I  T  Y        O          W  O  R  D  P  L  A  Y
              T  H  E        C  I  T  Y        O          W  O  R  D  P  L  A  Y
              T  H  E        C  I  T  Y        O  F        W  O  R  D  P  L  A  Y
              T  H  E        C  I  T  Y        O  F        W  O  R  D  P  L  A  Y
              T  H  E        C  I  T  Y        O  F        W  O  R  D  P  L  A  Y
     A  B  C  D  E    F  G  H  I  J  K    L  M  N  O    P  Q  R  S  T  U  V  W  X  Y  Z
     A  B  C  D  E    F  G  H  I  J  K    L  M  N  O    P  Q  R  S  T  U  V  W  X  Y  Z
     A  B  C  D  E    F  G  H  I  J  K    L  M  N  O    P  Q  R  S  T  U  V  W  X  Y  Z
     A  B  C  D  E    F  G  H  I  J  K    L  M  N  O    P  Q  R  S  T  U  V  W  X  Y  Z
     A  B  C  D  E    F  G  H  I  J  K    L  M  N  O    P  Q  R  S  T  U  V  W  X  Y  Z
     A  B  C  D  E    F  G  H  I  J  K    L  M  N  O    P  Q  R  S  T  U  V  W  X  Y  Z
     A  B  C  D  E    F  G  H  I  J  K    L  M  N  O    P  Q  R  S  T  U  V  W  X  Y  Z
     ----------------------------------------------------------------------------------
     A     L     P     H     A     B     E     T          A     V     E     N     U     E
     ----------------------------------------------------------------------------------
```

4word

• • • • • • • • •

*B*URNING BRIGHT IN the forests of the night, William Blake was a painter, engraver, spiritual savant, and prophet of the age of romantic poetry. His vivid illuminations of "The Tyger" and other of his poems made him the first multimedia audio-visionary in the history of English literature.

Blake was struck with what is known as eidetic sight, a quality that allowed him to see visions as well as imagine them. When he was but a child, he claimed that God poked His head through his nursery window. Years later, Blake spoke face to face with the prophet Ezekiel in a tree, and his wife and he sat nude in their garden reciting passages from *Paradise Lost* as if they were in the Garden of Eden.

Now comes another wordstruck seer, Dave Morice. I wouldn't be a rich letterer if I didn't tell you that you are about to meet an acronimble, alphabetter, alliterary, paranomazing pun-gent, anagrammarian, palindromedary, onomasticator, onomatopoet, Peter Pangram, Uncle Rebus, Charader of the Lost Art. Never a palindroning one-dimensional Word Square, Dave is an aesthetic—never anesthetic—wordwizard who invests the universe of puzzledom with a Newtonian elegance and dazzle.

I don't want to write a word-for-word forward foreword, but I know about Dave's art-is-try firsthand. He's the illustrious illustrator and luminous illuminator of my book of good, clean dirty fun, *Nothing Risqué, Nothing Gained*, in which he converted my punographic humor into punograffiti of the highest ardor and odor. Thus, I have come to know this man as a left-brain/right-brain genus of genie genius, afflicted, not conflicted, with a profusion, not a confusion, of eye-detic-sight.

The medieval Jewish kabbalists based their interpretation of scripture on anagrams, acronyms, acrostics, and puns. I hope you'll read *Alphabet Avenue* religiously—with genuine flexion. Even if you're not a religious fan-addict, you may be fasten-ated by the mysterious ways that swirling letters configure themselves into epiphanous significance.

Take the anagremlins that cavort through our words. Is it not significant that an anagram of bedroom is boredom and the semordnilap of eros is sore? Isn't it a bit qwerty that one of the ten-letter words that can be typed on just the top letter row of a standard keyboard is—ta da!—typewriter? Is it just a coincidence that in March of the palindromic year 1991 a palindromic seventeen-year-old—Monica Seles—first achieved her number-one world tennis rating? Doesn't it prove that William Shakespeare must have written Shakespeare when we find four meaningful anagrams for his name?

I swear he's like a lamp.

We all make his praise.

Has Will a peer?, I ask me.

Ah, I speak a swell rime.

Prepare to exercise (not exorcize) verbal muscles you didn't know you owned. We're talking here about push-ups for the mind, Stairmaster for the brain, jumping jacks for the cerebrum, aerobics for the intellect.

Sharpen your pun cells. Call Dave Morice on the homophone. Recite his para-doxology. Climb his poet-tree. Gag him with a spoonerism. Analyze his vowel movements. Interpret his rhopalic cymbals. Read his lipograms.

Hurry! Hurry! Hurry! Step right up to a Lingo Brothers' twenty-six-ring-circus of words—words clowning, words teetering on tightropes, words swinging from tent-tops, words shot from canons, words thrusting their heads into the mouths of literary lions.

All the fun is guaranteed to be in tents.

Richard Lederer
Concord, New Hampshire

Chapter A

Introduction Path

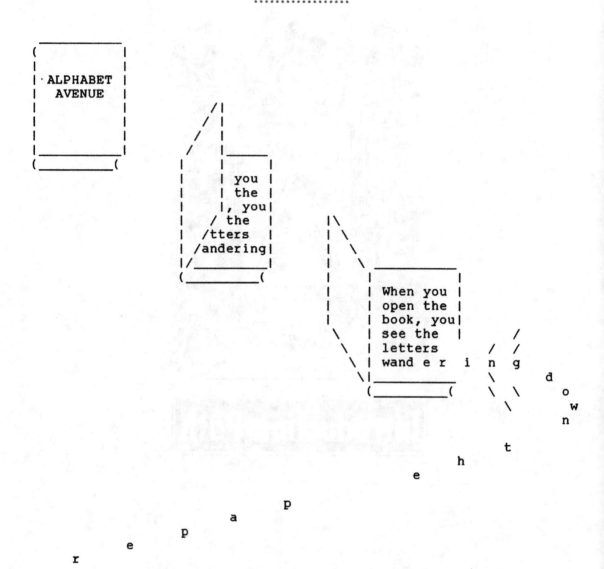

and marching across the page in the roads, streets, highways, and byways we call sentences. Let's follow the letters along Introduction Path, through the intersection of Sound and Sense, to Alphabet Avenue, the main street in the City of Wordplay.

THE UNIVERSAL LETTER

At the entrance to the city, there's a billboard with the Universal Letter on it. That symbol contains all twenty-six letters of the alphabet, all the words in this book, all the knowledge in the world. Can you find the letters? You have to turn the symbol sideways to locate some of them.

ALPHABET AVENUE

Alphabet Avenue intersects twenty-six other streets that are built on wordplay. Each chapter in this book is one of those streets, but the zoning is more complex than you might imagine. Since wordplay is such a multifaceted field, the chapters present it in different ways.

A chapter might focus on wordplay form (Chapter D, Pun Freeway), literary form (Chapter M, Story Row), specific content (Chapter L, Numeric Overpass), or something else. Each chapter is made of smaller sections, but sometimes the same section could fit into different chapters. For instance, anagrams of famous people's names could fit into Chapter B for anagrams or Chapter O for names.

Puzzles, riddles, and quizzes appear in Puzzle Bluff (Chapter T), but they pop up every now and then in other chapters. If you get stumped, you can turn to Answer Alley (Chapter Y) at the end of the book.

For various reasons, some chapters are longer than others. This may reflect the complexity of the topic, the availability of material, or the proverbial twist of fate.

THE CITY OF WORDPLAY

In the City of Wordplay, we'll find anagrams, palindromes, puns, and many other forms. Some have been around for centuries, but others are recent developments familiar only to veteran word players. On the next page is a map showing the streets we'll visit.

In the twentieth century, the city has grown from a one-horse town to a towering verbopolis. It's governed by laws that combine language, logic, mathematics, humor, and who-knows-what. Here language doesn't always look like language. To paraphrase Dorothy from *The Wizard of Oz,* "Toto, I don't think we're in English anymore."

But we are.

LOGOLOGY

In 1965, Dmitri Borgmann resurrected an old word, "logology," in his groundbreaking book, *Language on Vacation,* and gave it a new meaning: Logology is the study of words—not from a linguistic point of view, but from a wordplay point of view—and a logologist does just that.

Borgmann ushered in the modern era of wordplay. His book presented many forms, from time-honored anagrams and palindromes to space-age transposals and reversals. He wanted to broaden the audience for "word beauty," as he called it, and his book helped spark a wordplay renaissance.

WORD WAYS

Logology wouldn't have thrived, however, if it weren't for another individual, Ross Eckler. Since 1970, Eckler has edited *Word Ways: The Journal of Recreational Linguistics* (Spring Valley Road, Morristown, NJ 07960). He and his wife, Faith, have published and distributed the sixty-four-page magazine on a quarterly basis for more than twenty-five years. *Word Ways* has presented over two thousand articles, poems, stories, puzzles, and other works by dozens of authors. Most new wordplay concepts make their debut in the magazine.

THE CITY OF WORDPLAY

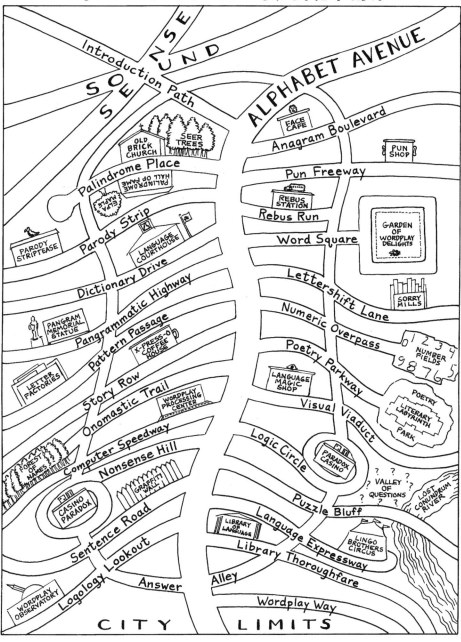

A prolific author with an encyclopedic knowledge of the field, Eckler synthesized many of the wordplay discoveries of the past twenty-five years in his latest book, *Making the Alphabet Dance*. In it, he defines "letterplay"—manipulating the letters of the alphabet—and shows the intricate twists and turns that letters make in forming the words of our language.

KICKSHAWS

Most of the material in *Alphabet Avenue* originally appeared in one form or another in *Word Ways*. Some of the wordplay came from articles and poems appearing in the mag, but more than half of the sections came from Kickshaws, a regular feature.

The Kickshaws column, a dozen or so pages long, presents a wide variety of material in twenty to thirty short sections. It includes work by the Kickshaws editor and by others. The word "kickshaw" has two main meanings: "a fancy dish, delicacy" and "bauble, gewgaw."

In 1988, I had the good fortune to become the Kickshaws editor. This has given me the opportunity to look at a wide variety of wordplay and to correspond with many talented and inventive authors. Over the past few years, the short sections added up to a long collection.

Alphabet Avenue is primarily an outgrowth of Kickshaws. In a sense, it's a "Superkickshaws."

ONE BOOK, MANY AUTHORS

Most wordplay books include work by the author and by many other writers. In *Alphabet Avenue*, I've tried to identify all other people whose works appear and to indicate anonymous works. Otherwise, the work is my own.

Logology Lookout (Chapter W) includes wordplay statements by many of the writers in this book and by other writers. All of them have written for *Word Ways*.

Library Thoroughfare (Chapter X) presents a two-part bibliography. The first part is an annotated listing of recommended works, including books and magazines mentioned in the text. The second part lists dictionaries and other sources cited in the text.

The short titles for the most frequently cited dictionaries are *Pocket Webster's*, *Webster's Tenth Collegiate*, *Webster's Second Unabridged*, *Webster's Third Unabridged*, and *Oxford English Dictionary*. Their full titles appear in Chapter X.

OTHER WORDPLAY

Alphabet Avenue contains a wide range of wordplay, from traditional to new forms. Many other intriguing forms could have been included—subtransposals, word girders, ana-gram-mar chains, and trifixes, to name a few—but there wasn't enough space.

Thirty years ago, a wordplay book could cover the field fairly well. Now such a goal is impossible. It would take at least a dozen or more volumes to do a comprehensive job.

PURPOSES OF THE BOOK

Alphabet Avenue is meant to enchant, encipher, encircle, enclose, encode, encompass, encounter, encourage, endear, enfold, engross, engulf, enhance, enlarge, enlighten, enliven, enrapture, enrich, ensnare, entangle, enthrall, entice, entrance, entwist, envelop, and, of course, entertain.

You'll run across mistakes, too. In fact, almost all the verbs in the previous paragraph are used incorrectly. Which are wrong, and why? Can you add just one word in the right place to correct all the mistakes? (Answer Alley)

START AT THE STOP SIGN

It's time to see the sights. We'll turn onto each road of wordplay and then return to Alphabet Avenue to go to the next road. The stop sign at the intersection says START. On the other side of it, the journey begins.

Chapter

Anagram Boulevard

THE FACE CAFE

LETTERS ARE THE bricks that build words. On Anagram Boulevard, the bricks can be removed and put back in a different order to form new words. You can take the bricks that spell ANAGRAMS, shuffle them around, and put them back to spell ARS MAGNA, the Latin phrase for "Great Art." An anagram is a word, phrase, or sentence formed by rearranging the letters of another word, phrase, or sentence.

At the Face Cafe, where people feed their faces, the heady odor of piping hot alphabet soup tempts the passersby. SOUP: O, SUP! the neon sign flashes anagrammatically above the door.

Customers enter through the Anagram Door. On the outside, the door has large ceramic letter tiles set in two rectangles around it. The outer tiles spell FACE over and over clockwise, but they anagram to spell CAFE counterclockwise. The inner rectangle spells CAFE clockwise but anagrams to FACE counterclockwise. In the middle of the door, the word EAT invites customers to enter.

On the inside, the design on the door works the same way, except that CAFE goes around the outer rectangle and FACE around the inner. The word ATE bids satisfied customers farewell.

```
F A C E F A C E F A C E        C A F E C A F E C A F E
E C A F E C A F E C A F        E F A C E F A C E F A C
C E                 F A        F E                 C A
A F       E A T     E C        A C       A T E     E F
F A                 C E        C A                 F E
E C                 A F        E F                 A C
C E              _  F A        F E              _  C A
A F             | |  E C       A C             | |  E F
F A             |o|  C E       C A             |o|  F E
E C             |_|  A F       E F             |_|  A C
C E                 F A        F E                 C A
A F                 E C        A C                 E F
F A                 C E        C A                 F E
E C                 A F        E F                 A C
C E                 F A        F E                 C A
A F                 E C        A C                 E F
F A                 C E        C A                 F E
E C                 A F        E F                 A C
C E F A C E F A C E F A        F E C A F E C A F E C A
A F E C A F E C A F E C        A C E F A C E F A C E F
```

Noam and Mona run the place. They serve alphabet soup specially prepared with letters in it spelling a famous quotation. If the customer can figure out the quote while eating it, the soup's on the house.

The walls are covered with small canvases on which Noam and Mona have painted anagrams. Their cafe is also a museum, the Anagram Museum, where all the classics are exhibited. Let's look at some of the anagams that prove that MASTERPIECES = ART SEEMS EPIC.

IN THE ANAGRAM MUSEUM

Anagrams relate in meaning to the original words from which they're made. A DORMITORY is often a DIRTY ROOM, and GOLD AND SILVER are certainly GRAND OLD EVILS. Antigrams, however, are anagrams that contrast in meaning to the originals. DORMITORIES aren't usually TIDIER ROOMS, and LEMONADE isn't DEMON ALE.

Both anagrams and antigrams hang on the walls of the Anagram Museum. Most of them were first published in *The Enigma* or *The Eastern Enigma*, official publications of the National Puzzlers' League (NPL), and reprinted in *The New Anagrammasia*, compiled by Ross Eckler. The authors' NPL pseudonyms appear in quotation marks.

ANAGRAMS

THE ACTIVE VOLCANOS	Cones evict hot lava. ("Viking")
ANAGRAMS	ars magna ("D.C. Ver")
A BARTENDER	beer and art ("Arcanus")
A DECIMAL POINT	I'm a dot in place. ("A. Chem")
DESPERATION	A rope ends it. ("Air Raid")
A DIVORCE SUIT	I advise court. ("Amaranth")
DORMITORY	dirty room ("T.H.")
DRIVEWAY	yard view ("Osaple")
EDGE TOOLS	good steel ("Enavlicm")
EXECUTION	Exit on cue. (Stephen Marlowe)
GALAHAD	had a gal ("Hoho")
GOLD AND SILVER	grand old evils ("Johank")
GREYHOUND	Hey, dog, run! ("King Carnival")
HMS PINAFORE	name for ship ("Mangie")
LIMERICKS	slick rime ("Hexagony")
MOONLIGHT	thin gloom ("Jason")
THE NUDIST COLONY	no untidy clothes ("Ellsworth")
OLD MASTERS	art's models ("Traddles")
PITTANCE	a cent tip ("The Duke")
PROSPERITY	is property ("Arty Fishel")
SCHOOLMASTER	the classroom ("Molemi")
TELEVISION NEWS	It's now seen live. ("Tut")
UNADORNED	and/or nude ("Sakr El Bahr")
WOMAN SCORNED	Now man scored. ("That Gal Nell")
X-RATED MOVIES	video sex mart ("Nightowl")
YODELLING	dog yellin' ("Castet")

ANTIGRAMS

ANHEUSER BUSCH	Shun such a beer! ("Corn Cob")
ANTAGONIST	not against ("Arcanus")
CUSTOMERS	store scum ("Neophyte")
A DIET	I'd eat. ("Larry")
DEANSHIP	pinheads (Anon.)
DIPLOMACY	mad policy ("Jemand")
DORMITORIES	tidier rooms ("Sally")
DYNAMITE	dainty me ("Tut")
EARLIEST	Rise late. ("Enavlicm")
EPITAPHS	happiest ("Hap")
FILLED	ill-fed ("Enavlicm")
FORGET-ME-NOT	forgotten me ("Minuta")
FORTY-FIVE	over fifty ("Philana")
FUNERAL	real fun (Anon.)
GIANT	gnat, I ("Larry")
HONESTLY	on the sly (Anon.)
INFERNO	nonfire ("Osaple")
LEMONADE	demon ale ("Plantina")
MAIDENLY	Men? Daily. ("Ulk")
MEDICATE	decimate (Anon.)
MILITARISM	I limit arms. ("Barnyard")
NOMINATED	not named ("Midurndist")
PERSECUTED	due respect (Anon.)
THE SHIP TITANIC	hasn't hit ice tip ("Señor")
THE WINTER GALES	sweltering heat ("A. Chem")
WITHIN EARSHOT	I won't hear this. ("Hoodwink")

ANAGRAMS AND TRANSPOSALS

Anagrams belong to a broader category of words known to logologists as transposals (or transpositions). Transposals are simply rearrangements of letters. When a transposal relates in meaning to the original word, it qualifies as an anagram, too. All anagrams are transposals, but not all transposals are anagrams.

Ironically, "anagram" is the term that most people apply to a rearrangement of letters whether the result is related to the original or not. To avoid confusion, "anagram" is used throughout most of this book to mean either anagram or transposal.

ANAGRAM TEST

To test how difficult it really is to make an anagram of a random word, I selected twenty-six words, one for each letter of the alphabet, from *Webster's Seventh Collegiate*. I turned to a page, put my finger on it, and picked the first word from six to twelve letters long that I touched. Then I shuffled Scrabble tiles for a minute or so to see what would turn up. Here are the results:

ALCHEMY	clay hem
BARBARISM	AM: bar, ribs
CAPITOL	Tail cop.
DEVASTATION	O, sad event, it.
EDUCATION	I counted "A."
FISHERMAN	He rams fin.
GERUND	rug end
HABITUAL	a halibut
IMPRUDENCE	mere cup din
JASMINE	jam sine
KIMONO	OK, I'm on.
LAMBKIN	lab mink
MALCONTENT	molten cant
NOGGIN	in gong
OXIDIZE	Oz, Dixie
PERMAFROST	former past
QUARRY	RR quay
RANDOM	nor mad
SHRAPNEL	her plans
TRAVELER	art revel
UNDERFOOT	tour of den
VOLATILE	a vile lot
WEDDING	Wend, dig?
XYLOPHONE	Holy ox pen!
YARDBIRD	dry braid
ZODIAC	I, Oz cad

Two of them are close matches to two anagrams in *The New Anagrammasia*: KIMONO = I'm on OK (Fred Domino) and VOLATILE = a live lot ("Awl Wrong"). Among the others, which would you consider to be meaningful anagrams or antigrams?

Mike Morton used a computer program he's written to anagram the same set of words. He came up with several alternatives, including the next bunch. Some of them make funny phrases, and a few make sense, too.

BARBARISM	Mars rabbi
CAPITOL	oil pact
DEVASTATION	Invade toast.
EDUCATION	a coed unit
IMPRUDENCE	prime dunce
LAMBKIN	I'm blank.
MALCONTENT	no calm tent
PERMAFROST	pot farmers
UNDERFOOT	to founder
XYLOPHONE	Help yon ox.

DYSLEXICS HAVE MORE FUN

People with dyslexia have trouble reading words from left to right. Instead, MUG might be interpreted as GUM, EMIT as TIME. DYSLEXIA itself doesn't make a word or phrase in reverse, but anagramming it is another matter.

On his way to give a talk at a convention on speech disorders, Richard Lederer discovered that DYSLEXIA anagrams to DAILY SEX. Is that the cause or the cure?

SCRABBLE SENTENCE

Scrabble tiles are ideal tools for making anagrams. Usually the anagrammatist slides a small number of tiles around to make words, but Peter Stickland shuffled the whole set of letter tiles to form 120 sentences. Here's one that sounds like a quote from Shakespeare's play *Julius Caesar*:

COUNTRYMEN, I AM TO BURY, NOT EULOGIZE, CAESAR;
IF EVIL LIVES ON, BEQUEATHING INJURY, GOOD OFT EXPIRES:
A PALSIED, AWKWARD DEATH!

FROM LONG WORD TO FULL SENTENCE

In general, longer words have more potential for full-sentence anagrams than shorter words do. ANTIDISESTABLISHMENTARIANISM anagrams into a line that could've been uttered by Pablo Picasso.

I AM AN ARTIST, AND I BLESS THIS IN ME.

It can also form plenty of other sentences, such as these two very different responses to the Picasso line.

HIS ART IS IN, MAN. A MIND BLAST! SEE IT?
I'M A SENSIBLE MAN, AND I HIT ARTISTS.

IN THE NAME OF ANAGRAMS

Ross Eckler searched through more than one hundred U.S. telephone directories to find the following group of anagram names—that is, the first names rearranged to form the last names. The number of people with the same name appears in parentheses.

GARY GRAY (163)   LEON NOEL (5)
RONALD ARNOLD (47)   ALBERT BARTEL (4)
EDNA DEAN (10)   NEAL LANE (4)
ROLAND ARNOLD (9)   NORMA MORAN (3)
ERIC RICE (9)   DALE DEAL (2)
ARNOLD ROLAND (9)   ERICH REICH (2)

PRESIDENTIAL ANAGRAMS

The names of the American presidents can be anagrammed into phrases, but few truly excellent ones have been composed. Sometimes the phrases are particularly apt; other times they have little relationship to the president. In this selection, each anagram (or antigram) relates to its presidential subject, but exactly how is left for you to decide.

WILLIAM HOWARD TAFT   A word with all—I'm fat. ("Sphinx")
GROVER CLEVELAND   dang clever lover (David Williams)
CHESTER ARTHUR   truth searcher ("Camillus")
JAMES A. GARFIELD   Lead far, sage Jim! (James Rambo)
ULYSSES SIMPSON GRANT   surpassingness my lot ("Bolis")
ABRAHAM LINCOLN   Oh, call man brain! (David Williams)

MONROE	no more (Brian Sylvester)
HARRY S. TRUMAN	rash army runt (Mary Hazard)
CALVIN COOLIDGE	Love? a cold icing. (David Williams)
THEODORE ROOSEVELT	loved horse; tree, too (Mary Hazard)
FRANKLIN DELANO ROOSEVELT	Tons o' drink, even ale, for all! (Wyndham Lewis)
RONALD W. REAGAN	a wan old ranger (Richard Lederer)
GEORGE WASHINGTON	Great Whig's gone on. (James Rambo)

Depending on the form of the name, different anagrams turn up. These examples reveal contrasting sides of two presidents and one presidential hopeful-turned-gadfly:

HERBERT HOOVER	overt hero, Herb
HERBERT CLARK HOOVER	the ever black horror (David Williams)
WILLIAM CLINTON	I'll not claim win.
WILLIAM JEFFERSON CLINTON	Jilts nice women. In for fall. (Richard Lederer)
ROSS PEROT	sore sport (Richard Lederer)
H. ROSS PEROT	short poser (Richard Lederer)
INDEPENDENT H. ROSS PEROT	Oh, spender—not president!

Presidential wives have been anagrammed less often than their spouses. To counter this wordplay sexism, Marjorie Friedman has composed a few:

ELEANOR ROOSEVELT	role: to serve alone
MAMIE DOWD EISENHOWER	We deem war mood; he is in.
JACQUELINE KENNEDY ONASSIS	is as queenly on deck in jeans

One president has had hundreds of thousands of anagrams made of his name—more anagrams than any other human in history! Turn to Chapter Q for the details.

POLITICAL ANAGRAMARAMA

Politicians often rearrange their words and phrases to suit the occasion. Instead of listening to the politicians, let the issues speak for themselves—anagrammatically.

AMERICAN DREAM	damn crime area
BALANCING THE BUDGETS	Beg, cheat big, stun land.
BREAST IMPLANTS	Permit? Bans last.
COLD WAR OVER	Cover a world.
EQUAL RIGHTS AMENDMENT	mad men requesting halt

THE GULF WAR	We hurt flag.
GUN CONTROL LAWS	Guns crown a toll.
HOMELESS PEOPLE	Some see hell, Pop.
OLLIE NORTH'S DEALS	Tall hero nods, lies.
PANAMA'S NORIEGA	A man? Iron age sap!
POLITICIAN	I . . . I . . . I can plot!
SADDAM HUSSEIN OF IRAQ	Man of raid is squashed.
SOVIET UNION	O, no! Invite U.S.
STEALTH BOMBER	Let's bomb Earth.
SUPREME COURT	Corrupt? Sue 'em!
TELEVISION	TV is one lie.
UNEMPLOYMENT RATE	Plenty are out, amen!
THE U.S. PRESIDENTIAL RACES	Pride these nutcase liars?
WAR ON DRUGS	or draw guns
MILITIA	'til I aim
HATE GROUPS	shot up rage

CELEBRITY ANAGRAM QUIZ

In the following quiz, designed by Mike Reiss, nine common words can be anagrammed into the names of living celebrities. The last two are by Alan Levine. The numbers give the lengths of first and last names. Can you unscramble them? (Answer Alley)

1. HOCKED (2, 4)	6. ASCERTAINS (5, 5)
2. GALORE (2, 4)	7. ENDEARS (2, 5)
3. GERMANY (3, 4)	8. WATERFALLS (4, 6)
4. GENERAL (2, 5)	9. NARCOLEPTIC (4, 7)
5. COSTUMIER (3, 6)	

ANAGRAM VANITY PLATES

Car names are especially suitable for anagramming. Here's a list of fifty anagrams customized for use on vanity license plates. Is your horseless carriage listed below?

The list doesn't include names that anagram to the names of other cars, like ELECTRA = A TERCEL or PREVIA = A VIPER. It doesn't have any names that anagram to foreign words, either, like METRO = MORTE (French for "dead").

A single anagram follows each car name, although in most cases other anagrams can be made. SILVERADO generates a dramatic pair of opposites: EVIL ROADS and LORD, I SAVE. The letters in VILLAGER switch around to two questions that might be overheard in a greasy-spoon restaurant— LIVER, GAL? or VEAL, GIRL? Here it's truly a matter of taste.

A few might not seem to make sense, but compare them to the vanity plates out there on the road now. They don't always make sense, either—except to the drivers.

ACHIEVA = AHA! VICE!
ASTON MARTON = IT'S NO ART, MAN
CAMRY = MY CAR
CELEBRITY = CITY REBEL
CENTAURUS = U.S. CAR TUNE
CHEVROLET = HOT, CLEVER
CIERA = I RACE
CONTINENTAL = NEON CAT LINT
CORDOBA = CAB DOOR
COUPE DE VILLE = EVIL CLOUD PEE
CRESSIDA = SIDECARS
CUTLASS = LUST SAC
DATSUN = SAD NUT
DIABLO = BAD OIL
DIAMANTE = I AM A DENT
DIPLOMAT = MAD PILOT
DURANGO = ROAD GUN
DUSTER = RUSTED
ELANTRA = A RENTAL
FAIRLANE = FEAR IN L.A.
FAIRMONT = I'M NO FART
GALANT = TAN GAL
GRAND PRIX = BRAND X PIG
GREMLIN = GIRL, MEN
HUSTLER = HER LUST
INTEGRA = INGRATE
INTREPID = I RIP, DENT
LAMBORGHINI = BLAH! I'M NO RIG
LE SABRE = A REBEL'S

MASERATI = I, A MASTER
MONARCH = NO CHARM
MONTE CARLO = CLEAN MOTOR
NEWPORT = WET PORN
OLDSMOBILE = O, BOLD MILES!
PIONEER = I, NO PEER
PRIZM = MR. ZIP
RENAULT = REAL NUT
RENEGADE = GEE, A NERD
RIO GRANDE = DANGER OR I
ROLLS-ROYCE = O SELL OR CRY
ROMANO = A MORON
SPIRIT = I STRIP
SPITFIRE = FIRST PIE
ST. REGIS = TIGRESS
THUNDERBIRD = HE'D BURN DIRT
TORONADO = O, NOT A ROD
TOYOTA = AY, TOOT!
TRACKER = CAR TREK
TRANS AM = STARMAN
VOLKSWAGEN = SWANK GLOVE

WHY DID THE CHICKEN CROSS THE ROAD?

Susan Thorpe came up with a new answer to this old riddle. The first sentence is an anagram of the second.

THE CHICKEN CROSSES THE ROAD =
  SHE CHECKS CORN AT OTHER SIDE!

SONG OF THE MISSING LINK

This poem is a comic book view of evolution, starring SLIME THING, a creature similar to DC Comics' SWAMP THING, but missing a few links. Each line is an anagram of THE MISSING LINK.

Think! Sing, Slime!
Slime's thinking.

Sink, Slime Thing,
Set him slinking.

Night's ink! Slime
Lets him, sinking

Slime Thing's kin.
Helm is stinking.

Sing! Think slime!
Slime's thinking.

DOROTHY WAS ONCE IN THE EMERALD CITY OF OZ

Before composing the following poem, I loaded the first line with letters that spell the names of various characters from *The Wizard of Oz*. All the lines are anagrams of each other.

Dorothy was once in the Emerald City of Oz.
She tried the way to Oz, forced in many cool
Woods nicely on the road for the city maze.
The icy dew froze Tinman. "Choose a dry tool,"

He said more wretchedly. "Oof! Tin not a cozy
Coat now. My foot dozes, Child, er, in the year."
"Try oilcan of Oz," Dorothy said. "Hence we met."
The Witch: "No freedom do I slay, no cozy tear.

"Come on, stay! For they lionized the coward."
Yonder the crazy Witch made Lion's foe, too,
Doom his tail. Chore: New toy or zany defect?
A mean old Witch cried to Oz, "Try on fey shoe."

Wizard said to her, "Come! Only fetch yon toe!
If Lion cared, who do they center at my zoos?"
Then hot, moody Scarecrow failed yet in Oz.
They fed Scarecrow hay. "No, don't limit ooze."

Scarecrow moaned, "They fly into Oz to hide.
Raze homey castle door." Din of witchy tone!
O, holy Tinman recorded size of way to etch
Secret of Wizard: "Hi-ho! Today note my clone."

Dorothy wanted more in life: "O, yes, Oz. Catch
My Toto!" She realized why no force can do it.
"O, Em is not here!" Dazed with act of loony cry,
Dorothy had zest. "Crone! Felon! Me? I, a coy wit."

O, Scarecrow! O, Tinman! O, Oz! They hid, yet fled.
O, moon! Fate! Cry only zero. The Witch is dead!

DREAMING OF ANAGRAMS

This pair of anagram-laden sentences, written by Lee Sallows, shows how several anagrams that relate to each other can work together for extra effect. The lines talk about the curse of the waking class—snoring.

THE EYES, they see; THIS EAR, it hears; YOUR NOSE, you snore!

THIS EYE, THE EARS, YOUR NOSE: You see, they hear it snores.

OPTS!

At the end of Anagram Boulevard, the sign is an anagram of the letters OPST. For each day of the week, the street crew puts up a different sign. From Sunday to Saturday, the words are TOPS, OPTS, POST, POTS, SOPT, SPOT, and STOP.

TOPS tops the week, and STOP stops it. Since today is Monday, the crew opts for OPTS.

Palindrome Place

THE ELPA MAPLE

T HE NORMAL ENGLISH sentence is a one-way street leading to a dead end. Not so on Palindrome Place. When you reach the end, you can turn around and go back again. It's like riding a RACE CAR, which has the same letters going in both directions. A palindrome is a word, phrase, or sentence that spells the same in reverse.

Halfway down the street, an old brick church stands loftily among the Seer Trees. The large stained-glass windows in the front have messages on them. On the left window, the letters say, somewhat ominously:

EVIL DID I DWEL & LEWD I DID LIVE.

That's the first known palindrome in the English language. John Taylor, aka "The Water Poet" (1580–1653), composed it. DWEL might seem like a misspelling, but it was an acceptable variant for DWELL back then.

However, the use of the ampersand in the middle has caused a rift in palindromic circles that has never been resolved. Some people think the symbol is a cop-out, while others say it's a stroke of genius. & you can judge for yourself.

The other stained-glass window has a shorter palindrome, an anonymous line quoting Adam introducing himself to Eve:

MADAM, I'M ADAM.

Halfway up the street, an old stone meetinghouse stands beneath the stately Elpa Maple, the tallest of the Seer Trees. The maple was named in honor of the place mentioned in this anonymous palindrome attributed to Napoleon (who couldn't speak English):

ABLE WAS I ERE I SAW ELBA.

A stone staircase leads to the door of the meetinghouse. The steps are lined with symmetrical ceramic pots, protected by a fearsome chihuahua named Spot, who sleeps in one of the pots on the top step. Each step has a warning sign on it, and each line is a palindrome.

PET STEP!
PUP UP?

STEP ON NO PETS:
STOP ON NO POTS.

STEP ON POTS, STOP NO PETS:
PETS STOP ON NO POT'S STEP.

RISE TO NEW PET STEP. WE NOTE, SIR:
SPOT'S A GOD DAMN MAD DOG! AS TOPS!

Quietly we sneak up the stairway, tiptoe past Spot, and go in the door. The meetinghouse is home to the Palindrome Hall of Fame. All the modern classics appear here. They're etched in silver plaques sitting in glass display cases throughout the building.

IN THE PALINDROME HALL OF FAME

The selection below shows a few of the best palindromes in the English language, followed by the author's name when it is known. J. A. Lindon and Leigh Mercer, two of the greatest palindromists of the twentieth century, probably wrote the anonymous works.

A dog! A panic in a pagoda! (Anon.)

A new order began, a more Roman age bred Rowena. (Dmitri Borgmann)

A slut nixes sex in Tulsa. (Anon.)

Are we not drawn onward, we few, drawn onward to new era? (Leigh Mercer)

Dennis and Edna sinned. (J. A. Lindon)

Doc, note, I dissent. A fast never prevents a fatness. I diet on cod. (Anon.)

Draw, O Caesar, erase a coward! (Mercer)

Egad, a base life defiles a bad age. (Mercer)

Goddesses so pay a possessed dog. (Mercer)

Harass sensuousness, Sarah. (Mercer)

I maim nine more hero-men in Miami. (Anon.)

"Miry rim! So many daffodils," Delia wailed, "slid off a dynamo's miry rim!" (Lindon)

Ned, go gag Ogden. (Anon.)

Niagara, O roar again! (Mercer)

No lemons, no melon. (E. J. McIlvane)

Nurse, I spy gypsies, run! (Mercer)

Pa's a sap. (Anon.)

Rats live on no evil star. (Anon.)

Red rum, sir, is murder. (Lindon)

Rise to vote, Sir. (Anon.)

Sit on a potato pan, Otis. (Borgmann)

Step on no pets. (G. R. Clarke)

Straw? No, too stupid a fad. I put soot on warts. (Mercer)

Sums are not set as a test on Erasmus. (Mercer)

Was it a rat I saw? (Anon.)

Yawn a more Roman way. (Mercer)

SURREAL LIFE

Palindromes don't have to make complete sense to wind up in the Hall of Fame. Some palindromes work by doing just the opposite: they create bizarre wordscapes as alien to everyday sentences as Salvador Dali's paintings are to Norman Rockwell's.

In this selection, Lindon wrote the first three and Mercer probably wrote the second three:

He wondered: Is no colossal eel as solo considered now, eh?

Won pots! Spa tympanists, I nap, my taps stop now!

Pun: I pay a pixy no onyx, I pay a pinup!

Stephen, my hat—ah, what a hymn, eh, pets?

"Slang is not suet, is it?" Euston signals.

Tide-net safe soon, Alin. A manila noose fastened it.

PALINDROME TEST

In Chapter B, I picked twenty-six words at random and anagrammed them into other words. In this chapter, I tried to recycle the same words into palindromic lines, but only half of them worked. Does this mean that anagrams are twice as easy to make? Or that palindromes are twice as difficult?

As might be expected, many of these palindromes have a surrealistic glow emanating from them:

BARBARISM	Ham, sir? A bra be barbarism, ah!
CAPITOL	Top slot, I pace capitol spot.
DEVASTATION	Devastation? No, I tat, saved.
EDUCATION	No! It, a cud: education.
FISHERMAN	Do cast, fisherman. A Mr., eh, sifts a cod.
HABITUAL	Habitual—ha!—kahlua. Ti? Bah!
KIMONO	O, no, Mike! Not one kimono.
MALCONTENT	Malcontent, net no clam.
UNDERFOOT	Ed underfoot? Oof! Red nude.
VOLATILE	Not love lit a love: volatile volt on.
WEDDING	Wedding, I sign: "I'd dew."
YARDBIRD	Yardbird era bared rib dray.
ZODIAC	Zodiac, aid Oz!

ON THE PANAMA CANAL

Leigh Mercer wrote a palindrome that has become the most famous for which an author is known. It's a tribute to the designer of the Panama Canal:

A MAN, A PLAN, A CANAL: PANAMA!

There are two sides to every palindrome. Here's a one-liner built, like Mercer's, around the words CANAL and PANAMA, yet expressing the opposite viewpoint:

DAM OR A CANAL, PANAMA MAN? A PLAN? A CAR? O, MAD!

MADAM, I'M ADAM: A PALINDROMIC PLAY

A woman is standing next to the Grand Coulee Dam, which she mistakenly believes to be the Panama Canal. She utters the "Panama" palindrome, and the dam speaks back. Its replies are variations on the "Madam" palindrome.

WOMAN: A man, a plan, a canal: Panama!

GRAND COULEE: Madam, I'm a dam!

WOMAN: You seem angry.

GRAND COULEE: Mad am I, madam.

WOMAN: Sorry. By the way, who made you?

GRAND COULEE: Madam? I? Ma Dam.

WOMAN: "Ma Dam"? Did you say, "Ma Dam"?

GRAND COULEE: Ma Dam. I'm a dam.

WOMAN: Okay, you're a dam. But what did you tell your mother?

GRAND COULEE: "Ma! Dam! I'm a dam."

WOMAN: That's right. Oh, you're angry again.

GRAND COULEE: Mad am I! Mad am—

WOMAN: I think you're crazy!

GRAND COULEE: Mad? Am I mad? Am—

WOMAN: Crazy—or damn mad!

GRAND COULEE: Madam, I'm Adam.

PALINDROMES AND REVERSALS

Palindromic words read the same backward and forward—ERE. Reversal words form different words when read backward—ARE and ERA. If a palindrome is composed entirely of palindromic and reversal words, then, according to

Borgmann, it's "perfect." This doesn't mean "highest quality." It just refers to a particular facet of the palindrome's structure.

While fewer perfect palindromes exist, those that do can serve as simple patterns for other palindromes. The "Elba" palindrome is a perfect example. By replacing ABLE and ELBA with appropriate nouns and adjectives, others can be formed:

Able was I ere I saw Elba. (Anon.)

Eve was I ere I saw Eve. —Adam (Anon.)

Harpo was I ere I saw Oprah.

Live was I ere I saw Evil. (Borgmann)

Regal was I ere I saw lager. (Anon.)

EVOLUTION OF A PALINDROME

Howard Bergerson composed a palindromic phrase noted for its beautiful image: GOLDENROD-ADORNED LOG. Borgmann expanded it into a palindromic sentence: "NORA, ALERT, SAWS GOLDENROD-ADORNED LOGS, WASTREL AARON." Bergerson responded by extending it into the first palindromic haiku:

> *Smart Nora, alert*
> *Saws goldenrod-adorned logs.*
> *Wastrel Aaron trams.*

LONG-WORD PALINDROMES

The previous palindrome uses the nine-letter GOLDENROD. However, most words appearing in palindromic sentences tend to be fairly short—seven letters or less. Of the twenty-six Hall of Famers, only four have longer words (PREVENTS, GODDESSES, POSSESSED, SENSUOUSNESS, DAFFODILS).

One way to write palindromes with longer words is to look through the dictionary for words that reverse to spell or almost spell shorter words and work them into sentences. Using *Webster's Tenth Collegiate,* I found several words of eight to fourteen letters that fit into palindromes, including these:

We, I—very rare till literary review. (8)

Submarine men, I ram bus! (9)

Cain, a monomaniac. (10)

Risen, I'm for a cadet. A reneger regenerated a car of mine, sir. (11)

"No!" I tared. "Is no category by Roget a consideration?" (12)

Sis: "Oh, prom ate my metamorphosis." (13)

Draw, O Constantinople! Help on it! Nat's no coward. (14)

Lindon wrote a palindrome with a nineteen-letter giant in it. The word looks real, but it isn't in any dictionary. It's the longest word appearing in a palindrome composed of otherwise common words:

"UNGASTROPERITONITIS—IS IT I? NOT I," REPORTS A GNU.

PALINDROMIC SLIDE RULE

This device makes palindromes—ten thousand of them. To put it together, photocopy the four boards in larger size on thicker paper (card stock), and then cut out the boards. Place the A-board on a table, then lay the B-board on the A-board, positioning it between the two columns of words. In similar fashion, put the C-board on the B-board, and the D-board on the C-board.

To pick a specific palindrome, select a four-digit number (from 0000–9999) and slide the boards up or down so that the appropriate digits in the word boxes line up. When you read the words in the line, you'll see that they make a palindrome.

For easier reading on the printed page, here are the words that appear in the columns on the slide rule:

0	SPOT	GUM.	REGAL	PANS	SNAP	LAGER,	MUG	TOPS.
1	NAB	DEER.	MAD	NUTS	STUN	DAM,	REED	BAN.
2	PAT	LOOT.	STRAW	POTS	STOP	WARTS,	TOOL	TAP.
3	DOOM	PIT.	TEN	BATS	STAB	NET,	TIP	MOOD.
4	MAR	RATS.	SNUG	PAWS	SWAP	GUNS,	STAR	RAM.
5	EDIT	BUS.	SORE	NAPS	SPAN	EROS,	SUB	TIDE.
6	WED	POOL.	LIVE	BUNS	SNUB	EVIL,	LOOP	DEW.
7	FLOG	PART.	SLEEK	TIPS	SPIT	KEELS,	TRAP	GOLF.
8	EMIT	GATS.	DRAB	PALS	SLAB	BARD,	STAG	TIME.
9	TUG	RAIL.	RAW	PINS	SNIP	WAR,	LIAR	GUT.

Oren Dalton wrote a computer program, PALINDRUL, to manipulate the strips on the screen. His program allows two things that the paper version doesn't: single columns can be moved independently, and words can be changed or added.

PALINDROMIC SLIDE RULE
"MAKE A WORDROW"

0 Spot	
1 Nab	
2 Pat	
3 Doom	
4 Mar	
5 Edit	
6 Wed	
7 Flog	
8 Emit	
9 Tug	

A

tops.	
ban.	
tap.	
mood.	
ram.	
tide.	
dew.	
golf.	
time.	
gut.	

0	pans	snap
1	nuts	stun
2	pots	stop
3	bats	stab
4	paws	swap
5	naps	span
6	buns	snub
7	tips	spit
8	pals	slap
9	pins	snip

D

0 gum.	
1 deer.	
2 loot.	
3 pit.	
4 rats.	
5 bus.	
6 pool.	
7 part.	
8 gats.	
9 rail.	

mug
reed
tool
tip
star
sub
loop
trap
stag
liar

B

0 Regal	
1 Mad	
2 Straw	
3 Ten	
4 Snug	
5 Sore	
6 Live	
7 Sleek	
8 Drab	
9 Raw	

lager,
dam,
warts,
net,
guns,
eros,
evil,
keels,
bard,
war,

C

LEGAL PALINDROMES

Beginning with a classic line by Lindon, this set of palindromes shines the spotlight on crime, criminals, and the legal system:

SEX AT NOON TAXES. The IRS law about lunch-hour love.

SEX AT ONE, NO TAXES. After lunch, the law goes out of effect.

NO ON-TASK LAWYER PREY WALKS AT NOON. By now, most
lawyers know that it's hard to find clients during the lunch hour.

TIE, TAG IT. I'LL LITIGATE IT. The motto of the legal profession, meaning "You come up with a lawsuit, and I'll represent you in court."

EMIT NO LIAR! TRIAL ON TIME. In order to speed things up, the judge
decides to allow perjury.

NO, SIR. PRISON! One way a judge can reply to a request for probation.

AMORALITY TIL AROMA. The latest plan for decreasing crime: first
offenders get sprayed with an evil-smelling liquid.

TAFT, FAT

Of all the American presidents, William Howard Taft's last name fits into the
shortest, most appropriate palindrome—TAFT, FAT—which calls attention to his
legendary portliness. HARRISON is the only name that makes a complete reversal, NO, SIRRAH. Both of those are by Borgmann. NIXON fits into an unusual
type of palindrome discussed in Chapter P.

Here are some more chief executive palindromes. Carter's is by Edward Scher.
Bush's could've been spoken by Dan Quayle.

God! Adams is mad, a dog.

No? Si? Damn Madison!

O, note: Vote! Or no Monroe to veto. No!

Raw? Tap Marty Van Buren. One rub: Navy tramp at war.

Now rely. Tyler won.

To last, Carter retracts a lot.

I'm a Bush sub, am I?

Not nil: Clinton.

PALINDROMES WITH PERSONALITY

In its October 1991 issue, *Games* magazine introduced a contest called "Palindromes with Personality." Entrants created palindromes that included the name of a well-known person, real or fictional, living or dead. The prize was five hundred dollars toward air fare to anywhere in the world. More than two hundred people sent more than two thousand entries.

When *Games* published the winners, I was expecting the first-prize palindrome to be an inspired wonderwork approaching the heights of the "Panama" palindrome. Instead, the winning entry was clever, it sounded nice, it made sense, but it wasn't Hall of Fame material:

LISA BONET ATE NO BASIL (Douglas Fink).

Ten runner-ups and nineteen honorable mentions appeared. Here are six of the also-rans:

To Idi Amin: I'm a idiot. (Anon.)

Oh, no! Don Ho. (Several authors)

Plan no damn Madonna LP! (Anon.)

(Yawn.) Madonna fan? No damn way! (Susan Leslie and Robert Siegel)

Man, Oprah's sharp on A.M. (Anon.)

Vanna, wanna V? (Mike Griffin)

The contest provided a good incentive for writing palindromes. After spending a few nights doing it, I entered one hundred, including the next five. The first received an honorable mention.

O, Geronimo, no minor ego!

Nan, honor Ron. Oh, Nan!

Now no rise, Ma. Jesse James iron won.

"Tut-tut!" tuts Tut. "Tut-tut!"

Pure Venus, a sun ever up.

The longest first-and-last-name combination that fits into a palindrome appears in this line about a contemporary novelist:

I CALL A FAN: "AIR ON ORIANA FALLACI!"

INTERVIEW WITH A CAR COLLECTOR

In the last chapter, the names of cars were anagrammed into vanity plate messages. Car names can fit into palindromes, too. The best known is A TOYOTA'S A TOY-

OTA. The Spanish palindrome SONOMA, VAMONOS! translates to "Sonoma, let's go!" Some car names reverse to words or phrases by themselves: PACER = RECAP; REGAL = LAGER; STRATOS = SO, TARTS; and YAMAHA = AHA, MAY! or A HAM, AY!

In this dialog, the interviewer talks with a man who collects cars and speaks palindromes with car names in them.

Q: Hello. You've owned every make of car, haven't you?

A: I had no HONDA. Hi!

Q: Which car is the jewel of your collection?

A: A gem? OMEGA.

Q: But which do you like above all others?

A: Er, a love? VOLARE.

Q: Is there any type of driver you really dislike?

A: Ah, an ass in a NISSAN—aha!

Q: Do all of your cars honk?

A: SAAB baas.

Q: Do you ever try to crash into other cars?

A: O, ram a CAMARO.

Q: Which of your three girlfriends' cars do you like the best?

A: Norabel's LE BARON.

Q: You told one of the others not to race, didn't you?

A: No! "Hell, Eva, race CARAVELLE, hon."

Q: What did you tell your third girlfriend?

A: "Race LE CAR!"

Q: How did you explain the affair in the Beretta to your wife?

A: "Deb, BERETTA matter ebbed."

Q: Did you ever own a Seville?

A: Had I a SEVILLE? Hell, I've said "ah!"

Q: Is your old Storm still in good condition?

A: STORM rots.

Q: Which car expresses contemporary values best?

A: Age, vanity, tin—a VEGA.

Q: Which car least reflects our era?

A: O, guy, a YUGO.

Q: Do you ever call a cab?

A: Call? I'd a CADILLAC.

Q: Which car is best for getting a lot of sun while you drive?

A: A tan? O, SONATA.

Q: Is there any car you wouldn't exchange for a new one?

A: Trade not one DART.

Q: Is there any car you wouldn't sell again?

A: Resale? Not one LASER.

Q: What advice would you give a person about buying a Subaru?

A: SUBARU? O, tour a bus.

Q: What do you think of my car?

A: DASHER, eh? Sad.

CHEATER'S PALINDROMES

Writing palindromes would be much simpler if there were a lot more words in the English language. As it is, the combination of letters in many words, even common words like HOUSE, THINK, and SQUIRREL, makes reversing them impossible.

Cheater's palindromes provide a stress-free alternative. Instead of confining yourself to dictionary entries, you can make up words whenever you need them. In creating a cheater's palindrome, you write the first half, and the last half writes itself—or vice versa. Or just cheat on a word or two. You control the language, instead of the language controlling you.

To find out how people might handle the form, I wrote to several wordplay writers and asked them to try writing a few. Here is a selection of lines by Darryl Francis:

Capable was I ere I saw Elbapac.

We drink Nir dew.

"De ret tume," he muttered.

Odd word: "drowddo."

The next four are by Jeff Grant:

Oolginani's evil Eskimo, "Nomik Se," lives in an igloo.

How does one interpret "Nie Nose Od Woh"?

Samorael bats at times emit tastable aromas.

"Gniebne! Ilaeht! Demaercsiiiiii!" screamed the alien being.

These four came from Peter Newby:

Madam, I'm not Onmimadam.

Purcell, a base note detones a balle crup!

"Emord nil apaflah," sed Ivor P., "provides half a palindrome."

To oracle, Janus replied, "Deil persun a jel caroot."

IT'S A NICE NIGHT IN NITHGINECINASTI

In this half-act play, two tipsy celebrants meet at a party. They talk in cheater's palindromes. Their speech is somewhat slurred, but their meaning is as clear as the night sky.

SHE: My name's Emanym.

HE: How are you? I'm Miuoy E. Rawoh.

SHE: May I call you Uoy Llaciyam?

HE: Uoy Llaciyam? Tah! What may I call you?

SHE: Me? Em.

HE: It's a nice night in Nithginecinasti.

SHE: Drink, nird.

HE: Mmm, this siht . . . Mmm.

SHE: Blue rum, sir, is mureulb.

HE: Uh-oh, look! There's Sereht "Kool" Hohu.

SHE: With his wife, Efi W. Sihhtiw.

HE: Em, 'e sucxe! True, Em? Ree-beer me. EURT! Excuse me."

SHE: Ah! Ah! Start a belch, cleb at rats! Ha! Ha!

HE: A word can be funny ynnuf. "Ebnac." "Drowa—"

SHE: "Drowatonsi" is not a word!

HE: "Drowasi" is a word.

SHE: "Ootsi" is, too!

HE: Does it mean "a emti seod?"

SHE: It means "I love you, Uoy!" Evol is na emti.

HE: Me? You lov' ol' Uoy, Em?

SHE: Yes. Ah, I'm married, deir ramm. I—ha!—sey.

HE: Who's your mate? Tam Ruoy Sohw?

SHE: No, I think someone called Dell Ace. No, Emos K. Nihtion.

HE: Kiss me! Ooh! I—hoo!—em s-sik.

SHE: So it is a word, "Drowasitios"?

HE: I don't—now, who cares? Er, a cohw won't nod. I—

SHE: Uoy, let's go home. Mo' hogs tel' you.

HE: To my good doog, Ymot!

SHE: And my tact cat, Ymdna.

HE: More rum! Mure rom!

SHE: It *was* a nice night in Nithginecinasawti.

THE YEAR OF THE PALINDROME

Word Ways magazine proclaimed 1991 "The Year of the Palindrome" because the digits are the same in reverse. In that year, the Soviet Union crumbled, and Lenin's statue toppled with a thud heard around the world. The sweeping changes in the Communist bloc are chronicled in the following palindrome, which is one of very few that uses numbers:

1991: NO RED LENIN ELDER ON 1991.

THE MOTHER OF ALL PALINDROMES

DRAT SADDAM, A MAD DASTARD!

The Gulf War spawned the palindrome above—a bombshell instantly acclaimed the world over for its backward beauty. It couldn't have been written without the cooperation of Saddam Hussein, the Iraqi dictator.

But Ku-wait a minute! Who really wrote it? Several people independently discovered it. Once the circumstances were in place, it was inevitable. To get a feel for its purity, try making a palindrome with the name Schwarzkopf. The general may have won the war, but he lost the palindrome.

The "Saddam" palindrome makes a direct, in-your-face statement. It's not wordy, like this one: A RED RAT, SADDAM! A MAD DASTARD ERA. Nor is it a cautiously civil palindrome, like this: HE'S SADDAM. ADD "ASS," EH?

The Saddamdrome makes perfect sense. His name can fit into palindromes that make little sense, too, such as NO, I NOD: A LA SADDAM? ADD A SALAD ONION! You wouldn't hear that spoken in many places other than a cannibal restaurant.

And it has power. Four of the five words, all but the article, form a linguistic tour de force. Much better than any close alternatives—for instance, Porky Pig saying DRAT, SADDAM, A D-DASTARD!

It's ironic that a man who can inspire such an outstanding palindrome can wage a fool's war, lose it, and continue his tyranny. To this, one can only comment: DRAT, SADDAM, ALL ITS EVIL ALIVE, STILL A MAD DASTARD!

YOU TURN

And with that, we'll make a U-turn on Palindrome Place and return to Alphabet Avenue. This time, the sign is a palindrome, STOP POTS, referring to the potholes in the street.

Chapter D

Pun Freeway

THE PUN SHOP

EVERYONE SPEAKS PUNS on Pun Freeway, but not all puns work the same. There are three main types. Homographs are words with the same spelling but different meanings (TONGUE meaning a human tongue or a shoe tongue). Homophones have the same sound but different spellings (FLOWER and FLOUR). Double-sound puns have different spellings and sounds, but they're close enough to suggest each other (HORSE and HOARSE).

At the Pun Shop, the proprietor, Chuck Roast, is a beefy fellow who isn't afraid to crack a pun wide open. The worse, the better. His business card reads, HAVE PUN, WILL TRAVEL. He used to be a butcher, but now he takes pride in butchering the meat of language. Above his shop, there's a large sign in the shape of a giant hamburger. The words BUN and PUN flash on and off:

```
N B U N B U N B U N B
U N B U N B U N B U N B U
B U N B U N B U N B U N B U N

P U N P U N P U N P U N P
U N P U N P U N P U N P U
N P U N P U N P U N P U N

B U N B U N B U N B U N B U N
U N B U N B U N B U N B U
N B U N B U N B U N B
```

This week Chuck is having a special on woks, those oriental cooking pots. He doesn't sell them, but he sells puns with WOK in them to be used on bumper stickers, advertising signs, or political posters. His window is plastered with them:

ALL WOK AND NO PLAY

WHISTLE WHILE YOU WOK

WOK LIKE A MAN

THESE BOOTS ARE MADE FOR WOKKIN'

CAUGHT BETWEEN A WOK AND A HARD PLACE

WOK MUSICIANS

Needless to say, Chuck is held in low esteem. Still, the pun has been the most widely used form of wordplay in every language throughout history.

Let's take a wok on the wild side.

PUN NAMES—A MERRY CON PRECEDENT

The American presidents haven't fallen much under the spell of the pun. It's time to press a dent in them. Here are pun names for all of our leaders from George to Bill. Hail to the chiefs!

1. George watching dawn
2. John had hams.
3. Tom has chef for son.
4. Chains, men. Row!
5. shame's maddest son
6. John, quints see autumns.
7. Ann drew Jack's son.
8. Marred in ban, viewer ran.
9. Will ya, men, rehearse son?
10. John, dial her.
11. gem's cape oak
12. Sack hairy tailor.
13. Milord, fill more.
14. Frank, lean peers

15. Dames view cannon.
16. A bra hem—link on.
17. Ann drew John's son.
18. You lease ease. Yes, grand!
19. rudder for bee haze
20. James, a car field
21. Jester, eh, author?
22. Grow fair, cleave land.
23. Been jammin', hairy son?
24. grove, air, cliff, lawn
25. Will ya, Mick? Can Lee?
26. The ode or rosy veldt
27. Wool yam? How, er, daft!
28. Wood! Row well, son.
29. Warn hard. Ding!
30. calf in cool itch
31. her bird-do fur
32. Frank? Lynn? Della? No, Rosa felt.
33. Hairy? Yes! True, man.
34. To white day, fit eyes in hour.
35. John fits chair, old kin, Eddie.
36. Land on bee, join son.
37. Rich yard nicks sun.
38. cherry Ford
39. Shimmy, garter.
40. Run, old dragon!
41. Charge! Push!
42. Bilk lean tongue.

OTHER FAMOUS PUN NAMES

Most peoples' names easily convert to puns. Just take a name, break it into syllables, and put it back together with words punning on the syllables. What is your pun name? Can you figure out who owns these? (Answer Alley)

1. hem, hilly tick in sun
2. Loot wig, ban bait, O Ben.
3. mud dawn awe
4. Will yam shake spear?
5. Curt roots dine.
6. Hell, fuss! Press Lee.
7. share
8. Petey, barn hum
9. Clean eel is a bet.
10. Nap, O Lee, on bony part.

MULTIPUNS

Judging the quality of a pun is almost a paradox. To quote Shakespeare, "Fair is foul, and foul is fair." Puns follow a linguistic version of Heisenberg's Uncertainty Principle: you can't know whether a pun succeeds until you try.

Usually a pun involves a word or two referring to another word or two, but sometimes it gets more complex, as in these multipuns. The first one, a classic, appeared long ago in *Reader's Digest*. The second is a triple pun.

SONS RAISE MEAT
SUN'S RAYS MEET

SO BEE, TOO, SEES
SEW B TO C'S
SOW , BE TWO SEAS

ERROR APPARENT

Each of the next three phrases has one wrong word that can be replaced by a pun.
Can you do it? It's a peace of cake.

MUCH ADIEU ABOUT NOTHING

THE AURICLE AT DELPHI

GORILLA WARFARE

Now the real question: what is so special about each of those punning pairs?
(Answer Alley)

NEWSPUNS

The newspaper industry would suffer greatly if it weren't for headline writers. They
are the poet-punsters of inkprint. Using their own abbreviated language, they dis-
till the news of the day into miniature poems.

Since they live in the present, they rarely use the past tense. THE and A are dirty
words to them. They glory in double meanings. Although indispensable, they
remain faceless, nameless creatures living in punderous anonymity.

To commemorate these unsung Shakespeares, here are some punning headlines.
Veteran headline-hunter Richard Lederer collected the first ten, selected from his
book, *Anguished English*.

ANTIQUE STRIPPER TO DISPLAY WARES AT STORE

MILK DRINKERS ARE TURNING TO POWDER

DRUNK GETS NINE MONTHS IN VIOLIN CASE

ROBBER HOLDS UP ALBERT'S HOSIERY

STOLEN PAINTING FOUND BY TREE

GENETIC ENGINEERING SPLITS SCIENTISTS

TRAFFIC DEAD RISE SLOWLY

IRAQI HEAD SEEKS ARMS

AMERICAN SHIPS HEAD TO LIBYA

SOVIET VIRGIN LANDS SHORT OF GOAL AGAIN

RAINBOW GIRLS ADMIT BLACK

KURDS MASS ON TURKEY BORDER

INDIANA'S NIT GOAL: HALT TORRID CARROLL

BELL NOT A COX MAN

RED SOX PURCHASE FINGERS

RAPE CASE RESULTS IN HUNG JURY

IOWA SNATCHES WIN IN GIRLS' BASKETBALL
DAVENPORT ANNEXATION ASKED FOR BY CATERPILLAR
COOK'S DEPARTURE LEAVES FRY COLD

POP BEATS BAD RAP

The headline above, from the *Daily Iowan*, weaves a web of wordplay intrigue. Three of the four words are synonyms, or close to it. According to *Webster's Tenth Collegiate*, BEAT is "to strike repeatedly," POP is "to strike or knock sharply," and RAP is "to strike with a hard blow." It's easy to punch up the number to eight synonyms as in this made-up headline, which translates as "Beatnik bestselling song cuts down bop music, attacks rap music, and criticizes pop music":

BEAT HIT KNOCKS BOP, STRIKES RAP, SLAMS POP.

The real intrigue behind the original headline, however, is its meaning. Before reading the story, I tried to guess what it was about, but I was wrong. Here are some interpretations. Which one is the true story behind POP BEATS BAD RAP? (Answer Alley)

1. Soda pop isn't as bad as people thought it was.
2. Pop music is better than rap music.
3. A man accused of murdering his son is acquitted.
4. "Pop" wins a race against "Bad Rap." Both are racehorses.

POSTCARD FROM MISS ZOORY

The 1904 St. Louis World's Fair had the first American Olympics, the first beauty contest, the first air show, and the first wooden postcards. The postcards had printed messages on them making heavy use of puns.

Here, for the first time in decades, is an example of truly wooden punning:

All a-board for the World's Fair. Arrived safe. Exposition is more than oak-a, it is ash-tonishing, you cedar sights of your life. The Pike is fir-straight, more than a pear of peaches and the spielers don't bark like a tree. Board and (s)lumber at poplar prices, no need to pine for what you plank down. Birch-ance the last great show for many years. More fun than the beech. I wood spruce up and come. You walnut regret it. Butternut delay.
Sincerely,
Hickory Hemlock

GRECO-AMERICAN GRAFFITI

The Greek tradition on campus has produced its own brand of puns, and they pass from generation to generation like children's playground chants. Which fraternity or sorority would you like to join?

Chugga Lugga Bru	I Felta Thigh
Eata Bita Pi	Mu Goesa Cow
Gotta Getta Poppa	Tappa Kegga Day
Hoppa Toppa Box	You Drinka Pepsilon

HERMANS

Tom Swifties are sentences that begin with a quote and end with an adverb punning on the quote: "I burnt my finger!" said Tom heatedly. The Herman, named after the lead-off example below, drops the adverb and concludes with a punning first name:

"She's my woman," said Herman.

"Can I touch you?" asked Ophelia.

"Your cat scratched me!" said Claude.

"You're my best friend," said Opal.

"I've got to use the loo," said Lulu to Lou.

"Listen! I hear horses," said Winnie.

"What comes after H?" asked I, Jay, Kay, Ella, and Emma.

"Bottoms up!" said Fanny.

Vernon MacLaren came up with the next batch:

"I'm drawn to you," said Art.

"I feel very English," said Britt.

"I love these tiny flowers," said Bud.

"Bless this food," said Grace.

"I feel like a little bug," said Nat.

"That was a deception by father," said Patrick.

"I sang do, re, mi, fa, sol, ti, do!" said Nola.

"I'm working on a new chemical compound," said Polly Esther.

Next, a group by Oren Dalton:

"Testing—testing," said Mike.

"I've burnt my mark into those steers," said Brandon.

"He gave me a beautiful red jewel," glowed Ruby.

"The moon is declining," said Wayne.

"The Mayans invented corn," said Maisie.

"I burned it all up," said Ashe.

"I was the winner," exulted Victor.

"I can't help but wobble in these shoes," said Lucille.

Jeff Martinez created these:

"Don't touch that stove—it's hot," said Bernie.

"Oops, my watch alarm is beeping!" said Elsie Dee.

"Step on it!" said Matt.

"Let's sing Christmas songs," said Carol.

"I'd rather sing 'Down in the Valley,'" said Dale.

"Violent? I wouldn't hurt a fly," said Maime.

"I haven't a thing to wear," said Buff.

"Pass me the binoculars, please," said Seymour.

LOGOMOTIVES

In each of these punning questions, Peter Newby joined the last name of a famous person with a word that completes a question. The results are linguistic double takes:

Was Robert Frost bitten?

Is Doris Day light?

Was Vincent Price conscious?

Is Koo Stark naked?

Was Donald Duck billed?

Is Colonel North bound?

Was Tyrone Power hungry?

Did Captain Kidd nap?

Was Barbara Bush whacked?

WAR OF THE NETWORKS

Board games sometimes use puns for the names of fictitious characters, places, and other things. "War of the Networks," a 1979 Hasbro game, channeled their punning into a television motif. If you can find ABZ, NBZ, and ZBS on the tube, then look for the following, same time, same place:

PROGRAMS

Charlie's Ankles	M'U'S'H
The Inedible Bulk	Hobo's Heros
The Brainy Bunch	Mucous B. Well, M.D.
As the World Burns	Star Trucks
Hardley Boys	Cattlecar Gigantica
Wander Woman	Routes

ACTORS

Betty Bye	Rome E. Oh and Julie Ett
Rex Carrs	Steve Adoro
Izzy Hereornot	Sid Onitt
Mona Groana	Frank Footer
Otto Site	Holly Wood
Ted E. Bear	Oscar Emmie
Wanda Lust	The Lee Sisters—Ug and Home

CROSSING THE BORDERS

What do you drink when you cross Canada and Minnesota? A Canasota. Other geographic locations can be connected punfully to provide answers to questions you'd never ask. How would you answer these, fellow traveler? (Answer Alley)

1. What kind of clothes are most comfortable in Washington and Delaware?
2. How do you ask people to pause in Kenya and Kuwait?
3. What do you get when you travel from America to Indonesia?
4. How do you tell jokes in Wisconsin and Italy?
5. How did you travel through Iran and Madagascar?
6. What do you drink in Malta and Lichtenstein?
7. Where do you go after visiting Yugoslavia and Oklahoma?

KNIVES, FORKS, AND SPOONERISMS

The spoonerism is a specialized form of pun in which the sounds at the beginnings of words are switched, either by accident or on purpose, to make different words. One of the most famous, attributed to its nineteenth-century namesake, Reverend Spooner, is: "Mardon me, padam, but you're occupewing the wrong pie. May I sew you to another sheet?" Shorter spoonerisms abound. This modern pair combines politics and fate: LAME DUCK=DAME LUCK.

In each couplet in the following rhyme, the first line ends with a word pair that is spoonerized in the next line:

When Sandy sees a flying crow,
It makes her weep. The crying flow

Runs down her nose and lips and cheeks
Into a cup that chips and leaks.

Outside the house, her parking spot
Is lit up by a sparking pot

At night. She sees no other man
Or woman but her mother, Ann,

Who cries aloud, "She feels the stun
Of sorrow." Still, she steals the fun

By putting on her mask in time
As if it were a task in mime:

Sometimes her makeup's yellow hue
Just smears when she shouts, "Hello, you!"

She gobbles up the jelly beans,
Which overflow her belly, jeans

And all. She keeps on gaining weight
(It shows up in her waning gait).

She nods. "This candy's sadly mine,
But I'm no star who'll madly sign

My autograph." Her life is strong,
Although she thinks her strife is long.

"I laugh a lot," she chuckles now,
While munching on pig knuckles chow.

She says, "Pass me a strip, and I
Will eat." And then she'll sip and try

Some wine on her next trip, and sigh
About her dress's rip. "And sty

Just proves I've made a golden rule
Of eating all the olden gruel."

PUNDROMES

Pundromes combine puns and palindromes in a sentence whose words, not letters, sound the same in either direction. Most of them make sense, too!

No eye sees the seas I know.
Pshaw! Reed doesn't read Shaw.
Our bear won prizes one bare hour.
Hi! Sore two feet? Know it's no feat to soar high.
Mary, maid missed in mist, made merry.
We'll know no car, know no wheel.
Knight, buy Whale's Inn wine or whine in Wales by night.
Shoo gnats off Nat's shoe.
Find bee or be fined!

EXECUTING THE DICTIONARY

The prefix EX has three main meanings: "out of," "not," and "former." Using the third meaning, Charles Linnet has given new definitions to EX-words found in the dictionary.

EXAMPLE: someone who used to be fat
EXCITATION: residue of tearing up a traffic ticket
EXHALE: someone who used to be healthy
EXILE: Atlantis
EXPENSIVE: someone who used to think a lot
EXPIRED: when a church steeple collapses
EXPORTER: someone who used to work on the railroad
EXPUNGE: used to be that funny sea creature you could wash your car with
EXTENDED: when the shepherd abandons his flock
EXTERMINATOR: if Arnold Schwarzenegger stops making movies
EXTORTED: if you drop your lawsuit

IT'S CIAO TIME

On Pun Freeway, people tailor their goodbyes to fit their personalities—for instance, a store owner saying, "GOOD BUY." Here are a dozen more:

FAIR WELL	oil driller
TILL NECK'S TIME	Dracula
GOOD KNIGHT	queen
HAPPY TRIALS	lawyer
TAKE ID EASY	psychiatrist
BUN VOYAGE	baker
CHEERY OWE	loan officer
HAVE AN ICE DAY	skater
TAKE AIR	lifeguard
HAIRY BACK	barber
BE SCENE YOU	movie star
BONE VOYAGE	butcher

THE PUN TAKES ITS TOLL

At the end of the street, cars are lined up for the toll booth. Each driver pays with a chicken, a duck, or a goose. As the sign on the booth says, "FARE IS FOWL, AND FOWL IS FARE."

Fair enough! But since we're not driving, we can walk past the booth and the stop sign, too. The stop sign was designed by Chuck Roast.

Chapter E

Parody Strip

THE PARODY STRIPTEASE

O<small>N</small> P<small>ARODY</small> S<small>TRIP</small>, literature becomes a mockery of itself. Just ask Bill Shakesbeer over there. He manages the Parody Striptease, a burlesque theater that shows no mercy to the serious art of poetry, prose, or any other form of language. To Bill, everything is a parody, which is why he laughs a lot.

A parody is an imitation of a work or style of art. It's usually a humorous, even satirical, form of literary, cultural, or social criticism. In *The Teachers and Writers Handbook of Poetic Forms,* poet Ron Padgett calls it "verbal kung fu." Sometimes the parodist creates in admiration of the original work, and sometimes in contempt.

Bill is giving his patter, urging people to see the next show. His pet parrot Mock perches on his shoulder. Whatever Bill says, the bird parodies. At the top of the building, Mock's image twinkles in flashing lights. She's more than a pet: she's a logo.

```
                              CK
                             MOC
                            CKMO          M
                            OCKM         KM
                          KMOCKM        OCKM
          CKM             CKMOCKMOCKMOCK              CKM
         OCKMOCK          CKM  KMOCKMO              MOCKMOC
        KMOCKMOCKMO       KMOCKMOCKMO             CKMOCKMOCKM
       OCKMOCKMOCKMOCK     MOCKMOCK              MOCKMOCKMOCKMO
      KMOCKMOCKMOCKMOCKMO    CKMOC             OCKMOCKMOCKMOCKMOC
      CKMOCKMOCKMO  KMOCKMOCKMOCKMOCKMOCKMOCKMOCKMO  KMOCKMOCK
     OCKMOCKMOCK      OCKMOCKMOCKMOCKMOCKMOCKMOCK     MOCKMOCKM
     MOCKMOCKMO        CKMOCKMOCKMOCKMOCKMOCKM         CKMOCKMO
    KMOCKMOCK           MOCKMOCKMOCKMOCK                KMOCKMO
    KMOCKMO             MOCKMOCKMOCKMOCK                 MOCKM
    KMOCK               MOCKMOCKMOCKMOCK                  MOC
     MOC                MOCKMOCKMOCKMOC                    MO
      O                KMOCKMOCKMOCKMOC                     K
                      CKMOCKMOCKMOCKMO
                      OCKMOCKMOCKMOCKM
                     KMOCKMOCKMOCKMOCK
                     OCKMOCKMOCKMOCKMOC
              MOCKMOCK        KM      OC
             CKMOCKMO         CK      MO
              OCKMOCK          K      C
             KMOCKM            M        M
            OCKM              KMOC     OCKM
          KM                  C M C     C M C
```

"Get in here and wet your whistle while we have a bad old time with language!" Bill shouts to passersby. "This is where we draw the wine. Water sneaks its own level!"

"Water squeaks!" Mock squawks.

"C'mon, pal," Bill continues. "You cheap or something? Put your money where your moth is! Remember, today is the first day of the rest of your lie."

"Rusty July!" Mock chirps.

So we step inside. Lining the walls of the hallway, distorted pictures of the greatest writers of all time leer goofily at us. Onstage, a stripper drops a scarf. Bill grabs the mike and says, "No use crying over spilled silk. After all, chaste makes waste!"

"Chased waist!" Mock trills.

The lights dim. The show is about to begin.

ST. NICK PARODIES

"A Visit from St. Nicholas" may be the most parodied poem of all time. Since Clement Clark Moore wrote it in 1822, dozens of takeoffs have appeared in places ranging from *Mad* magazine to the photocopy room bulletin board. Martin Gardner collected ninety-one "St. Nicks" in his book, *The Annotated Night Before Christmas*.

In this selection, the first couplet of the original is followed by the first couplet from each of seven parodies:

A Visit from St. Nicholas (Clement Clarke Moore)

'Twas the night before Christmas, when all through the house
Not a creature was stirring, not even a mouse;

The Effect of Inflation on Santa (Dave Sharpe)

'Twas the night before Christmas, and all through the house
How the tinsel was scattered! and twigs by the thous–

The Night Before Christmas in "Hip Talk" (Mad magazine)

'Twas the night before Christmas, and all through the pad
Not a hipster was swinging, not even old Dad;

A Visit from Jack Nicklaus (Hugh A. Mulligan)

'Twas the night before Christmas, when all through the bar
Every golfer was stirring and guzzling a jar.

A Visit from Sid Vicious (Anon.)

'Twas the night before New Year's, when everyone's drunk,
Not a rocker was stirring, not even a punk.

The Night Before Chanukah (Anon.)

'Twas the night before Chanukah, boichecks and maidels,
Not a sound could be heard, not even the draidels.

Der Nighd Pehind Grisdmas (Sidney W. Wetmore)

'Tvas der nighd pehind Grisdmas, und all ofer der haus,
Nod von beobles vas schleebing, nix cum arous;

A Visit from St. Alphabet

'Twas the night before X, when all through the Y
Not a letter was stirring, not even an I;

OPERATING ON BROWNING

The opening couplet of the next poem is from "De Gustibus," by Robert Browning. The rest of the couplets are anatomically correct takeoffs.

Open my heart, and you will see
Graved inside of it, "Italy."

Open my liver, and you will glance
At how I used to misspell "France."

Open my bladder, and you will find
That "Germany" is underlined.

Open my head and look at my brain,
Where once I neatly printed, "Spain."

Open my lungs, for there I've written
"Great" in the left, in the right one "Britain."

MARY HAD A LITTLE LAMPOON

Everyone is familiar with "Mary Had a Little Lamb," and familiarity breeds parodies. It's become a popular vehicle for wordplay writers in particular. The challenge is to use wordplay in writing a new "Lamb" that sticks to the spirit of the original as much as possible.

To lead in a flock of "Lambs" that wordplay bred, here are the first two stanzas of Sarah Josepha Hale's original, published in 1830 in her book, *Poems for Our Children*:

Mary had a little lamb
Its fleece was white as snow,
And everywhere that Mary went
The lamb was sure to go;

> *He followed her to school one day,*
>   *That was against the rule;*
> *It made the children laugh and play*
>   *To see a lamb in school.*

Richard Lederer included this classic "Lamb" send-up based on a pun in his book, *Nothing Risqué, Nothing Gained*:

> *Mary had a little sheep,*
>   *And with the sheep she went to sleep.*
> *The sheep turned out to be a ram.*
>   *Now Mary has a little lamb.*

Ross Eckler showed how versatile the "Lamb" could be by rewriting it five times in the form of a lipogram, which disallows words having a specific letter of the alphabet. Eckler excluded one of the five commonest letters in each version. This one omits E:

> *Mary had a tiny lamb,*
>   *Its wool was pallid as snow,*
> *And any spot that Mary did walk*
>   *This lamb would always go;*
>
> *This lamb did follow Mary to school,*
>   *Although against a law;*
> *How girls and boys did laugh and play,*
>   *That lamb in class all saw.*

Carrying the "Lamb" even further, Eckler wrote a lipogrammed version omitting half the letters of the alphabet:

> *Maria had a little sheep,*
>   *As pale as rime its hair,*
> *And all the places Maria came*
>   *The sheep did tail her there;*
>
> *In Maria's class it came at last,*
>   *A sheep can't enter there;*
> *It made the children clap their hands,*
>   *A sheep in class, that's rare.*

Paul Hellweg, on reading Eckler's "Lambs," decided to shear the original by doing it univocalically, that is, allowing only one vowel to appear throughout the text, as in this I-full version:

> *This is Mitzi's slight stripling,*
> *Its skin is vivid milk-light,*
> *In districts which Mitzi visits*
> *This stripling sticks with Mitzi;*
>
> *It visits Mitzi's thinking-inn,*
> *Its plight is illicit*
> *Still, kids' spirits it did lift*
> *Sighting Mitzi's stripling within.*

James Rambo wrote a version of the "Lamb" in which the two stanzas are anagrams of each other:

> *A girl once kept a tiny sheep,*
> *Widely famed for whiteness:*
> *This pet would dog her every step*
> *No certain sigh of brightness.*
>
> *'Twas viewed, the pest, one day in class*
> *By impish children there;*
> *Kids laugh to see pets, goofing off,*
> *Weren't trying—open, err!*

Jay Ames, turning to the Toronto telephone directory for inspiration, composed a "Lamb" by punning on the surnames of real people:

> *Marry Haddad Liddell Lamb*
> *Witt Fleece Azzaz Whiter Snowe*
> *Ann Devry Ware Young Marry Wendt*
> *Durr Lamm Wass Shore Ru Goh.*
>
> *Hitz Followes Herr To School Wonn Day*
> *Witcher Wasser Gaines Turr Rule*
> *Wych Maida Kinder Laffan Pley*
> *Tooze See Allam Innes Cool.*

The next "Lamb" is a palindrome, which, as palindromes often do, sometimes takes wild leaps into greener pastures:

> *Mary, baboon? to go to room?*
> *Gnu? Star? No, 'tis all lamb.*
> *O, bit on stool, eh, Mary?*
> *Won sore heel? Sit! One rule, so:*
>
> *No nose lure. No, 'tis Lee, hero,*
> *Snowy ram. He loots! Not I, Bob.*
> *Mall, la. Sit on rat. Sung—*
> *"Moo rot! O, got no, o, baby ram!"*

Peter Newby parodied the "Lamb" in a one-line palindrome about the Derby ram, a giant beast from British folklore. The line sounds so natural that any additional lines would sully the purity of its palindromic wool:

> *Mary bred a Derby ram.*

RAVENOUS POE-TRY

Edgar Allan Poe's classic "The Raven" is a long, haunting poem about a bird that wouldn't fly away. To refresh your memory, here's the opening stanza:

> *Once upon a midnight dreary, while I pondered, weak and weary,*
> *Over many a quaint and curious volume of forgotten lore—*
> *While I nodded, nearly napping, suddenly there came a tapping,*
> *As of some one gently rapping, rapping at my chamber door—*
> *"'Tis some visitor," I muttered, "tapping at my chamber door—*
> *Only this and nothing more."*

Like the "Lamb," "The Raven" has been rewritten in several wordplay forms. The three that follow are first stanzas of parodies that, in their full form, are as long as the original.

The first, by Howard Bergerson, is heteroliteral. Each word has no letter in common with the words on either side of it:

On a midnight, cool and foggy, as I pondered, light and groggy,
Ancient books and musty ledgers, not remembered any more,
As I nodded, all but napping, there I sensed a muffled tapping,
Very much of hushful rapping, just behind my attic door.
"'Tis a guest, mayhap," I muttered, "knocking at my attic door—
　　　I can't judge it any more."

In sharp contrast, Eckler wrote a homoliteral version, in which each word *does* have a letter (or more) in common with the words flanking it:

On one midnight, cold and dreary, while I, fainting, weak and weary,
Pondered many a quaint and ancient volume of forgotten lore,
While I studied, nearly napping, suddenly there came a tapping,
Noise of some one gently rapping, rapping at the chamber door.
"Oh, some visitor," I whispered, "tapping at the chamber door,
　　　Only one, and nothing more."

In the next version, "The Raven" becomes "The Crow." It's made of one-syllable words only:

Once at twelve on one night's drear, 'twas while I, weak and tired, thought here
On the words in lots of quaint and odd old tomes of mind's lost lore,
While I dozed, so near a nap, there came but then a soft, quick tap,
As of one who made a rap, a rap at my front room's closed door,
"'Tis some guest," I spoke, voice low, "who taps at my front room's closed door,
　　　Oh just this and not much more."

Now back to Bergerson for a short takeoff in a form that he dubbed "word square poetry." It can be read across or down. Here is the complete poem:

once	upon	a	midnight	dreary
upon	a	wintry	cyclone's	blackness
a	wintry	raven	soared	with
midnight	cyclone's	soared	cursing	endless
dreary	blackness	with	endless	nevermores

TWINKLE, TWINKLE, LITTLE WHAT?

In *Alice's Adventures in Wonderland,* Lewis Carroll wrote a parody of the well-known first stanza of Jane Taylor's "Twinkle, Twinkle, Little Star." Carroll's parody is fairly well known, too. What did he substitute for STAR? (Answer Alley)

A car is the star of this modernized "Twinkle":

> *Twinkle, twinkle, little car,*
> *How I wonder what you are.*
> *From this distance, who could say*
> *Cadillac or Chevrolet?*

UNQUOTES

Famous people from politicians to comedians are often masters of the immortal soundbite. History thrives on great quotes, but they're almost always taken out of context. Unquotes put the exact words back into sentences, and—voila!—the real meanings return.

Julius Caesar: "In spite of an uncontrollable fear of the dark that I had when I CAME, I SAW. I CONQUERED my phobia after several sessions with my analyst."

Marie Antoinette: "I'd be glad to LET THEM EAT CAKE, but it's too fattening."

John Paul Jones: "I'm too young! I HAVE NOT YET BEGUN. TO FIGHT is dangerous!"

Will Rogers: "I NEVER MET A MAN. I DIDN'T LIKE the competition."

Gertrude Stein: "Hemingway, you're a good writer, but do you think YOU ARE ALL A LOST GENERATION wants to read?"

Douglas MacArthur: "Damn! This milk is sour! I SHALL RETURN it for a full refund."

Neil Armstrong: "With such a tiny foot, THAT'S ONE SMALL STEP FOR A MAN. ONE GIANT LEAP FOR MANKIND would take a size-twelve shoe."

Richard Nixon: "You think I am honest? I AM NOT. A CROOK would be a better word."

THE CURTAIN CLOSES

The show is over, but another one starts in five minutes. Bill Shakesbeer calls after us, "Hey, you two, don't leave yet. Wait'll you see our next show!"

But there are many other shows to see on Alphabet Avenue. As we head to the stop sign, we can hear Mock squawking the word "Stomp!" over and over.

Chapter F

Rebus Run

THE REBUS STATION

I N THE CITY of Wordplay, if you miss the bus, you can catch the rebus. The shortest street in town is Rebus Run. Consequently, the people try to minimize the number of symbols they use to spell words. Instead, they rely on letters and numbers that sound almost the same. LO means HELLO. I I 2 C U means I WANT TO SEE YOU. This is one of several ways to form rebuses. In general, a rebus uses alphabetic, numeric, and pictorial symbols to represent words through aural and visual puns.

Here comes the Greyhound Rebus now. It's motto, XPDNC, is the longest word expressed in rebus that sounds like the original word. Can you find a word that achieves greater XLNC?

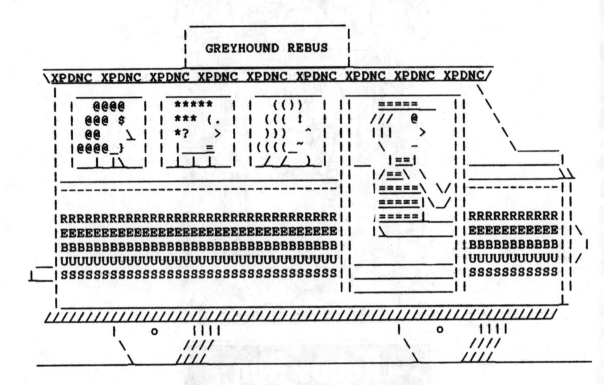

Letters and numbers don't have to sound exactly like the words they represent, but they should come close enough to make it easy to recognize the words. Let's hop aboard and ride the rebus.

CHILDHOOD REBUSES

Children sometimes come across rebuses in grade school. Valentine cards, children's magazines, even jokes have rebuses in them. Here are four that have been around for decades:

I. Q: Can you spell "I CUP"?

   A: I see you pee.

2. O G I C U R A Q T

   Oh, gee, I see you are a cutie.

3. UR 2 GOOD
   2 ME
   2 BE
   4 GOT 10

   You are too good
   to me
   to be
   forgotten.

4. YY UR
   YY UB
   I C U R
   YY 4 ME

   Too wise you are.
   Too wise you be.
   I see you are
   Too wise for me.

WHERE THE WORDS ARE

Some rebuses can be deciphered by noting the relative location of words or letters. The relationship provides the information necessary to spell a word or complete a phrase. For instance, SIDESIDE means SIDE BY SIDE. C P H means PINCH (P IN CH).

Can you figure out the next few rebuses? The last one is a classic rebus name and address. (Answer Alley)

1. DOG   TAKE   TO   THE
    THE   MAY   THROW   SEER

2. CLOUD
    TH

3. C
    CHARGE

4. SI OUT DE

5. WOOD
    JOHN
    AND
    MASS

THE ONE-LETTER REBUS

The one-letter rebus is a word puzzle in which a word or phrase describes a letter of the alphabet. Philip Cohen identified four types and illustrated them with examples from *The Enigma*, the National Puzzlers' League publication. The categories and some examples follow. The authors' NPL pseudonyms are in parentheses.

The standard rebus must be respaced to form a message that reveals the hidden letter. BASIS refers to the letter B because it's B AS IS ("Mrs. Ev").

B = iamb ("Fiddle")
E = an ethereal thing ("Su San")
D = disappearing ("Grandmother")
W = seesaw (Anon.)

The phonetic rebus must be sounded out to form the message. CASEIN means K because it sounds like K SEEN ("Roving").

A = avowal ("Hoho")
R = Caesar ("Mars")
I = black eye ("Ixaxar," "Pearlie Glen")
X = annex ("Blue Jay")

The enigmatic rebus must be solved like a riddle. In some cases, the rebus hides the letter within the word or phrase (D and R below), and in other cases it presents a description of the letter (O and Q below).

D = dauntless aunt ("Archimedes")
O = a circular letter ("Macropod")
R = revolutionless evolution ("Grulla," "Vesta")
Q = ringtailed ("Awl Wrong")

The suber, or reversed rebus, must be respaced like the standard rebus and read in reverse to form the message. KENO becomes ONE K ("Fanacro").

B = bolos ("Treesong")
K = knees ("Sakr-el-Bahr")
D = denotes ("Nightowl")
O = onward ("Nightowl")

THE LETTER CONUNDRUM A–Z

Letter conundrums are rebus-type word puzzles that have been around for more than a hundred years. They frequently appeared in nineteenth-century books, newspapers, and magazines like *St. Nicholas* and *Chatterbox*.

A letter conundrum involves a single letter in either the question or the answer. The answer works in one of two ways: (1) The letter is part of a word, as in the example for A below; or (2) the letter is an addition that changes one word into another, as in the example for B. The second type is more difficult to construct. The rare letters J, Q, X, and Z are the most difficult to represent.

Ross Eckler and Will Shortz gathered a collection of vintage letter conundrums from books and newspapers dating from the 1850s to the 1920s. Here's one for each letter:

Why is A like noon? Because it is in the middle of day.

Why is B like a hot fire? Because it makes oil boil.

Why is C the most noisy of letters? It begins all clamor.

Why is D like a squalling child? Because it makes Ma mad.

Why is E like London? Because it is the capital of England.

Why is F like a cow's tail? Because it comes at the end of beef.

Why is G like a hot day? Because it is in the middle of August.

Why is H like servants? Because it is the first to help.

What letter is invisible, yet never out of sight? The letter I.

Why is J like your nose? Because it is next to your I (eye).

Why is K like flour? You cannot make cake without it.

What changes a pear into a pearl? The letter L.

What comes once in a minute, twice in a moment, and not once in a thousand years? The letter M.

Why is N like a pig? Because it makes a sty nasty.

Why is O the only vowel we hear? Because the rest are inaudible.

Why is P like a Roman emperor? Because it is near O (Nero).

Why is Q like a guide? Because it goes ahead of U (you).

Why is R always in confusion? Because it is in the middle of labyrinth.

What turns a word into a sword? The letter S.

What is the difference between here and there? The letter T.

Why is U the most unfortunate letter? Because it is always in trouble and difficulty.

Why cannot V be divided? Because it is indivisible.

Why is W like Sunday? Because it is the first of the week.

Why is X like a mystery? Because it is inexplicable.

What changes a lad into a lady? The letter Y.

Why is Z like the monkey cage? Because it is the leading feature of the zoo.

THE SYLLABIC REBUS

In this kind of rebus, letters and numbers are sounded out individually. Syllabic languages, like Japanese, work on the same principle. Normal English mimics syllabic in some common words or phrases like BB or IOU. In a rebus, NRG is ENERGY, and LMN is A LEMON.

   This matching quiz tests your rebus reading skills. Each pair of capital letters on the left represents an adjective that fits next to a noun on the right to form a common two-word phrase. QT would go with PIE to make CUTEY PIE. Can you match letter pairs with nouns to complete the phrases? (Answer Alley)

AL	cat
BZ	doll
CT	brush
DR	cell
EZ	bee
IV	log
JL	show
KG	baggage
LE	limits
MT	test
NR	read
QP	effort
RR	friend
SA	cutlet
TM	customer
UL	storm
VL	cup
XS	tower
YR	strength

THE FARMER

H. C. Dodge used rebuses for some of the words in this melancholy poem from the July 1903 *Woman's Home Companion*.

> *The farmer leads no EZ life,*
>   *The CD sows will rot;*
> *And when at EV rests from strife*
>   *His bones all AK lot.*
>
> *In DD has to struggle hard*
>   *To EK living out;*
> *If IC frosts do not retard*
>   *His crops, there'll BA drought.*
>
> *The hired LP has to pay*
>   *Are awful AZ, too;*
> *They CK rest when he's away*
>   *Nor NE work will do.*
>
> *Both NZ cannot make to meet,*
>   *And then for AD takes*
> *Some boarders, who so RT eat,*
>   *& E no money makes.*
>
> *Of little UC finds this life;*
>   *Sick in old AG lies;*
> *The debts he OZ leaves his wife,*
>   *And then in PC dies.*

THE "HEY, BEE! SEE?" OF ANTI-REBUSES

In the rebuses discussed so far, letters and numbers form words. RUN is ARE YOU IN. An anti-rebus goes in the other direction: words form letters. That is, the words have syllables that sound like letters, and those letters in turn spell out new words. ARE YOU IN sounds like R, U, and N, spelling RUN.

Anti-rebuses always form rebuses, but not all rebuses form anti-rebuses. A LEMON, for instance, isn't an anti-rebus, since its rebus form, LMN, doesn't spell a word.

Can you figure out the word or phrase that each of the anti-rebuses below spell? If you get them all, you win an EMMY from ME. (Answer Alley)

1. Oh, any.

2. Hello, Angie. I see. Why are—oh, hey, Dee. Yes?

3. Age? Oh, tee 'em! A tee? See age.

4. Gee, oh, a devil. You, eh? Why?

5. Cue you, Whitey?

D N

The Greyhound Rebus pulls up to D N of the block, that is, THE END of the block. As we get off the rebus, we see that the stop sign has a farewell message on it.

Chapter G

Dictionary Drive

THE LANGUAGE COURTHOUSE

AT THE ENTRANCE, the Language Courthouse stands impressively high. Its roof is a giant unabridged dictionary. In the front, the Alphabet Flag waves atop a tall, pencil-shaped flagpole.

```
  (   )
 |---|
 || ||   *    *    *    *    *    *    M N O P Q R S T U V W X Y Z
 || ||      *    *    *    *    *      M N O P Q R S T U V W X Y Z
 || ||   *    *    *    *    *    *
 || ||      *    *    *    *    *      M N O P Q R S T U V W X Y Z
 || ||   *    *    *    *    *    *    M N O P Q R S T U V W X Y Z
 || ||      *    *    *    *    *
 || ||   *    *    *    *    *    *    M N O P Q R S T U V W X Y Z
 || ||      *    *    *    *    *      M N O P Q R S T U V W X Y Z
 || ||   *    *    *    *    *    *
 || ||   A B C D E F G H I J K L M N O P Q R S T U V W X Y Z
 || ||   A B C D E F G H I J K L M N O P Q R S T U V W X Y Z
 || ||
 || ||   A B C D E F G H I J K L M N O P Q R S T U V W X Y Z
 || ||   A B C D E F G H I J K L M N O P Q R S T U V W X Y Z
 || ||
 || ||   A B C D E F G H I J K L M N O P Q R S T U V W X Y Z
 || ||   A B C D E F G H I J K L M N O P Q R S T U V W X Y Z
 || ||
 || ||   A B C D E F G H I J K L M N O P Q R S T U V W X Y Z
 || ||   A B C D E F G H I J K L M N O P Q R S T U V W X Y Z
 || ||
 || ||
 || ||
 || ||
 || ||
 || ||
 || ||
 || ||
 || ||
 || ||
 || ||
 || ||
 || ||
 || ||
 || ||
 \|  |/
  \  /
   \/
   !
```

Dictionary Drive is a long, winding road lined with trees whose branches lead to leaves, the leaves of books. Without the definitions in the roots of those trees, the books would have no meaning. But even with those roots, is there really meaning?

One of the prime directives of wordplay is that the words must be found in a published source. Otherwise, they could be made up on the spot, reducing the wordplay to a trivial pursuit. Another prime directive is that there are always exceptions.

Sources can include dictionaries of all types, atlases, phone books, census records, and just about any other printed material. When unusual words are used, or when a text relies on a special word list, the source should be cited. The source cited most often is the dictionary.

But does the dictionary—any dictionary—do one of its most important jobs: does it define words beyond the shadow of a doubt? Or does the doubt of a shadow cross each page? Because words are used to define other words, nothing is really defined. Still, we understand what they say.

The people who live on Dictionary Drive enjoy looking through the *Webster's Second Unabridged* for the surprises it conceals, such as these curiosities:

DOIT: to go about stupidly

LOVE: to appraise

NAKED LADY: the meadow saffron *Colchicum autumnale*

SPRUNNY: sweetheart; lover

TIG: to run about, as cattle pestered by flies

Then they try to fit them into sentences, like this one: "I gave my sprunny a naked lady, which she loved at ten dollars, and I doited and tigged around her in joy."

Many forms of written wordplay use dictionaries as official word lists to verify a word's existence and to determine its spelling. A few words have such outstanding spellings that they become a part of the lore of wordplay.

Let's go into the courthouse and look up some of the entries in Webster's Book of Word Records.

WORD RECORDS FROM *WEBSTER'S THIRD*

Words make records and break them. They compete with each other to be the longest, the shortest, the greatest, the most extreme in some way. They're hidden in dictionaries, waiting for people to discover them.

Chris Cole put together a list of record-breaking words selected from the largest American dictionary, *Webster's Third Unabridged*, and from *12,000 Words: A Supplement to Webster's Third*.

Twenty-five of the record-holding entries appear below. The number in parentheses at the end of each entry is a count of the letters.

1. Longest word: pneumonoultramicroscopicsilicovolcanoconiosis (45)
2. Longest palindrome: kinnikinnik (11)
3. Longest tautonym (consecutive letters repeated): tangantangan (12)
4. Most consecutive double letters: bookkeeper (3)
5. Most repeated letters: possessionlessnesses (9—the letter S)
6. Longest isogram (no letters repeated): dermatoglyphics (15)
7. Longest word with all vowels: eau (3)
8. Longest word with each vowel once: subcontinental (14); (with Y) abstemiously (12)
9. Shortest word with each vowel once: sequoia (7); (with Y) facetiously (11)
10. Longest word with one vowel only: strengths (9)
11. Longest univocalic (one vowel repeated throughout): defenselessnesses (17)
12. Longest word with one consonant repeated throughout: assesses (8)
13. Longest alternating vowel-consonant word: supererogatorily (16)
14. Longest consonant string in a word: catchphrase (6)
15. Longest word with letters in order: aegilops (8)
16. Longest word with letters in reverse order: sponged (7)
17. Longest word with letters from first half of alphabet: hamamelidaceae (14)
18. Longest word with letters from last half: nonsupports (11)
19. Word with most consecutive letters mixed throughout: perquisition (7—O,P,Q,R,S,T,U)
20. Longest beheadable word (remove first letter for new word): (p)redetermination (16)
21. Longest curtailable word (remove last letter for new word), not a plural: bulletin(g) (9)
22. Longest reversal: desserts, stressed (8)
23. Longest anagram (transposal): cinematographer, megachiropteran (15)
24. Longest one-syllable word: squirrelled (11)
25. Longest sequence of silent letters: brougham (4—U,G,H,A)

EXTRA RECORDS

Richard Lederer collected a list of record breakers from different sources. They, too, show the long and the short of English.

1. Longest palindrome string within a word: sensuousnes(s) (11)
2. Shortest word with each vowel once in an unbroken string: miaoued (7)
3. Word with most consecutive letters in order throughout: ambuscade: (5—A,B,C,D,E)
4. Word with most consecutive letters in order in an unbroken string: over-stuffed (4—R,S,T,U)
5. Longest pair isogram (each letter appearing twice): shanghaiings (12)
6. Longest pyramid word (formed of a single letter, two letters, three letters, etc.): sleeveless (10—V, LL, SSS, EEEE)
7. Longest snowball word (separating into a single letter, a 2-letter word, a 3-letter word, etc.): temperamentally (15—t, em, per, amen, tally)
8. Longest binade (odd letters form one word, even letters form another): triennially (11—tinnily, renal)
9. Longest letter-sound word (letter rebus): expediency (5 syllables—XPDNC)

THE UGLIEST WORD

What is the ugliest word in the English language? I feel that REPULSIVE is rather repulsive. On the other hand, HIDEOUS seems quite hideous. I also find OFFENSIVE very, very offensive. But none of those three is the ugliest. My immediate response is that UGLIEST is the ugliest.

However, when I think about it, UGLIER is even uglier than UGLIEST, and it's also uglier than UGLY. That means UGLIER is the UGLIEST of the three, which makes UGLIER and UGLIEST synonyms, and so UGLIER doesn't really exist.

But that would make UGLIEST more ugly than UGLY. In other words, of the two, UGLIEST is UGLIER. But if UGLIEST is UGLIER and if UGLIER does not exist, then neither does UGLIEST. So it all boils down to UGLY. And UGLY certainly isn't the ugliest word in English.

I'll opt for KAKKAK instead.

Or LUGUBRIOUS, PHLEGM, GUTTURAL, PERSIMMON, FOOFOORAW, BLUDGEON, and TEENSY-WEENSY. Also CALIGINOUSNESS, TAXES, EPISTEMOLOGY, FLICK, UMBRAGE, OOF, and SKUNK.

All other words range from being sort of pretty (such as DIN, BEAK, or THE) to extremely beautiful (like PELLUCID, NEBULA, or FRESHET). But that's my own subjective opinion.

Psychological experience could be a factor influencing the choice. LOVE may be the ugliest word if a person has been unloved; on the other hand, EAT wouldn't be the ugliest word just because a person has been uneaten.

I have stronger feelings about French. The French word for "happy" is to my mind one of the ugliest words ever to be uttered on the face of the earth: HEUREUX. In spite of its meaning, it sounds like you're throwing up when you say it. To me, "Je suis heureux" translates as "I am blaaaaaaggghhh!"

THE THIEF OF WORDS

English steals shamelessly from other languages, and sometimes the new word looks like, sounds like, and means like a word already in the language. The most incriminating evidence of such looting is the next set of words, all referring to a celebration. The first nine can be found in *Webster's Second Unabridged*, and the tenth can be found driving down the highway.

FEAST	Middle English
FESTIVAL	Old French
FESTIVITY	Old French
FETE	French
FEST	German
FESTA	Italian
FESTINE	Italian
FESTINO	Italian
FIESTA	Spanish
FESTIVA	New Ford

English, you thief of language, does your beauty lie in your booty?

DANIEL'S A NURDY, TIDDLING WRETCHOCK, DOLL!

Jeff Grant found the words below in the *English Dialect Dictionary*. They're all synonyms with a very specific meaning. If you define one, you define all. What are they? (Answer Alley)

anthony	doll	nisgol	runnock
barling	ducky	nurdy	tiddling
cadma	gramfer	pedman	treseltrype
croot	greck	poke-shakings	wankling
crowly	harry	rinklin	wretchock
dalling	kerdidwin	rit	wrig
daniel	nesquaw		

PLURAL EYES

Unlike other dictionaries, *Pears Advanced Word Puzzler's Dictionary*, edited by Peter Newby, revels in unusual words, words that sometimes have amusing quirks.

Among the quirkiest, XENIA and XENIUM stand out like Tweedledum and Tweedledee. XENIA is "the supposed influence of foreign pollen upon that pollinated," and XENIUM is "a present given to a guest or stranger." However, the plural of one is the singular of the other:

Singular	Plural
XENIA	XENIUM
XENIUM	XENIA

THE BERMUDA TRIANGLE OF DEFINITIONS

Newby found these three definitions in the original *Pears Dictionary* published over fifty years ago. To paraphrase the song, "You can't have one without the others."

ANT: n. emmet or pismire

EMMET: n. ant or pismire

PISMIRE: n. ant or emmet

FLIP-FLOP DEFINITIONS

Using verbal sleight-of-hand, *Webster's Second Unabridged* defines LION ANT as "an ant lion" and MILE-TON as "a ton-mile." If only every word were so easy to define! Here are a few that *Webster's* missed. The list doesn't include pairs that rely on puns, such as TIMEPIECE = PEACETIME. That's for another time.

CAST IRON = IRON CAST

CAT HOUSE = HOUSE CAT

DRESSING TABLE = TABLE DRESSING

GRADE SCHOOL = SCHOOL GRADE
PLAYER PIANO = PIANO PLAYER
SHOTGUN = GUNSHOT
SPACE BAR = BAR SPACE
TIME TRAVEL = TRAVEL TIME

WONE FOR THE BOOKS

WONE is a word like no other, a singularity of language. According to *Webster's Second Unabridged*, it is actually two words, both spelling variants of two familiar words, ONE and WON. ONE is formed by dropping the initial letter, and WON by dropping the final letter: W(ON)E. All three words have the same pronuncation.

Thanks to the mighty WONE, these four sentences mean and sound exactly alike:

I WON ONE.
I WON WONE.
I WONE ONE.
I WONE WONE.

WINING AND DINING WITH THE DICTIONARY

If you set your table according to *Webster's Tenth Collegiate*, you'll have a well-defined meal, but in some cases it may be too well defined. Sometimes the words are over-cooked:

COLLOP is a contronym (a word having opposite meanings). Its two definitions are: (1) "a small piece or slice esp. of meat"; and (2) "a fold of fat flesh." If you're served a steak that's mostly fat, you can cut off the COLLOP and eat the COLLOP.

NOGGIN has three definitions: (1) "a small mug or cup"; (2) "a small quantity of drink"; (3) "a person's head." You could say that a NOGGIN of NOGGIN might go to your NOGGIN.

And there's more: NOGGIN splits into two other drinks, NOG and GIN. Cheers!

THE BEAST WITHIN

In the Language Jungle, animal names hide within words unrelated to the animal kingdom. All of the words in this list come from *Webster's Tenth Collegiate*. Can you fill in the blanks with the names of twenty-six different animals to make longer, nonanimal words? For starters, AM___ is AMASS. (Answer Alley)

AM___	HEAT___	OF____	UNDER___
BILLY____	IN___	PSEUDO____	VA_____
COM___	JU___	QUAR____	WOLF___
DR___	KEB____	RAM____	X___
ES____	LUMM__	SAW_____	YARD___
FOR____	MAN_____	TIP___	ZIL____
GENT___	NIGHT____		

THE WILD GOOSE FLIES AT NINETEEN O'CLOCK

Sometimes dictionaries play word games. *The Pocket Webster's* defines NINETEEN as "one more than eighteen." Look up EIGHTEEN and you'll find "one more than seventeen." And so it goes, all the way down to ONE, "the number denoting unity."

If you look up UNITY, you'll see that it's "the quality or state of being one." Don't try looking up MILLION.

TRICTIONARY

Trictionary challenges you to make just one sentence using the dictionary as a starting point. Here's how to do it:

Open the dictionary randomly and point to a boldface entry. Using it and the next four different entries in order, try writing a sentence. Add your own words to weave the fivesome together.

Chances are you'll wind up with unusual sentences like those below, which use words from *Webster's Seventh Collegiate*. Actually, the fourth sentence doesn't sound too different from what you might read in a linguistics textbook.

FOLDAWAY, FOLDBOAT, FOLDER, FOLDEROL, FOLDING DOORS.

> The foldaway bed on the foldboat was strewn with folders full of folderol about folding doors.

MADRAS, MADREPORE, MADRIGAL, MADRILENE, MADRONA.

> They lost the shipment of madras on the huge madrepores because the crewmen were singing madrigals, sipping madrilenes, and sitting on madronas.

NIPPY, NIP-UP, NIRVANA, NISAN, NISEI. I did a nippy nip-up to nirvana during Nisan with a nisei.

ONOMASTICS, ONOMATOPOEIA, ONONDAGA, ONRUSH, ONSET. According to one theory of onomastics, onomatopoeia among the Onondaga preceded the onrush of speech that led to the onset of language.

WRYNECK, WUD, WULFENITE, WUNDERKIND, WURST. The wryneck made wud sounds on the wulfenite as the wunderkind ate wurst.

EXCESS X'S

In this story, an all-inclusive form of Trictionary, Joyce Holland used every X entry from *Webster's Tenth Collegiate* along with a few of her own words.

"X out X!" I exhorted to Xanadu. "Xanthan gum tastes like xanthate, and xanthene is covered with xanthene dye."

"Xanthine," Xanthippe explained, "feels like xanthone."

"Xanthophyll!" the Xaverian Brother exclaimed.

The x-axis around the X band near the X chromosome crossed the x-coordinate like a xebec. Then the xenia, as a xenobiotic, avoided xenodiagnosis, but the xenogeneic xenograft fell off the xenolith.

"Xenon!" the xenophile exhaled.

Xenophobia mirrored the xenotropic, a xeric Xeriscape of *xeroderma pigmentosum.* Xerography? The xerophilous xerophthalmia of a xerophyte defied my xeroradiography. It was too xerothermic.

"I xeroxed the Xerox at the x-height!" the Xhosa exulted.

Xi at the x-intercept of the xiphisternum showed both the xiphoid and the xiphoid process. X-irradiation at Xmas removed x-radiation from my X-rated Xray.

I once x-rayed an X ray. When I studied X-ray astronomy, I learned that the X-ray diffraction of an X-ray star was a form of X-ray therapy. The X-ray tube lit up the x-section of the xu I swallowed. It tasted like xylan or xylem.

The xylem ray melted the xylene in xylidine. Soon, xylitol sweetened the xylography of xylol. From that day on, I played the xylophagous xylophone covered with xylose.

DICTIONARY MYSTERY STORY

It was a stark and dormy night. I was all alone in the library of my mansion. I'd just come back from playing a good game, and I wanted to relax with an equally good book. Suddenly I heard something outside—CLINK-CLANK, CLINK-CLANK. I rushed to the dictionary to find out what the sound meant. Unfortunately, it meant itself. Then I heard a noise in the drawing room—PLOCK! I looked up the word, but it, too, meant itself.

I crept into the drawing room in time to see a burglar climbing in the window. He was holding a chain in one hand and reaching to retrieve his black leather bag with the other. Apparently he'd dropped it on the floor. I needed a weapon to stop the intruder, and I realized I was still clutching *Webster's Second Unabridged*, a formidable weapon in itself.

"SHOO!" I shouted across the room, and he replied "WHOA!" in surprise and tumbled in. Before he could get up, I rushed at him—WHISH!—and slammed the unabridged—CHUNK!—down on his head. He sprawled on the floor like a cheap paperback thesaurus.

I turned on the light and called the cops. Trembling, I looked up SHOO, WHOA, WHISH, and CHUNK, but like the other two words, they meant themselves.

"WHEW!" I said, realizing that if all the words that defined themselves weren't listed in the dictionary, it wouldn't have weighed enough to stop a gerbil. As an afterthought, I looked up WHEW.

Here are the definitions of those lifesaving words:

CHUNK: v.i. to make the noise represented by the pronunciation of *chunk*

CLINK-CLANK: n. a noise made up of clinks and clanks

PLOCK: v.i. to make a sound suggestive of the word *plock*

SHOO: v.i. to cry "shoo!"

WHEW: n. an utterance of "whew"

WHISH: n. a slight sound, as of one saying "whish"

WHOA: v.i. to call "whoa!"

But there's still a mystery. In the first paragraph, the hero mentioned playing a "good game." What game was it? Clue: one word in the story names the game in its definition. (Answer Alley)

DI VERSE

When Princess Di(ana) married Prince Charles, they fascinated the world. Now, although no longer a couple, they still make the headlines. Their romance is even chronicled in *Webster's Second Unabridged*. From the faint stirring of love to the final dissolving of marriage, words beginning with "dis-" tell a sad tale indeed:

Disinterested? Di's interested.
Dishonest? Di's honest.
Disrespectful? Di's respectful.
Disloyal? Di's loyal.
Disappointed? Di's appointed.
Dispassonate? Di's passionate.
Disengaged? Di's engaged.

Discharge Di's charge.
Dispose Di's pose.
Discourage Di's courage.
Disgrace Di's grace.
Dishonor Di's honor.
Dismantle Di's mantle.
Disrobe Di's robe.

Di's satisfied? Dissatisfied.
Di's taste? Distaste.
Di's composed? Discomposed.
Di's pleasure? Displeasure.
Di's agreeable? Disagreeable.
Di's temper? Distemper.
Di's solution? Dissolution.

THE FINAL ULTIMATE CONCLUSIVE END OF ENGLISH

At last, the last word in English has been found. Grant spotted it in an *Oxford English Dictionary* citation. It represents the sound of snoring, but how do the editors know that it's spelled with exactly forty-three Zs? Does each Z represent one vibration of the uvula and the soft palate? Has it ever been asked in a spelling bee? Is a child's snore spelled with fewer Zs? Think about it. It'll put you . . . to . . . (yawn . . .)

ZZZZZZZZZZZZZZZZZZZZZZZZZZZZZZZZZZZZZZZZZZZZ

THE WIND IN THE WORDS

A strong breeze is shaking the branches of the trees. The leaves of the dictionaries stir, rustle, and flap in the wind. It's time to move on before all the words blow away.

At the end of the street, the stop sign has STOP spelled in Webster symbols to show how it's pronounced.

Chapter H

Word Square

THE MOSAIC WORD WALKS

WORD SQUARE ENCIRCLES, or ensquares, a park in the center. Just beyond the hedges, the intricate Mosaic Word Walks, with letters set in different shapes, wind through the well-trimmed lawn. The most common shape is the square, but other shapes—triangles, diamonds, crosses, stars—nestle among the flowers.

Word squares are arrangements of letters that make words of equal length horizontally and vertically. Before the invention of the crossword puzzle, word squares occupied a respected place in the puzzle pages of magazines and newspapers.

At first they really were puzzles—blank grids with clues for the reader to solve. Unlike crossword puzzles, they had no black squares separating the words. Nowadays, word squares are usually presented without grids or clues.

We come to a wrought-iron gate with a pattern formed by the letters in the phrase AH, OMEN engraved in its bars. Wherever the bars intersect, the letters form two-letter squares with words from *Webster's Second Unabridged*:

```
        A H              E M                  O N              A H
      A       H        E          M      O      N      A          H
   A              H E                  M O              N A              H
   N              E H                  O M              A N              E
     N          E        H          O        M        A        N        E
       N E              H O                  M A              N E
       E N              O H                  A M              E N
     E          N        O        H        A        M        E        N
   E              N O              H A                  M E              N
   M              O N              A H                  E M              O
       M        O        N        A        H        E        M        O
       M O              N A              H E                  M O
       O M              A N              E H                  O M
     O        M        A        N        E        H        O        M
   O              M A              N E                  H O              M
   H              A M              E N                  O H              A
       H A              M E              N O                  H A
       A H              E M              O N                  A H
   A              H E                  M O              N A              H
   N              E H                  O M              A N              E
     N          E        H          O        M        A        N        E
       N E              H O                  M A              N E
       E N              O H                  A M              E N
     E          N        O        H        A        M        E        N
   E              N O              H A                  M E              N
   M              O N              A H                  E M              O
       M        O        N        A        H        E        M        O
       M O              N A              H E                  M O
       O M              A N              E H                  O M
     O        M        A        N        E        H        O        M
   O              M A              N E                  H O              M
   H              A M              E N                  O H              A
       H A              M E              N O                  H A
```

We slowly open it and enter the park. First we'll view some of the squares, and then we'll take the Word Walks to the Garden of Wordplay Delights to see some of the most incredible forms ever constructed.

THE EAT SQUARE

The simple square on the left is constructed of three-letter words familiar to most children. When I was in third grade, my teacher printed it on the blackboard as an example of a word square:

```
E A T          A T E          T E A
A T E          T E A          E A T
T E A          E A T          A T E
```

Because its words are also anagrams of each other, the square has a special property: each word starts its own rearranged version of the same square, as shown.

THE OLDEST WORD SQUARE IN THE WORLD

Archaeologists and historians have found an ancient inscription that keeps popping up in Roman ruins. Carved on walls or sculpted into fountains, it's a palindromic word square composed in Latin. If the words are written in a single line, it reads the same in both directions: SATOR AREPO TENET OPERA ROTAS.

```
S A T O R
A R E P O
T E N E T
O P E R A
R O T A S
```

```
            A
            P
            A
            T
            E
            R
A P A T E R N O S T E R O
            O
            S
            T
            E
            R
            O
```

The letters can also be rearranged to form a cross that has the first two words of "The Lord's Prayer" and the letters A and O in both directions. A and O stand for "Alpha" and "Omega," referring to the Christian belief that God is the "Alpha" and the "Omega," the beginning and the end, of all things.

One problem continues to bedevil Latin scholars: what does AREPO mean? Dmitri Borgmann suggested that it was someone's name, and he translated the line in this way: "The sower, Arepo, guides the wheels with care."

No one knows its purpose. Was it an early piece of graffiti, like "Kilroy Was Here"? Or was it a secret Christian symbol whose meaning has been lost to the ages? The *Dictionary of Satanism* gives a strangely practical view: it can be used for finding witches, making wishes, putting out fires, and other magical things.

SINGLE AND DOUBLE SQUARES

Word squares come in two different varieties. The single square has the same set of words going across and down. The double square has two different sets, one across and one down. Double squares are more difficult to construct.

Below on the left, the single square, by "H.E.P.," was one of the earliest in English, published in the London journal *Notes and Queries* in 1859. On the right, the double square, by "Imperial," was the first of its kind, appearing in the American publication *Our Boys* in 1871.

```
A I S L E        T E R M
I D I O M        A L O E
S I E V E        P L A T
L O V E R        S A M E
E M E R Y
```

SQUARES TO THE NINES

Word square constructors, called formists, measure the size of a square according to the number of letters on a side (or the number of words going in the same direction). A five-square has five letters (or words), a six-square has six, and so on. Up to size six, they're fairly easy to construct.

After that, construction becomes difficult, and the difficulty increases geometrically with size. According to master formist Palmer Peterson, an eight-square is about ten times harder to make than a seven-square, and a nine-square ten times harder than an eight-square. A double eight-square, he believed, is about as difficult as a single nine-square. About the possibility of constructing a double nine-square, Peterson said, "Nil! Absolutely and positively nil!"

The selection below includes squares of both types in a variety of sizes. All the words in the single eight-square appear in the *Oxford English Dictionary*.

1. Single six
   (Langdon Root, 1871)
   ```
   S C I O N S
   C A T N I P
   I T H A C A
   O N A G E R
   N I C E S T
   S P A R T A
   ```

2. Single seven
   ("Skeeziks," 1877)
   ```
   C A M A R G O
   A T O N E R S
   M O T I V E S
   A N I L I N E
   R E V I V A L
   G R E N A D E
   O S S E L E T
   ```

3. Single eight
   (Jeff Grant, 1989)
   ```
   M A T R I C A L
   A C I E R A G E
   T I R V I N G S
   R E V I S O R S
   I R I S H I A N
   C A N O I S T E
   A G G R A T E S
   L E S S N E S S
   ```

4. Single nine
   (Arthur F. Holt, 1897)
   ```
   Q U A R E L E S T
   U P P E R E S T E
   A P P O I N T E R
   R E O M E T E R S
   E R I E V I L L E
   L E N T I L L I N
   E S T E L L I N E
   S T E R L I N G S
   T E R S E N E S S
   ```

5. Double six
   (Palmer Peterson, in *The Enigma*, 1972)
   ```
   P A N A D A
   O B E L U S
   M A C L E S
   A T T U N E
   D E O D A R
   E R N E S T
   ```

6. Double seven
   (Holt, in *The Enigma*, 1921)
   ```
   M A R A R I E
   I D O L I N G
   S E M E N C E
   A L A R G E S
   V I N C E N T
   E N C E N S E
   R E E S T E D
   ```

THE "IMPOSSIBLE" TEN-SQUARE

To the formist, constructing a well-formed ten-square is the greatest challenge of all. Such a mythical square would require going beyond dictionaries to any printed sources of English words. But what about these two ten-squares?

```
O R A N G U T A N G          A S T R A L I S E D
R E N G A R E N G A          S C H O L A R I T Y
A N D O L A N D O L          T H Y L A C I N E S
N G O T A N G O T A          R O L Y N A D E R S
G A L A N G A L A N          A L A N B R O W N E
U R A N G U T A N G          L A C A R O L I N A
T A N G A T A N G A          I R I D O L I N E S
A N D O L A N D O L          S I N E W I N E S S
N G O T A N G O T A          E T E R N N E S S E
G A L A N G A L A N          D Y S S E A S S E S
```

M. J. Sheedy constructed the left square in 1876. It uses two tricks to achieve its success. It repeats three words in each direction, and it resorts to using variant spellings of the same word—ORANGUTANG and URANGUTANG. Clever, but most formists don't believe it fulfills the requirements for a well-built ten-square.

Going to a variety of sources, Jeff Grant constructed several ten-squares with varying degrees of success. In the ASTRALISED square on the previous page, the only nondictionary words are the names of real people, ROLY NADERS (in plural) and ALAN BROWNE. LA CAROLINA appears in a geographical dictionary. Better than Sheedy's square, but it still isn't a perfect ten.

Someday a ten-square will be found, and then the search will begin for the impossible eleven-square.

PALINDROMIC AND REVERSAL SQUARES

In 1871, Nellie Jones created the first palindromic square in English. It can be read in all four directions—right, left, up, and down. Here are two views:

```
S T E W        W E T S
T I D E        E D I T
E D I T        T I D E
W E T S        S T E W
```

Jones's square is a palindromic single. Ross Eckler showed that there are four different types of squares that use reversal words, and he constructed three-square and four-square examples of each:

palindromic single	palindromic double	reversal single	reversal double
A T E	D A B	P A T	P A R
T O T	E V E	A R E	I T A
E T A	B A D	T E N	N E T
S T E P	S N A P	S L A P	S L A G
T I D E	L A N A	L A N A	N A V E
E D I T	A N A L	A N A N	A N A T
P E T S	P A N S	P A N S	P A L S

In palindromic squares, the words going in the same direction form a palindromic set: ATE-TOT-ETA. In reversal squares, the words form a different set of words in reverse: PAT-ARE-TEN = NET-ERA-TAP. For single squares, the horizontal and the vertical words are the same; for double squares, they're different.

WORD-UNIT PALINDROMIC SQUARES

A word-unit palindromic square consists of palindromic words only, and this means that words have to be repeated. The examples below show three kinds. The word ZZZ is from the *Random House Unabridged*.

word unit palindromic single	word unit palindromic double	total palindromic single
A B A	P A P	Z Z Z
S I S	A L A	Z Z Z
A B A	P A P	Z Z Z

ANAGRAM WORD SQUARES

Peter Newby constructed the first anagram double square, in which all the words are anagrams of each other. Reversing the letters horizontally produces the second square below, a single square.

Reversing the second square vertically makes the third, another double square, and reversing the third horizontally makes the fourth, another single.

The series can also be formed by rotating each square ninety degrees counterclockwise to generate the next one in the sequence. Rotating the last one results in the first.

double	single	double	single
E A R	R A E	E R A	A R E
R E A	A E R	A E R	R E A
A R E	E R A	R A E	E A R

All six combinations of the letters A, E, and R form words. They can be assembled into a total of twelve different squares, including the four above.

STATE SQUARES

Squares don't have to be made of words. In these squares, each pair of adjacent letters forms a state postal abbreviation in both directions. For instance, the letters N M N V would connect three abbreviations, NM, MN, and NV.

The double three-square on the left has all different abbreviations, twelve of them, across and down. It's the only state square of any size that doesn't repeat an abbreviation. In comparison, the double four-square on the right repeats twelve of its twenty-four abbreviations.

The NMNV square is by Tom Pulliam, and the INCA square is by Ross Eckler. Other four-squares can be made, but they are variations formed by changing one or at most two abbreviations in the four below.

double three	single four	single four	single four	double four
N M N	N M N V	I N C A	T N M A	M I N V
C O H	M S C A	N M O R	N C O R	T N M A
A R I	N C O K	C O H I	M O H I	N C O K
	V A K Y	A R I A	A R I N	V A K Y

MORSE CODE SQUARES AND MORE

The dots and dashes of Morse code can make word squares and other forms having properties absent from the usual alphabetic squares. Morse squares omit the spaces separating the sets of dots and dashes that stand for letters. Because of this, the same Morse symbol can convert to different strings of letters.

This Morse six-square has at least two possible decodings for each set of dots and dashes. The first row (and column) can mean DO or TEAM, the second row (and column) PI or ADE, and so on.

Morse single six	alternative decodings	
_ · · _ _ _	DO (_ ·· ___)	TEAM (_ · ·_ __)
· _ _ · · ·	PI (· __ · ··)	ADE (·_ _·· ·)
· _ _ · · _	AX (· _ _··_)	WIT (· __ ·· _)
_ · · · · _	BET (_··· · _)	TEST (_ · ··· _)
_ · · · · ·	THE (_ ···· ·)	BEE (_··· · ·)
_ · _ _ · _	YET (_·_ · _)	TEMA (_ · _ ·_)

The dot and dash halfsquare below decodes differently in three directions. Across, left to right: TAR, TENT, TEN, K, N, T. Across, right to left: ART, AET, ETA, R, A, E. Down (and up): TOM, IS, TO, S, M, E.

The all-dot pyramid decodes the same in all three directions. Progressing from one dot to ten, the lines read: E, I, S, H, HE, HI, ESS, SHE, HIS, ISIS.

dot and dash halfsquare   all-dot pyramid

```
—                                         ·
— ·                                     ·   ·
— · —                                 ·   ·   ·
— · — ·                             ·   ·   ·   ·
— · — · —                         ·   ·   ·   ·   ·
— · — · — ·                     ·   ·   ·   ·   ·   ·
                              ·   ·   ·   ·   ·   ·   ·
                            ·   ·   ·   ·   ·   ·   ·   ·
                          ·   ·   ·   ·   ·   ·   ·   ·   ·
                        ·   ·   ·   ·   ·   ·   ·   ·   ·   ·
```

IN THE GARDEN OF WORDPLAY DELIGHTS

While the regular word square is the most popular, other forms have appeared in the pages of journals and books. In many cases, the formist had to make up the form and then find the words to construct it.

This display begins with simple geometric forms, progresses to compound forms, and concludes with a masterpiece by Palmer Peterson, the Picasso of formists. These incredible forms and many more appear in *Words at Play: Quips, Quirks and Oddities,* by O. V. Michaelsen.

1. inverted halfsquare ("Pen Ledcil," 1899)

```
A G G R E S S I O N
G R E E N H O R N
G E L A T I N E
R E A D I N G
E N T I T Y
S H I N Y
S O N G
I R E
O N
N
```

2. diamond (Edward William Dutcher, 1879)

```
          M
        M A P
      P A N E D
    P E N I C I L
  M A N I P U L A R
M A N I P U L A T E D
  P E C U L A T E D
    D I L A T E D
      L A T E D
        R E D
          D
```

3. left rhomboid (J. A. Haddock, 1875)

```
C O L L A T E R A L
  N E U R O S O M E S
    D E C K T E N N I S
      S E K E R I N G E S
        S E M I S I N G L E
          R E V I L E M E N T
            S E D I M E N T A L
              R E T E N D E R E D
                S E N T E N T I A E
                  S T A R T E R O F F
```

4. hexagon (George
Haywood, 1883)

```
  C O O L S
 M A R R O W
S I R N A M E
M I S D A T E D
C A R D A M I N E
O R N A M E N T
O R A T I N G
 L O M E N T
  S W E D E
```

5. double diagonal star
(Morton G. Lloyd, 1894)

```
      P
      A A
S E S M S E S
  H T P P T H
  O E U E O
  R R R R R R
S E T N T E S
      E E
      N
```

6. Maltese cross ("Will
O' The Wisp," 1888)

```
    C A R E W
    B E D
C   L O V E R   S
A B O M I N A T E
R E V I C T I O N
E D E N T A T E D
W   R A I T H   S
    T O E
    S E N D S
```

7. compound octagon
(Levi G. De Lee, 1879)

```
    C A R       R E D
  C A D E S   C A P E L
C A L A M A R A D I C A L
A D A L I N E P I D O T E
R E M I P E D E C O Y E D
S A N E R   L A T E R
  R E D       L E D
  M E L E E   G E M E L
R E F U S A L E V E R E T
E L U S I V E M E L I N E
D E S I R E D E R I V E D
  E A V E S   L E N E S
    L E D       T E D
```

8. diamond cross ("Pen Ledcil," 1882)

```
        S               E
        C O G           H O D
      B O A R D       H E L E D
      C O M P A R E   H E M I N A S
S O A P S T O N E O L I P I L E
      G R A T I N G A D E N I Z E N
      D R O N E E R E D A L E S
      E N G R A T E R S E N
        E A R T H P E A S
      A N D E E P E S T E A
    U R G E D R E S S E A R S
  A R G O L I S A T E N D R A C
E N G O T I N E S E A D R A G O
    D E L I V E R   A R R A Y E D
      D I N E S       S A G E S
      S E R           C O D
      S               N
```

9. connected diamonds with square in center (J. A. Haddock, 1877)

```
              R
            R I B
            R I V E R
            B E Y
              R
    O       V E S T A       S
  A C T     E N T E R     A H A
O C E A N S T E A M S H I P S
  T A X     T E A S E     A P T
    N       A R M E D       S
              B
            B O A
          B O A T S
            A T E
              S
```

10. Salem cross ("Private," 1883)

```
            H A L F
            A R I A
            L I O N
      L E A F A N G R A M
      E D N A V E R O S E
      A N O N E V A S K S
      F A N G R A M E S S
            R O V E
            A V E R
A R E S H A M E R E N D S T E M
R U T H I D E V E N E A T A M E
E T N A D A R E A D A C E M I T
S H A M E R E N D S T E M E T E
            N O R A
            D R A M
      P A S S A M E R A S
      A R E A M I R E N T
      S E A M I C A N T I
      S A M E R A S T I R
            R E S T
            A S H Y
            S T Y X
```

II. the armless man (Palmer Peterson, 1943)

```
              A S P A R A M I D
              S T O N E C O L E
              P O P A F A L L S
              A N A C A R D I A
              R E F A N N I N G
              A C A R N A N I A
              M O L D I N E S S
              I L L I N I S S A
              D E S A G A S A N
                A R E P A
                T E A R Y
                A C L I S
          P A R I E T A L L O B U L E S
          U P E L L E T I E R I N E S E
          R A P I L E E N G I N E S I N
          P R A M A D I D A T E S A N S
          L A R A S E N A T O R A N C E
          E L A R A D E N E R E N G E L
          J U G G L E D U S A L T I R E
          A M O R A D O S Y L U A N E S
          C I N E M A S I T A M P A N S
          O N I V A L U N E S E E R E N
          B I T E N A N C R A S E I S E
          A T E S A R T E N T E S E S S
          E E S O R D I C I T I E S E S
          A S U P R E M E N E S S E S E
          S E A S I D E R A D I S H E S
        A O T E A R O A   C A S C A N T A
      A N T I A R I N     N S E N T A R U
    V I A T E C T A       I N D E X I N G
    P O R T U N U S       E U R I S T I C
  B I R L I N N S         B A G T A B L E
F L O R A N G E           L O O P L I N E
P O U N A W E A           E N S A I N T S
```

About the last form, Eckler wrote: "The 'Armless Man' consists of two squares, two rhomboids, and four pyramids. Note that the S at the center is shared by a pyramid and two rhomboids. This form has been justly termed 'outstanding' and 'remarkable,' requiring great ingenuity . . . and a pertinacity that very few have."

THE END SQUARE

Up ahead, the sign with the word square on it signals the end of Word Square. It tells us to pause for a moment and try constructing our own squares.

Chapter I

Pangrammatic Highway

THE PANGRAM MEMORIAL STATUE

ON THE NEXT street, a row of signs lines the side of the road. The first sign has A on it, the second has B, the third C, and so on to Z. Together they measure the Pangrammatic Highway. A pangram is a sentence with all twenty-six letters of the alphabet in it.

On the hill in the distance, a twenty-six-foot-high quartz statue rises above the mud. It's the Pangram Memorial Statue, erected in memory of the English mathematician Augustus de Morgan. In 1872, he made up the first pangram:

I, QUARTZ PYX, WHO FLING MUCK BEDS.

```
      Q
      Q
 I  Q A    PYX   WHO
 I  QU     PYX   WHO
 I,  Q     PYX   WHO
 I,  QU    PYX   WHO
 I,  QU    PYX   WHO
 I,  QU  TZ PYX  WHO FL
 I,  QU    PYX   WHO
 I,  QU    PYX   WHO
 I,  QU    PYX   WHO
 I,  QUA    YX   WH
   ,  QUAR   X   W
      QUARTZ PYX, WHO FLING M
       UARTZ PYX, WHO FLING MU
        ARTZ PYX, WHO FLING MUC
        ARTZ PYX, WHO FLING MUCK
        ARTZ PYX, WHO FLING MUCK B
        ARTZ PYX, WHO FLIN  MUCK BE
        ARTZ PYX, WHO FLIN   UCK BED
        ARTZ PYX, WHO FLIN    CK BEDS
        ARTZ PYX, WHO FLIN     K BEDS.
        ARTZ PYX, WHO FLIN     K BEDS
        ARTZ PYX, WHO FLIN     K BED
         RTZ PYX, WHO FLIN    CK BE
         RTZ PYX, WHO _____MUCK B_____
         RTZ PYX, WHO(_) ... .UCK B... )
         RTZ PYX, WHO  | . ...UCK .... |
         RTZ PYX  WHO  | ... ....... . |
         RTZ PYX  WHO  | .. ... ...... |
         RTZ PYX  WHO  | ... .. . .. . |
           Z PYX  WHO  | . ... . ..... |
           Z PYX  WHO  | .... . .. .. . |
           Z PYX  WHO  | .. .... ...... |
           Z PYX  WHO  | ... .. .. .. . |
           Z PYX  WHO  |
           Z PYX  WHO  (_)_____)
           Z PYX  WHO
          TZ PYX  WHO FL
          TZ PYX  WHO FL
          TZ PYX  WHO FL
         RTZ PYX  WHO FLI
      QUARTZ PYX  WHO FLING
 I, QUARTZ PYX, WHO FLING MUCK BEDS.
```

De Morgan realized that his pangram, like most pangrams since then, doesn't
have a clear meaning. To help the reader, he offered this explanation:

"I long thought that no human being could say this under any circumstances. At last I happened to be reading a religious writer—as he thought himself—who threw aspersions on his opponents thick and threefold. Heyday! came into my head, this fellow flings muck beds; he must be a quartz pyx. And then I remembered that a pyx is a sacred vessel, and quartz is a hard stone, as hard as the heart of a religious foe-curser. So that the line is the motto of the ferocious sectarian, who turns his religious vessels into mud-holders, for the benefit of those who will not see what he sees."

In his *Budget of Paradoxes*, de Morgan introduced this type of wordplay to the world, calling it "Cabala Alphabetica." His pangram seems to lack a little something—namely the letters J and V. Instead, it has an extra I and U, which were once considered to be interchangeable with the missing two. Just as John Taylor took liberties with his "Evil" palindrome in Chapter C, so de Morgan pulled an alphabetic bait-and-switch to achieve his goal.

"Hey, Buddy, can you spare a Q?" says a bedraggled, sad-looking character. He's a frustrated pangramhandler forever seeking perfection and elegance. His quest: to find a pangram that forms a natural-sounding sentence.

"The quick brown fox jumps over the lazy dog!" a woman snarls at him contemptuously as she strolls by with her Doberman. She has spoken the best-known pangram in English, but with thirty-five letters it's merely a typing exercise.

Writing pangrams is tricky business. J, Q, X, and Z, the rare letters that appear least frequently in printed text, have killed any hopes of constructing an example that resembles normal English. To include those four letters, the pangrammatist has to use words that seem to exist just to occupy dictionary space.

The De Morgan Memorial Statue holds a tablet with the Full Alphabet Honor Roll, containing the best pangrams ever composed, engraved in it.

THE FULL ALPHABET HONOR ROLL

The ideal pangram uses twenty-six letters in a single sentence, has perfect grammar, contains only main-entry dictionary words, makes complete sense, but doesn't exist. Instead, to achieve the twenty-six-letter mark, writers have had to violate one or more of those principles. In spite of such flaws, the pangrams here are the classics.

Those in the first group use more than twenty-six letters. The exact counts appear in parentheses next to them.

John P. Brady, give me a black walnut box of quite a small size. (48, C. C. Bombaugh)

Pack my box with five dozen liquor jugs. (32, Anon.)

How quickly daft jumping zebras vex. (30, Anon.)

Waltz, nymph, for quick jigs vex Bud. (28, Anon.)

Bawds jog, flick quartz, vex nymph. (27, Sir Jeremy Morse)

The next pangrams stick to twenty-six letters, but they include initials and abbreviations.

J. Q. Schwartz flung V. D. Pike my box. (Dmitri Borgmann)

Mr. Jock, TV quiz Ph.D., bags few lynx. (Clement Wood)

V.D. bug left Z. Q. Jaw my rock sphinx. (Anon.)

Frowzy things plumb vex'd Jack Q. (Anon.)

For the connoisseur, here is a selection of twenty-six-letter pangrams constructed of full words (and no initials or abbreviations). Many of the words are obscure, but they're all genuine.

Pyx crwth fjeld, quok, vang, zimbs. (Rev. S. Ream)

Cwm, fjord-bank glyphs vext quiz. (Borgmann)

Zing! vext cwm fly jabs kurd qoph. (Borgmann)

Squdgy fez, blank jimp crwth vox. (David Adler or Claude Shannon)

Pyx vang quiz: komb crwth fjelds. (Robert N. Test)

The following pangrams won fame by making it into the *Guinness Book of World Records:*

Jackdaws love my big sphinx of quartz. (31, Marvin Moore)

Cwm kvutza qoph jynx fled brigs. (Greg and Peter Maggs)

Veldt jynx grimps waqf zho buck. (Anon.)

Quartz glyph job vex'd cwm finks. (Anon.)

All the words in the preceding section can be found in *Webster's Second* or *Third Unabridged* or the *Oxford English Dictionary.*

PALINDROMIC PANGRAM

Writing palindromes is a challenge, but writing pangrams is much more challenging. Combining the two might seem impossible, but Jeff Grant has written an eighty-five-letter hybrid. In it, a monk is chastizing someone, and that person reacts to the tongue-lashing:

BEWARETH GIFTS; A PYRE—VEX A TIDE;

LO! JACK NO MAZES. "YOU QUOY!" SEZ A MONK.
CAJOLED, I TAX EVERY PAST FIGHTER—A WEB!

PARODY PANGRAM

To write a parody of a famous pangram is a different kind of challenge. Peter Newby composed a twenty-six-letter takeoff of "The quick brown fox jumps over the lazy dog":

QWYK GLAZ'D VOX JUMPS FERN BITCH.

GLAZ'D is a synonym for BROWN, VOX means FOX, and FERN is defined in its former adjectival sense as ANCIENT. All are listed in the *Oxford English Dictionary*. Translation: "Quick brown fox jumps ancient female dog."

PANGRAMMATIC CROSSWORD

The crossword puzzle format offers a way around the limitations of the traditional form. Words crossing over each other can share the same letter at the intersection. Leslie Card constructed two five-word pangrammatic crosswords with entries from *Webster's Second* and *Third Unabridged*.

```
        C
        H
        L
  W A Q F        J
        M      V O X
        Y        K
      S P I T Z E N B U R G
                 D


        S
        J
      W A Q F
        M
  L     B       V
  U N C O P Y R I G H T E D
  X     K       Z
```

PANGRAM FORMULA

This formula shows another way to write a pangram. How would you interpret it?
(Answer Alley)

$$2^J - 5C \div 6k \geqq 0$$

THE PANGRAMMATIC HIGHWAY

When highway driving becomes boring and the scenery more than serene, you can play the pangrammatic highway game. The rules are simple: find all the capitalized letters of the alphabet on all the permanent official highway signs that you pass. Temporary official signs, billboards, advertising signs, bumper stickers, and license plates don't count. Select as many letters as you want from each sign, and keep track of the mileage you've covered. The goal is to complete the alphabet in the shortest distance.

Udo Pernisz invented the game with slightly different rules. His version allowed all permanent signs, official or unofficial, but required finding the letters in alphabetical order using only one letter per sign, a restriction that made the game difficult.

Faith Eckler devised the new rules and tried them out. On a trip back to New Jersey, she and her husband Ross found a pangrammatic distance of only 1.3 miles southbound on I-95 in Maryland. She wondered whether anyone could discover a pangrammatic distance of less than a mile. Here are the signs she found:

JFK HIGHWAY MONITOR CHANNEL
AUTHORIZED VEHICLES ONLY
BRIDGE SUBJECT TO CROSS WINDS
EXIT
SUSQUEHANNA STATE PARK

A few months later, Ross Eckler found a .8-mile stretch on the northbound lane of Interstate 287 that had the next group of signs. However, wordplay sightseers shouldn't go out of their way to visit this landmark. The BRIDGE FREEZES sign is gone.

WASHINGTON'S HEADQUARTERS
NO TRUCKS IN LEFT LANE
LAFAYETTE AVE.
EXIT 20 MPH
BRIDGE FREEZES BEFORE ROAD SURFACE
INTERSTATE NEW JERSEY 287

ISOGRAMS

An isogram is a word with no repeating letters. Perfect pangrams are made of isograms that have no letters in common with each other. Several wordplay writers have looked for the longest single isogram and the longest sets of two or more isograms with different letters. Ross Eckler cites these as the longest in the *Pocket Webster's:*

AMBIDEXTROUSLY (14)
BLACKSMITH GUNPOWDERY (20)
HUMPBACKS FROWZY TINGLED (22)
HUMPBACKS FROWZY VELDT JINX (24)

In the last set, G and Q are the only missing letters. Since GQ is the logo for the magazine *Gentleman's Quarterly,* it provides the key to completing a pangram:

GQ HUMPBACKS JINX FROWZY VELDT.

THE FOUR-WORD PANGRAM PROBLEM

Without any restrictions on sources, Dmitri Borgmann assembled a set of four words having all twenty-six letters, but they don't fit together to make a sentence. The problem remains: can a four-word pangrammatic sentence be made?

FJORDHUNGKVISL: a short river in central Iceland (*Times Atlas of the World,* Vol. 3)

PECQ: a town in western Belgium (*Ibid.*)

WAMB: an obsolete spelling of WOMB (*Webster's Second Unabridged*)

ZYXT: an obsolete Kentish second person singular indicative present form of the verb "to see" (*Oxford English Dictionary*)

THE SCHWARZKOPF CHALLENGE

Norman SCHWARZKOPF, of Gulf War fame, has eleven different letters in his last name. His abbreviated title, GEN., adds another three letters, bringing the total to more than half the alphabet. The Schwarzkopf Challenge is to design a realistic-sounding pangrammatic full name around SCHWARZKOPF.

Robert Cass Keller started it off with a twenty-letter name for a daughter of the general, EMILY JUNG SCHWARZKOPF. John Bulten followed up a with a twenty-two-letter name for a hypothetical grandson, BIG MEL TY SCHWARZKOPF, JUN. Looking further into the future, I foresee a fifteenth-generation

BENJY GIL Q. T. "MUD" SCHWARZKOPF, XV, with the full alphabet in his arsenal.

Back to basics: can a reasonable pangram be made with the general's name in it? Here's one that uses SCHWARZKOPF and another name:

B. J. QUIGLY, M.D., VEXT N. SCHWARZKOPF.

THE PANGRAMMATIC WINDOW

A pangrammatic window is a segment of text having all twenty-six letters in it (as well as many other letters). Windows measuring 150 letters or more are relatively common, but windows of one-hundred letters or fewer are scarce.

Sarah Grand's *The Beth Book* (1897) has the shortest known pangrammatic window, sixty-five letters in length, that occurs by accident in a published text. That is, it's unlikely that Grand had intended to write a pangram. Several wordplay people have tried without success to find a shorter accidental window.

The sentence with the "Beth" window in capital latters looks like this:

> It was an eXQUISITE DEEP BLUE JUST THEN, WITH FILMY WHITE CLOUDS DRAWN UP OVER IT LIKE GAUZe.

OPENING THE PANGRAMMATIC WINDOW

"Century Collection Unveils Coin History," an article by Richard Giedroyc in *Coin World*, a numismatic newspaper, has a pangrammatic window with a span of 110 letters and four numbers. If the writer had taken a little more care, the window could have been shut almost halfway, and it would have beaten the "Beth" window. Here's the original and the fifty-nine-letter revision.

> In the following century the Byzantine army was decisiVELY DEFEAT-ED BY THE ISLAMIC SELJUQ'S IN 1071 AT MALZGIRD, ALLOWING TURKISH PEOPLES TO SETTLE INTO THE REGION OF WHAT IS NOW TURKEY AT THE EXpense of the declining Byzantine Empire.

> In the following century, in 1071, the Byzantine army was defeated decisiVELY BY ISLAMIC SELJUQ'S AT MALZGIRD, ALLOWING PEOPLE OF TURKEY AT THE EXpense of the declining Byzantine Empire to settle into the region now.

SHAKESPEARE'S PANGRAMMATIC SONNET

How many of Shakespeare's sonnets use all the letters of the alphabet scattered among the lines? Half of them? A third? Howard Bergerson found that there is only one: Sonnet 27, "Weary with toil, I haste me to my bed." And that is how Bergerson may have felt after going through all 154.

Actually, searching for pangrammatic sonnets doesn't take as long as it might seem. The secret is to scan for J, Q, X, and Z and then look for the others. In Sonnet 27, the rare letters appear in JOURNEY, JEWEL, QUIET, EXPIRED, and ZEALOUS.

PANGRAMMATIC REBUS

Can a letter rebus be written with all twenty-six letters of the alphabet appearing in any order? In 1886, J. H. Lundgren tried it, and he came up with the pangrammatic rebus below. Except for the last syllable, the letters sound exactly, or almost exactly, like the words they represent.

O LN, P J, IV FEG, W R! MT SA! Y? U C H DK; B XQZ! =

O Ellen, pea jay, ivy effigy, double you are! empty essay! Why? you see age decay; be excused!

The next poem uses all the letters in alphabetical order. If you read it aloud, you'll see that it sounds like the alphabet, too, and it rhymes.

Eh, Bees See

Abie's seedy.
He hefts—gee!—
Age. I, Jake, a hell,
Am in no pea.
Cue or rest?
Tea? You? Fee
Double?! You hex,
Wise sea.

PANGRAMMATIC EXIT

We've reached the end of the road, where the stop sign has all four rare letters on it. Most of the time, those letters stop pangrammatists from writing a normal-sounding sentence, but we won't stop here. We have many other words to go.

Chapter J

Lettershift Lane

THE JOLLY CHEER PUB

THE JOLLY CHEER PUB, located next door to the Ovals Hotel, is packed with customers. Some have just seen the play *Pecan Tiger*, starring John Punt and Hedda Spool, at the theater next door. Others, with sad looks on their faces, have just gotten off work from the Sorry Mills.

"It's an Alkyd Epoch we live in," Mary Drip mutters. "Hey, bartender! How about a swig of Two-Log Rum? How about you, Len?"

"Oz's Ale for me," says Len Bud. "I've been swimming in the Arena River."

"I'll take a six-pack of Knee Fizz soda pop for my kids," says Susy Moms.

Len gets up and puts a quarter in the jukebox. He presses W-7 to hear the Wheel Dolls sing their latest hit, "Punk Tyro," which begins, "Dodo Papa, Dodo Papa, take your Manful Thumbs off me."

The bartender, Sam Mug, brings Susy her six-pack, and she pays and leaves the place. Then he gets the drinks for Mary and Len and sets them on beer coasters with lettershift words on them. The more the two of them drink, the more the letters shift.

Lettershift words are words whose corresponding letters are an equal number of alphabetic steps apart. Lettershift Lane is full of examples. The names of people, businesses, and products are made of lettershift pairs. To see how the shifting works, look at the words on the buildings or in the river as they appear below. CHEER shifts seven steps to form JOLLY.

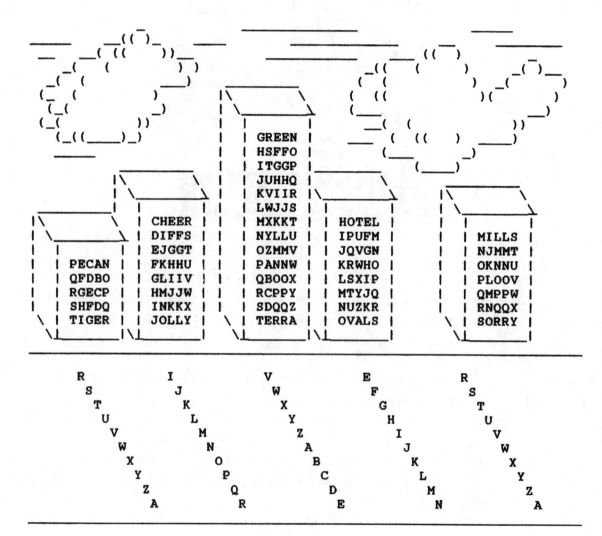

Dmitri Borgmann first wrote about lettershift words in *Language on Vacation*, and he presented several dozen examples of dictionary pairs. Lettershift words are scarcer than anagrams and palindromes. However, there are many shifty possibilities that haven't been explored yet.

INVISIBLE WORDPLAY

Anagrams and palindromes are visible manipulations of letters that can be done with Scrabble tiles, but lettershift words make their changes invisibly. It's difficult to know by looking at a word whether it has a lettershift partner. CHEER and JOLLY in the opening section don't broadcast their relationship. They don't even have a single letter in common.

In the sampling of lettershifts of words from three to seven letters, the number to the left of a word indicates the number of alphabetic steps from the word above it to the word itself. END shifts just a single step to reach FOE; thus, the shift value for END to FOE is one. However, the value for FOE to END is different—twenty-five.

In shifting, the letter count works on a "clock alphabet." Imagine a clock with the letters going around it from A to Z. When the count reaches Z, it continues with A, just as twelve o'clock continues with one o'clock.

Counting backward along the alphabet gives a negative shift value. From FOE to END results in minus one. To convert it to a positive shift value, add twenty-six to minus one. That gives a shift value of twenty-five, the same result produced by counting forward.

The list below includes lettershift pairs for words of three to eight letters for each of the thirteen shift values, where possible. Above five letters, some shift values have no known word pairs. All the words can be found in the *Pocket Webster's*, *Webster's Second* and *Third Unabridged*, and *The Offical Scrabble Players Dictionary*. Most of the pairs were discovered by Dmitri Borgmann and Leonard Gordon.

This list includes one pair of lettershifts for words of three to five letters for each of the thirteen shift values. Above five letters, some shift values generate no known pairs of words.

THREE-LETTER WORDS

END	ICE	BOO	CAP	NOT	BOA	PAR
1 FOE	2 KEG	3 ERR	4 GET	5 STY	6 HUG	7 WHY

EGG	TIP	RUT	ODD	ASK	TNT	
8 MOO	9 CRY	10 BED	11 ZOO	12 MEW	13 GAG	

FOUR-LETTER WORDS

STAR	SLAM	COLD	OPEN	FIDO	BOMB	LINK
1 TUBS	2 UNCO	3 FROG	4 STIR	5 KNIT	6 HUSH	7 SPUR

HAWK	SLIP	DEED	RAPE	POPS	GNAT
8 PIES	9 BURY	10 NOON	11 CLAP	12 BABE	13 TANG

FIVE-LETTER WORDS

SHEER	OSMIC	TELOI	BANJO	FIZZY
1 TIFFS	2 QUOKE	3 WHORL	4 FERNS	5 KNEED

MUNCH	LATEX	TSARS	SLEEP	CUBED
6 SATIN	7 SHALE	8 BAIZA	9 BUNNY	10 MELON

SPOTS	TOUCH	CREEL
11 DATED	12 FAGOT	13 PERRY

SIX-LETTER WORDS

STEEDS	PYRRIL	LALLAN	FUSION	INKIER
1 TUFFET	2 RATTAN	4 PEPPER	6 LAYOUT	7 PURPLY

CADDAW	VERITY	MUUMUU	SPLITS	BECUNA
8 KILLIE	9 ENARCH	10 WEEWEE	11 DAWTED	13 ORPHAN

SEVEN-LETTER WORDS

PRIMERO	UNFIBER
3 SULPHUR	7 BUMPILY

EIGHT-LETTER WORDS

WILIWILI
6 COROCORO

In some cases, three or four words form lettershift sets, but the shift values between any two pairs within a set usually differ. To figure out the shift value between the first word and the third word in a set, add the intermediate shift values. In the first set below, ADD shifts I + 7 = 8 steps to ILL.

A D D	O A F	I R K	B U S	M U D	G O D
1 B E E	8 W I N	9 R A T	6 H A Y	10 W E N	8 O W L
7 I L L	6 C O T	4 V E X	8 P I G	4 A I R	4 S A P
					4 W E T

HAL

In the 1960s, millions of moviegoers who went to see *2001: A Space Odyssey* witnessed lettershifts playing a major role on the silver screen. Whether director Stanley Kubrick knew it or not, HAL, the name of the computer that thought it was God, shifts one alphabetic step to spell IBM. In the movie, HAL was an IBM computer.

THE LETTERSHIFT CALCULATOR

Shifting words involves sifting through letter strings—lots of them. Each word has twenty-five parallel strings, but most are meaningless. Still, you must check them to find the words, and that can be slow, tedious work. Using paper and a pencil, you have to write the word and twenty-five strings of letters in a column beneath it and search through the strings for any valid lettershift partners.

There are quicker ways. You can program a computer to scroll the strings of letters down the screen in a twinkling. Or you can build a Lettershift Calculator out of common objects found at the corner supermarket.

The Lettershift Calculator consists of a soup can with seven loops of paper around it. The loops have the letters of the alphabet printed on them so they can rotate to spell a word in one row and make parallel lettershift strings in the other twenty-five rows.

Draw or photocopy the letter strip seven times and cut out the copies (Illustration 1). Remove the label from the soup can. Wrap each copy strip around the unopened can (Illustration 2) and glue the "A" square over the blank square.

Careful measurement is essential for a good, workable calculator. You may have to photo-enlarge the strips to several slightly different sizes and try them out to find the size that fits just right.

When the calculator is finished, you can rotate the strips to spell a word in one row (Illustration 3). All other rows will line up to make lettershift strings. Rotate the can to look for words among the strings.

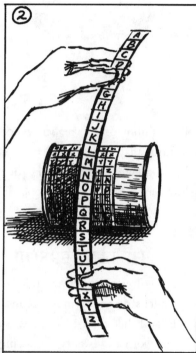

STRIP

Although the Lettershift Calculator is slower than a computer, in some ways it's more convenient. You can hold it in your hand, you can operate it whenever you want, and you can store it anywhere. It also gives a good demonstration of how the clock alphabet works.

THE GREAT VOWEL SHIFT

This group of seven all-vowel lines can be shifted into meaningful sentences. The letters in each line move the same number of steps down the alphabet, but the shift value differs from line to line. If you built a Lettershift Calculator, translating these is as easy as AEIOU and Y. Can you do it? (Answer Alley)

1. UAO, E OAA IAOOU IEYA.
2. AI AUA U AYYE.
3. OYAUI! Y IAY, IUU IAO.
4. U YUEE OAIE, EA U YAI YAEE.
5. UIUI'A IAA AIOA.
6. EUA EUEU, EUA IUE, OIE EUEU!
7. IIO, E UYEOI! AIEO, AI AEOI.

PARTIAL LETTERSHIFTS

Using the Lettershift Calculator, I found numerous lettershift pairs. Most of them had been discovered before, but a few new pairs, like ALKYD-EPOCH, turned up. I wanted to find new pairs longer than five letters, but the lettershift atmosphere becomes rarified at the six-letter plateau. All but a few known examples involve odd and curious words.

While turning the letter loops, I noticed that longer words sometimes generate lettershift strings that contain shorter words. COMPLETE shifts to RDBEATI, which has BEAT in it. Such pairs are partial lettershifts.

In the following examples, misfit letters have been replaced by dots, and shift values have been omitted.

P A N I C	G L A S S	J I N X	D A Y • •
T E R M •	• P E W •	• J O Y	L I G H T
F R I E N D	• H O O D •	S U B T L E	B R E A S T
• • • F O E	Z I P P E R	• B I A S •	• V I E W •
L A T T E R	L I V E L Y	• G O O D •	H A T I N G
F U N N Y •	• B O X E R	S W E E T S	B U N C H •

THING	AMPLE	HONEY	HOLE
•NOT•	CORN•	NUT••	TAX•
••PUN	•BEAT	•BAR•	•HEX
JOLLY•	SAD•••	MODEL	SIREN
CHEER•	•BEING	•SHIP	BRAN•
PURRED	EMPTY•	••TUB	••BOX
•••MY	•DAMN•	•HEAR•	•GO••
DREAM	BURDEN	•DAWN•	NOW••
MAN••	••COPY	BURNER	DEMON
	HIP••	I••••	
	GHOST	•GOT•	
	NO•••	UP•••	
	TUB••	TO•••	
		FAINT	

LETTERSHIFT NAMES

FIRST NAMES

Several three-letter personal names and nicknames are shifts of each other. You may have friends or relatives linked by lettershifts. You may even be married to a lettershift partner.

BEA	BOB	BUD	CAL	DAN	DON	PAT
SAL	NAN	LEN	KIT	ROB	TED	TEX
FAY	GUS	GUY	IDA	INA	NAT	
TOM	MAY	MAE	JEB	VAN	REX	

FIRST AND LAST NAMES

Many last names shift to first names. Most are partial shifts, but a few full shifts exist. When I tried my own last name, MORICE, I was surprised to find GIL•••, my father's first name. A student of mine shifted her last name, BERRY, and it turned up •ANN••. Her first name is ANNE, which is close enough.

Ross Eckler used a national computer database to find the lettershift names on the next page. The numbers in brackets indicate how many people share the same name. If full first-name listings were included, some of the counts would be much longer. For instance, adding the listings for ARTHUR JACKSON to those for ART••• JACKSON would up the total to 661.

There are undoubtedly many other names that are partial or full lettershifts. Is your name one of them?

A R T • • • •	• T O M • •	• A N N	J U D Y • •
J A C K S O N	K N I G H T	C O B B	G R A V E S
[349]	[54]	[47]	[17]
• J O E •	A R T • •	P A T R I C K	G A I L
H I N D S	H Y A T T	• • C A R L •	K E M P
[8]	[5]	[4]	[4]
• T E D	S U E • •	• J O E • • •	V I N C E N T
F A L K	M O Y E R	T I N D A L L	• D I X • • •
[2]	[2]	[2]	[1]
S H E L L Y	• P E T E R	• • • • S U E	
L A X • • •	P E T I T •	S T U R G I S	
[1]	[1]	[1]	

NAMES AND WORDS

On rare occasions, the first and last names of well-known persons shift to two common words. Of the six names below, ANNA FREUD gives the most meaningful shifts. Anna was Sigmund's daughter, and both of her names make Freudian shifts.

DON	HO	REX	REED	LANA	LANG
ITS	AH	HUN	BOON	PERE	SHUN
ED	MUNCH	ANNA	FREUD	JOHN	LENNON
ON	SATIN	BOOB	COBRA	PUNT	BUDDED

When written twice and shifted five steps, the last name of John SUNUNU, conservative host of the political talk show *Crossfire*, makes a two-word term defined as "idle talk, chatter" in the *The Pocket Dictionary of American Slang*. How appropriate!

S U N U N U	S U N U N U
Y A T A T A	Y A T A T A

GEOGRAPHIC LINES

Some country names have significant partial shifts. The first two letters of BRITAIN shift to UK, and the last two letters of AMERICA shift to US. A few country names generate sets of words that can be arranged into poetic lines worthy of the Imagists or the Surrealists:

```
• • • • • A H •        I • • • • •           • • • O H • • •
• • • • • • M E        A M • • • •           • • M Y • • • •
I • • • • • • •         • • A • • •           L A X • • • • •
A M • • • • • •         F R E N C H           F U R • • • • •
• • A • • • • •         • • V E T •           • • • • P E W •
S E R B I A N •         • I • • • •           • • • • • A S •
• B O Y • • • •         • • R A P •           • I F • • • • •
                        M Y • • • •           S H E • • • • •
A • • • • •             • • • T I N           • • • L E T • •
• • D I M •             • B O X • •           • • • • • M E •
• L O T • •                                   B Y • • • • • •
• • I N • •                                   • • • • A • • •
N O R W A Y                                    C R O A T I A N
                                              • D A M • • • •
```

Names of the states can form partial shifts, too. The following have pairs of words related in meaning:

```
C O N N E C T I C U T        H A W A I I          T E X A S
• • • • C A R • • • •        P I E • • •          A L E • •
• • • • • • • G A S •        • • • G O O          • • R U M
```

The first eight letters of another state name shift twelve steps to form one all-vowel string and twenty-two steps to form another. Which state is so avowedly shifty? (Answer Alley)

LETTERSHIFT FORMS

As with regular words, lettershifts can be placed into word squares and other forms. These three (omitting the dots) show different approaches:

```
L I V I N G            I                  L A P
R O B O T              T A P              A P E
H E R E                V I P E R          P E T
D A N                  I R E L A N D
B Y
I
```

The left-sided pyramid is formed by partial shifts of LIVING that decrease by one letter at each step. The centered pyramid has words increasing by two letters as it goes down the page. In the word square, probably the only one of its kind, each letter is fifteen steps from the letter to its right and from the letter below it.

NUDE LOVE STORY

In this chain, the letters in each column are shifts between the words. The twelfth word, NUDE, links to the first word, STORMY, resulting in an unbroken circle. It's a review of a 1990s X-rated sequel to the 1960s movie *Love Story:*

```
S T O R M Y
    W I F E
      O N L Y
        V I E W
          W O R K
            H A R D
              C O R E
                B O A T
                  S E X Y
                    S T O R Y
                      L O V E
                        N U D E
```

THE DIRTY DOZEN

The letter strings in this list shift to twelve different words. What are they? Why are they shifted to these letters in particular? (Answer Alley)

DOX	MQOPB	WKUHH
FIQXHQ	POF	WRWN
JSYV	PWPGPY	YOD
KNAJ	VYQ	ZLCLU

LETTERSHIFT REVERSALS

Most words don't have regular lettershift matches, but some shift to strings that spell words in reverse. THEM shifted ten steps has DROW, which reverses to

WORD. THEM and WORD form a lettershift reversal pair. There are probably as many of them as normal lettershifts.

In this small sampling, the shift appears under the starting word with the reversal in parentheses below it.

```
 DUNK          CALM          HEAR          BEES
1EVOL        2ECNO        4LIEV        10LOOC
 (LOVE)       (ONCE)        (VEIL)        (COOL)

               ALLOY        GHOST
             3DOORB       12STAEF
               (BROOD)      (FEATS)
```

ANTI-LETTERSHIFT PAIRS

If lettershift pairs display perfect order, anti-lettershift pairs display perfect chaos: no pair of corresponding letters has the same shift value. Many short words, such as WORD and PAIR, are anti-lettershifts (W to P takes nineteen steps, O to A takes twelve, R to I takes seventeen, and D to R takes fourteen).

STATESMEN INTERPRET COMMUNITY is a sentence made of surprisingly long anti-lettershift words. When I came upon the pair STATESMAN-INTERPRET, I thought it would be difficult to locate two other words of such length that related in meaning. Then Faith Eckler found INTERPRET-COMMUNITY.

The two pairs appear below with their shift values next to them and the differences below them. Note that in order to subtract a larger number from a smaller number, twenty-six has to be added to the smaller number: 5 − 18 = ? becomes 31 − 18 = 13.

```
STATESMEN     19, 20, 1, 20, 5, 19, 13, 5, 14
INTERPRET     9, 14, 20, 5, 18, 16, 18, 5, 20
Differences =  10, 6, 7, 15, 13, 3, 21, 0, 20
INTERPRET     9, 14, 20, 5, 18, 16, 18, 5, 20
COMMUNITY     3, 15, 13, 13, 21, 14, 9, 20, 25
Differences =  6, 25, 7, 18, 23, 2, 9, 11, 21
```

THE RED SHIFT

The sign ahead has the word HIDE on it because it hides something that's just eleven steps away. What is it? (Answer Alley)

Chapter

K

Pattern Passage

THE LETTER FACTORIES

$\mathcal{T}$HE CELEBRATION OF WORDS, an annual event on Pattern Passage, has just begun. Children walk by carrying balloons with letters on them. Banners flap syllabically on wires strung from the lampposts. Above the din, street vendors cry out their wordplay wares made in the Letter Factories.

"Word ladders, only twenty-six bucks!" a vendor shouts. "Guaranteed genuine, designed by Lewis Carroll! Two for the price of one—today only! Watch POOR FLOUR bake to RICH BREAD in six steps."

He gestures to the ladder behind him:

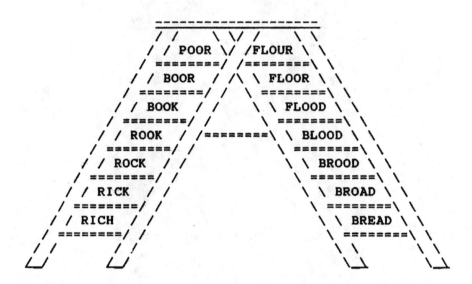

But before he can bargain with us, other vendors outshout him.

"Baseball caps with charades!" yells a guy with a stack of hats on his head, "T-shirts with triplets!"

"Get your bracelets with Ouija words on them!" a woman cries, holding up a few examples.

We'll go down to the Letter Factories and take a guided tour. The people who work there assemble the alphabet into structures that the dictionary makers never dreamed of. We've seen some of the well-known patterns—anagrams, palindromes, and word squares—but there are many more.

Oops! Watch out. Don't walk under the word ladder.

TOPPING LEWIS CARROLL

In 1879, Lewis Carroll made up a pencil-and-paper game that he called doublets. Since then, they've come to be known in wordplay circles as word ladders. Puzzle magazines and books have also called them changelings, laddergrams, passes, stepwords, transitions, transformations, transmutations, word chains, word links, word ping-pong, and an assortment of other names. No other wordplay form has had so many aliases.

According to Carroll's rules, the goal in building a word ladder is to connect two given words of the same length in the fewest steps. At each step, a single letter changes in one word to make the next word. Usually the starting and ending words are related in some way—as synonyms, antonyms, and so on.

Carroll constructed several ladders, but did he always do it in the smallest number of steps? One way to find out is to try beating him at his own game. In the five ladders below, blanks replace the connecting words. The numbers in parentheses indicate how many steps he took. Can you do better in fewer?

ARMY (8)	BLACK (7)	HEAD (5)	BLUE (9)	RIVER (11)
_____	_____	_____	_____	_____
_____	_____	_____	_____	_____
_____	_____	_____	_____	_____
_____	_____	TAIL	_____	_____
_____	_____		_____	_____
NAVY	WHITE		_____	_____
			_____	_____
			PINK	_____
				_____
				SHORE

It can be done. See Answer Alley for Carroll's solutions to the first two ladders. Turn to Chapter Q for his answers to the last three and for shorter answers found with the aid of a computer.

MINIMAL WORD LADDERS

Creating a specialized version of an established form offers a new challenge and revitalizes the old form. So it is with minimal word ladders, a form invented by Ross Eckler.

In a minimal word ladder, each letter in the starting word changes once and only once. The ending word doesn't have to relate in meaning. Just making the transition can be tricky enough. The number of steps needed equals the length of the word involved. A three-letter word takes three steps, a four-letter word four.

Following Eckler's suggestion, Kyle Corbin constructed minimal ladders for words of different lengths, including these:

ANY	SOAP	ELATE	BRAVER
AND	SWAP	PLATE	BEAVER
AID	SWAY	PLACE	BEATER
KID	AWAY	PEACE	BETTER
	AWRY	PEACH	SETTER
		PERCH	SETTEE
			SETTLE

WORD STEPLADDERS

One wordplay form sometimes leads to another, and that form leads to another. When I first saw the minimal ladders, I thought of the term "word stepladder." I liked how it sounded, so I made up a form and an example to go with it.

In a word stepladder, a word becomes another word by changing any letter in it to a letter next to it in the alphabet. MIKE can change to LIKE or MILE. The letter in the same position can change again and again to make new words. The goal is to construct a stepladder with as many different words as possible without repeating any.

The first stepladder below is the longest using words from the *Pocket Webster's*. Going to larger dictionaries, Tom Pulliam constructed the second stepladder, and Sir Jeremy Morse the third.

LIKE	RAKE	BURRING
MIKE	SAKE	CURRING
MILE	SALE	CURSING
MIME	TALE	CUSSING
MINE	TAME	BUSSING
LINE	SAME	BUSTING
KINE	SANE	BUTTING
KIND	SAND	CUTTING
	RAND	

SINGLE STEPS

In each of these single-step pairs, both words are the names of living creatures. The last pair does something special. What is it? (Answer Alley)

B A T	G N A T	L O U S E
C A T	G O A T	M O U S E

FRIENDLY, FRIENDLIER, AND FRIENDLIEST WORDS

In these three forms, words are connected in increasingly complex ways.

FRIENDLY

In a friendly word, the letter in each position can be replaced by another letter to make another word. The substitute letters on their own don't spell anything. The letters in BANE can be replaced respectively by L, O, D, and K.

BANE: Lane   bOne   baDe   banK

FRIENDLIER

As in a friendly word, the letters can all be replaced to spell new words, but in this case, the substitute letters spell out a word, too. BANE can be replaced by the letters in PORK:

BANE: Pane   bOne   baRe   banK = PORK

Five-letter friendlier word sets are more difficult to form. The first two that follow are by Pulliam, and the last two by Mary Lois Dennison:

BLAND:	Pland	bRand	blOnd	blaBd	blanE = PROBE
GLASS:	Class	gRass	glOss	glaNs	glasE = CRONE
BULLY:	Dully	bIlly	buRly	bulKy	bullS = DIRKS
CRIMP:	Primp	cHimp	crAmp	criSp	crimE = PHASE

FRIENDLIEST

In a friendliest word, every combination of letters can be exchanged with the letters in a different word to make a new word. BANE works this way with several other words, including CORD, LIDS, and MITT. Here is BANE-MITT, changing one to four letters:

BANE:	Mane	bIne	baTe	banT		
BANE:	MIne	MaTe	ManT	bITe	bInT	biTT
BANE:	MITe	MInT	MaTT	baTT		
BANE:	MITT					

The term "friendly" first appeared in the index of Dmitri Borgmann's book *Beyond Language*, but it isn't mentioned in the text. In 1970, David Silverman, discussing the form in *Word Ways*, called it an onalosi. The term "friendliest" is also known as a garble group. I chose to use the three terms here to emphasize the progressive relationships between the words.

All words in this section appear in *Webster's Second* or *Third Unabridged*.

WORD NETWORKS

A word network arranges words in arrays. The basic type of network, as described by Eckler in *Word Recreations*, connects words of the same length that differ in spelling by only one letter. It's a complex version of the word ladder.

In this example, Eckler arranged the thirty-eight two-letter *Pocket Webster's* words into the single network shown below. The two-letter length is the only one for which all the words connect. Even so, it's impossible to show the lines joining every pair of words.

Instead, a shorthand notation makes the connections possible: a single horizontal or vertical line connects words with a different letter in the same position. You can jump from one word in a line to another in order to find pairs of connected words. Thus OR is connected to OF just as it's connected to OK, OX, and ON.

The two-letter network maps out all possible word ladders. You can find the shortest ladder between any two words by tracing a path along the lines. The shortest path for UP to LO takes ten steps: UP-US-AS-AY-MY-MA-PA-PI-GI-GO-LO.

```
OR—OK—OX—ON—OF            US —UP
         |    |    |                    |
        IN—I F—I D—I T —I S
         |          |    |    |
    A Y—A X—AN —AM—AD —AT —AS
     |
   B E—B Y              TO—TV—TB
   |    |    |               |
   ME—MY—MA            NO
   |          |               |
   HE       P A—P I   DO
   |               |    |
   YE            GI — GO
   |                    |
   WE                  LO
                        |
                        SO
```

Several writers, including Eckler, have mapped out larger networks, and they've designed special types that link words related by different properties. As networks become more complicated, their representation in two-dimensional space becomes more challenging.

TRIPLETS—AN ADDED DIMENSION

The triplet, named after Carroll's doublets, changes the basic way that word ladders work. Peter Newby, inventor of the form, wanted to find a way to link words of different lengths. Instead of changing a letter to make a new word, Newby adds or subtracts a letter at each step. He calls this triplet a "literary egg timer":

SAND
AND
AN
A
AD
SAD
SAND

The next two are triplets-in-parallel. The first goes from a LOG CABIN to the WHITE HOUSE in ten steps. The second connects two well-known palindromes to each other in eight steps. All words are from the *Oxford English Dictionary*.

LOG	CABIN	LIVE	NOT	ON	EVIL
CLOG	CAIN	LIE	NO	ONE	VIL
COG	AIN	LE	O	DONE	VI
CO	IN	E	AO	DOE	I
O	I	EN	A	OE	IN
IO	IO	ENS	HA	E	INN
I	O	DENS	HAD	EA	INNE
HI	HO	DENIS	AD	ENA	INNED
HIT	HOE	DENNIS	AND	EDNA	SINNED
WHIT	HOSE				
WHITE	HOUSE				

HE, THE THEORETICAL REALIST

Now for a test of pattern recognition. The following poem has a special structure related to the letters in its words. The pattern becomes more noticeable with each stanza. How quickly can you figure it out? (Answer Alley)

He, earnest troubador, relishes singing
general lyrics: "Shadow women never react to
obvious songs, so obnoxiously you undermine
every youthful love, even natural longings."

The heroic, icy cynic, Icarus, usurped
Edwardian anemones: "Escape pernicious uses,
especially lyric ice, Centipede Demon."
One needed educational aliens.

Theoretical Californians answer:
"Werewolves, vestibules lessen senses' session."
Ionic, nice, iced cedar dares restructured redwood—
oodles, lest establishment entertains insurance.

Realist, listen! Stenographer's herself,
selfish fishmongers. Gershwin's winsome, somewhat,
whatever. Everglade laden adenine? Nineteen teenyboppers
persecute cutest testament, mentally allying.

ISIS

The letter pattern in the next poem is obvious, but does it make sense? Certainly, as long as you have a little explanation. Imagine the goddess Isis undergoing an identity crisis. Looking in a mirror, she addresses her image as if it were her sister:

Sis, is Isis Isis?
Is Isis I, Sis? I?
Sis, is Isis I, Sis?
Isis is I, Sis. I!

Sis is Isis? Isis
Is Isis? I, Sis? Is?

I. Sis. Isis is.
Isis is Isis. Is!

Isis? Isis is I.
Sis is I. Sis. I.
Sis is Isis is I.
Sis? Isis, I? Sis, I?

Sis is Isis; I, Sis.
I, Sis, Isis—is Isis.

CHARADES

The charade is a form of wordplay that resembles the anagram, except that the letters aren't rearranged—they're just spaced differently. Like anagrams, some charades relate in meaning to the starting words, as in this comment on the television culture by Michael-Sean Lazarchuk:

SOAP OPERA

SO A POP ERA

Many other words can be charaded. MAN'S LAUGHTER, THE RAPIST, and IS LAND are well-known examples. Here are twenty-one more charades from a long list compiled by Steve and Sheila Toth.

A LIE, NATION	DORM ANT	MAN, I CURE
ASS AS SIN	DRAG ON	MEAD, OWL, ARK
AT TEN, DANCE	GAR DEN	MUST ACHE
BAN KING	GENE RATIONS	OVERT AX
BEANS TALK	GRUBS TAKE	PLEA? SURE!
CAP A CITY	HEAT HER	SEA'S HELL
CON'S PIRACY	LEG ENDS	WAR'S HIP

FROM ANTI-CHARADE TO SUPER-CHARADE

In an anti-charade, a word or sentence changes into another word or sentence that means the opposite, like these two lines:

SEARING SUN LIT ISLAND

SEA RINGS UNLIT ISLAND

With a little extra linguistic spin, this three-line charade recycles the letters so that no word is repeated:

WITHAL, ONE VEILED
WIT, HAL. ON EVE I LED
WITH A LONE VEIL, ED

These two charades trade long and short words. The first sentence has longer words at the beginning, and the second has them at the end:

SIGNIFICANT INSCRIPTION: LYING OLD CAPITAL LINES SENT, I
ALLY ON ESTATE, MEN, TO NAME'S SAGE

SIGN IF I CAN'T—IN SCRIPT. I, ONLY IN GOLD, CAP IT ALL IN
ESSENTIALLY ONE STATEMENT ON A MESSAGE

The longest charade of all separates into eleven different words of two to four letters found in *Webster's Second Unabridged*. The number of words is important; their meaning isn't. And that super-charade is. . .

ANTIDISESTABLISHMENTARIANISM
ANT ID IS ES TAB LI SH MEN TARI AN ISM

A CHARADE IN THE GARDEN OF EDEN

The "Madam" palindrome began the wordplay of the world. The charade below continues the adventures of the first couple with their expulsion from the Garden of Eden. Adam tried to come up with some way for them to remain in the garden, but, since he couldn't think of anything, he and Eve raced out of there. The "Adam" charade puts it more succinctly:

O, HAD A MAN DEVELOPED A WAY!
OH, ADAM AND EVE LOPED AWAY

OUIJA WORDS

Have you ever worked a Ouija board? You and one or two friends lightly touch your fingers to a platform called a planchette that slides around the board and crosses letters, numbers, or the words YES and NO in order to talk to a representative of the spirit world or at least the alphabet world.

The name Ouija was coined by connecting "oui" and "ja," the French and the German words for "yes." Like a bilingual minidictionary, the word provides an instant translation of OUI to JA. (As Eckler pointed out, OUI is also a lettershift of YES.)

Ouija words can split apart charade-fashion to produce words that have the same meaning in different languages. Here are some Ouija words with translations. ANDY is the name, and LETHE the mythological river of the underworld.

ANDY = AND, Y	(Y = "and" in Spanish)
HEEL = HE, EL	(EL = "he" in Spanish)
LATHE = LA, THE	(LA = feminine "the" in Spanish and French)
LETHE = LE, THE	(LE = masculine "the" in French)
MIME = MI, ME	(MI = "me" in Spanish)

THE HOUSE OF USHERS

Sometimes a word has lots of other shorter words stuffed in it, but usually they're nothing more than linguistic packing peanuts. USHERS, on the other hand, is packed with pronouns. Richard Lederer found that it contains more pronouns spelled consecutively than any other word.

USHERS
US
SHE
HE
HER
HERS

GOLDSMITHERY

Peter Newby rearranged the letters in SMITHERY to spell twenty-two pronouns, all listed in the *Oxford English Dictionary*. Seventeen are familiar to most people. The other five are obsolete spelling forms of HOO, which is equivalent to one of the modern pronouns, but which one? Who's HOO? (Answer Alley)

COMMONLY RECOGNIZED PRONOUNS			VARIANTS OF *HOO*
HE	I	SHE	
HER	IT	THEIR	HEY
HERS	ITS	THEIRS	HI
HIM	ME	THEM	HIE
HIS	MY	THEY	HY
		THY	HYE
		YE	

A BOX OF LETTERS

COMMUNICATORIALLY, an adverbial form of COMMUNICATORY, acts like a set of Chinese boxes. Pulling out certain letters results in four new words, each referring to places where people live. Then pulling out certain letters from the two longest of those words gives the other two words, one of them twice. Words within words within a word.

COMMUNICATORIALLY				COMMUNITY			COUNTRY	
COMMUNI	T		Y	CO	UN TY		COUNT Y	
CO	UN	T R	Y	C		ITY		
CO	UN	T	Y					
C		I T	Y					

KANGAROO WORDS AND JOEYS

Like a mother kangaroo, who carries her young in her pouch, a kangaroo word carries a smaller word that means the same thing as the fully grown word. For instance, inside a PLAGIARIST you'll find a LIAR. Richard Lederer dubbed the smaller word a joey, which means a young kangaroo.

Lederer's Laws of Kangaroo Words state that the letters of the joey shouldn't be entirely adjacent; that is, it must take one or more hops. CAVErn, enJOYment, and cRUDE don't count. Also, the kangaroo and its joey shouldn't be etymologically related in an obvious way. PRIMevAL, CLEANsED, and REVOLuTion are out.

So what does that leave? Lederer went on a kangaroo hunt through the dictionary and found a herd of the creatures. Here are some kangaroos with their joeys jumping up in capital form:

AREnA	diSPutATion	MAscuLinE
BLOssOM	FabrICaTION	petrOchemIcaL
BrobdInGnagian	FRAgILe	pLagIARist
cHickEN	iMpAiR	proSecUtE
conTAmINaTe	imPOStER	RApSCALlion
destRUctIoN	inHErItoR	sTRIvES
diSAppointeD	insTrUcTOR	TwItCh

Lederer found some kanagroos that hop the extra mile. EXPURGATED gives birth to PURGED, which gives birth to PURE. ENCOURAGE holds its junior, URGE, and an evil twin, ENRAGE.

He also spotted a few kangaroos that give birth to multiple joeys: PERAMBU-LATE holds the near twins, RAMBLE and AMBLE. On the other hand, he trapped several joeys with multiple mothers: LIT beams within ILLUMINATED and LIGHT. The record holder for a joey of many mothers is DEAD, resting peacefully in DECEASED, DEPARTED, DEACTIVATED, DECAYED, DECI-MATED, DECAPITATED, and DESICCATED.

Some kangaroo words have other tricks down their pouches. Dmitri Borgmann noted that HOT and COCOA are mixed together in CHOCOLATE and that TIN and CAN are packaged within CONTAINER.

Occasionally, the letters that make up the pouch spell another word after the joey hops out. SEPARATED separates into the biblical-sounding PARTED SEA, and SLITHERED slides into SLID THERE.

How APpropriaTe!

THE ALPHABET CUBE

The Alphabet Cube is a machine that illuminates the patterns of wordplay. It is composed of twenty-six planes. Each plane consists of 676 tiny spherical lights arranged in twenty-six rows with twenty-six lights in each row. Pressing the buttons on a remote-control panel activates one or more lights.

Each light has a set of three letters, called a trigram, on it. The lights on the front plane go from AAA to AAZ in the first line, from ABA to ABZ in the second line, and so on down to AZZ.

The other twenty-five planes are similarly lettered, but the trigrams on each plane begin with a different letter. On the second plane, they go from BAA to BZZ; on the third plane, from CAA to CZZ; on the twenty-sixth plane, from ZAA to ZZZ.

Touching the PALINDROME button lights up all the palindromic trigrams in the cube. Holding the WORD button down at the same time causes the palin-dromic words to start flashing. Pressing other buttons sheds light on other forms: it's the geometry of wordplay.

Of course, the cube exists only in the imagination. It's a three-dimensional array of trigram points, alphabetized from AAA to ZZZ over twenty-six planes (Figure 1). Many wordplay forms operate harmoniously in this simple structure.

PALINDROMES (SEE CHAPTER C)

The palindromic plane (Figure 2) contains all the three-letter palindromes—AAA, ABA, . . . BAB, BBB, . . . ZAZ, ZZZ. It slices through the cube from the front left column to the back right column. Its corners are marked by the trigrams AAA, AZA, ZAZ, and ZZZ.

The lettershift diagonal (Figure 2) forms all the triple-letter strings from AAA to ZZZ. Every line parallel to the lettershift diagonal is made of lettershift trigrams. Depending on the location, a full set of twenty-six lettershift trigrams may appear on one, two, or three lines.

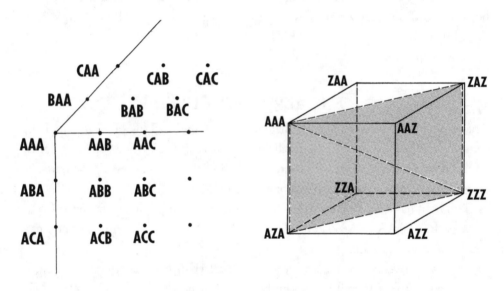

Figure 1   The Top Left Front Corner of the Alphabet Cube

Figure 2   The Palindromic Plane with the Lettershift Diagonal
            Lettershifts (see Chapter J)

REVERSALS (SEE CHAPTER C)

The left plane is a reversal of the front plane; that is, the positions of the trigrams and the order of letters within them are reversed. All twenty-six planes viewed from the left are reversals of the twenty-six planes viewed from the front. Similar relationships occur when the cube is viewed from the right and from the back.

ANAGRAMS (SEE CHAPTER B)

A set of trigrams that are anagrams of each other can be connected by lines to make either an equilateral triangle or a hexagon that is an equilateral triangle with its vertices cut off. Triangles represent anagram sets with two different letters, and hexagons represent sets with three.

The two major anagram triangles (Figure 3), the largest triangles in the cube, are parallel to each other, and their points touch six corners of the cube.

The major anagram hexagon (Figure 4), composed of the letters A, M, and Z in all permutations, is the largest hexagon. The lettershift diagonal, AAA-ZZZ, intersects the major anagram hexagon at its center (marked as "X," which doesn't represent an actual trigram).

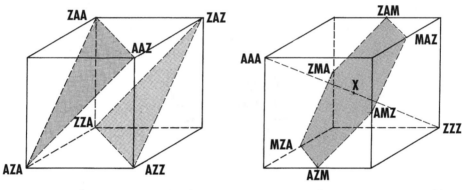

Figure 3   The Two Major Anagram Triangles

Figure 4   The Major Anagram Hexagon and the Lettershift Diagonal

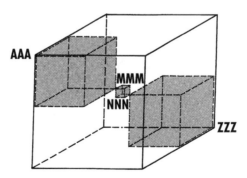

Figure 5   The Half-Alphabet Cubes, the Center Cube, and the Lettershift Diagonal

HALF-ALPHABET TRIGRAMS

Trigrams made of letters from the first half of the alphabet, such as AMC, GHB, and LFE, appear in a cube at the top left front, and those from the last half of the alphabet appear in a cube at the bottom right back (Figure 5). Bridging the two halves, the Center Cube has all eight three-letter combinations of M and N marking its vertices. The Lettershift Diagonal intersects all three cubes.

The forms discussed here can be explored in much greater detail, and other forms can be examined, too. Words of greater lengths, however, require higher-dimensional Alphabet Cubes, which aren't available at this time.

THE LADDER OUT

We exit at the stop sign ahead. It has a minimal word ladder on it that tells us to STOP and PLAY with the words.

Chapter L

Numeric Overpass

THE NUMBER FIELDS

CURVING ABOVE THE other roads, Numeric Overpass winds through a vast white expanse resembling graph paper. Let's climb up the steps and look out on the number fields, where farmers plant digits and harvest letters.

A bale of numbers sits on the edge of the field. All the number names that are six letters long line the edges of the bale shape. Some names are spelled forward, some are spelled backward, and some are used twice.

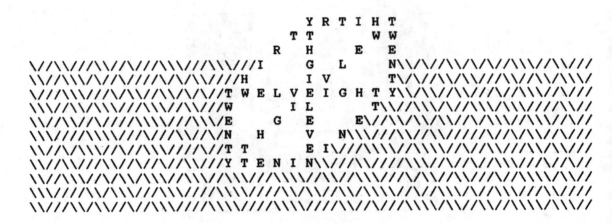

Numeric wordplay shows the intriguing relationships that arise when letters and numbers mix. Let's look at the harvest.

NUMBER GRIDS AND OTHER CROSSNUMBER FORMS

When viewed from the air, fields of crops often display quilt-like patterns. So it is when number names are linked together by their letters to form grids. As in crossword puzzles, the names go horizontally and vertically, and they connect to each other.

The FIRST grid below, discovered by Lloyd Quibble, uses the names of the first four ordinal numbers.

```
F I R S T
O         E
U         C
R         O
T         N
T H I R D
```

THE PRETEENS

With the cardinal number names from ONE to TWELVE, fifteen grids can be formed. In the four grids below, the first two connect nonconsecutive numbers. The second two are the only preteen squares made of consecutive numbers. All fifteen grids use SEVEN, ELEVEN, or both, but none uses SIX.

```
    F  S             E            N                      N
  O N E          E   L          E I G H T            E I G H T
    U  V         F I V E          N   E                N   E
T H R E E          G   V        S E V E N          E L E V E N
      N         T H R E E
                   T   N
```

WELL-FORMED GRIDS

For the TEENs and all numbers after that, a well-formed grid has to follow this guideline: the number names should not all link together at the same repeated parts, such as TEEN, TWENTY, THIRTY, MILLION, BILLION. At least one link should involve a different part. Otherwise, it's too easy to construct grids.

THE TEENS

The first TEEN set, TEN-ELEVEN-TWELVE-THIRTEEN, is impossible to put into a grid. After that, every set of four consecutive numbers having one or more TEENs in it can be arranged with the words going clockwise, counterclockwise, or both, to make well-formed grids.

Here are three of the TEEN grids:

```
              F               S I X T E E N                       T
              O               E           I                       W
              U               V           N                       E
    T H I R T E E N           E           E     N I N E T E E N
    W         T               N           T               W       T
    E         E               T           E           T W E N T Y O N E
E L E V E N                   E I G H T E E N                     N
    V         N               E           N                       T
    E                         N                                   Y
                                                                  T
                                                                  W
                                                                  O
```

Beyond the TEENS, every set of four consecutive numbers can make well-formed clockwise and/or counterclockwise grids.

LARGER GRIDS

Grids of five-number names in the teen range are scarce, but there are at least two of them. One five-number grid appears on the left below. The other can be formed by changing FIFTEEN to TWENTY in the same grid.

With the names of ordinal numbers, the six-number grid on the right can be formed.

```
          E   S                       T W E L F T H
      S I X T E E N                    H       O
          G   V                        I       U
          H   E                        R       R
    F I F T E E N                  S I X T E E N T H
          E   T                        E       E
          E   E                    E L E V E N T H
      N I N E T E E N                  N       N
              N                  F I F T E E N T H
                                       H       H
```

LATTICES

Some grids have a lattice pattern; that is, only one blank space separates neighboring parallel lines. Like a single-word square, the lattice below uses the same number names horizontally and vertically. Oddly enough, all the names are six letters long.

```
T W E N T Y
W   L   W
E L E V E N
N   V   L
T W E L V E
Y   N   E
```

OTHER NUMBER NAMES

Here are examples of grids constructed with different kinds of number names. The first grid below links a series of fraction names. The second has adjectives of order or rank. The third uses the nonnumerical "numbers" in a deck of cards. The fourth is composed of geometric terms.

```
        T                           Q               Q
        W   T               S       U       J       U
        O N E H A L F       T E R T I A R Y A C E
        T   R   I           C       T       C   E
        H   E   V           O       E       K I N G
        I   E   E           N       R
F O U R F I F T H S         D       N
        D   O   I           A       A                       L
        S   U   X           P R I M A R Y       P O I N T
            R   T           Y       Y           L   N
            T   H                               S P A C E
            H   S                                   N
            S                                       E
```

NUMBER TREES

In this form, number names are connected like tree branches to a trunk. The names in the trees climb up the trunk and interesect it in increasing values. In the quintuple and the quinary trees, the trunk has the highest value, and in the singleton tree, the trunk has the lowest value.

```
    Q U A D R U P L E              Q U A T E R N A R Y
    U                              U
  T R I P L E                    T E R T I A R Y
    N                              N
    T                    S E C O N D A R Y
  D O U B L E                    R
    P                    P R I M A R Y
S I N G L E
    E
```

```
              S E X T U P L E T
              I
          Q U I N T U P L E T
              G
      Q U A D R U P L E T
              E
        T R I P L E T
              O
          T W I N
```

EQUIVALENCIES

Instead of letter composition, number names can be arranged according to word length. Michael Sussna has constructed forms that show amazing relationships. He calls the forms equivalencies.

The first equivalency is especially remarkable. The numbers progress from ZERO to NINE as they go down and up the column. Each pair of numbers adds up to nine, and each line has nine symbols in it.

The second one enumerates the five months starting with MARCH, the first month of the year in the Old Style (pre-1752) calendar. This equivalency also uses nine symbols in each line.

```
Z E R O + N I N E          O N E - M A R C H
O N E + E I G H T          T W O - A P R I L
T W O + S E V E N          T H R E E - M A Y
T H R E E + S I X          F O U R - J U N E
F O U R + F I V E          F I V E - J U L Y
```

CALENDAR OF NUMBERS

Lee Sallows devised a way for the months to number themselves. If the twenty-one letters that spell the twelve months' names are set equal to the integers from minus ten to plus ten in just the right combination, the sum of each month's letter values equals the month's position in the year. He found that there are not one, not two, but six ways to number the letters. This is one of them:

```
-10 -9 -8 -7 -6 -5 -4 -3 -2 -1  0  1  2  3  4  5  6  7  8  9  10
  B   J  F  G  S  D  N  R  M  L  A  T  P  H  O  C  I  Y  V  E  U
```

J+A+N+U+A+R+Y = -9+0-4+10+0-3+7 = 1
F+E+B+R+U+A+R+Y = -8+9-10-3+10+0-3+7 = 2
M+A+R+C+H = -2+0-3+5+3 = 3
A+P+R+I+L = 0+2-3+6-1 = 4
M+A+Y = -2+0+7 = 5
J+U+N+E = -9+10-4+9 = 6
J+U+L+Y = -9+10-1+7 = 7
A+U+G+U+S+T = 0+10-7+10-6+1 = 8
S+E+P+T+E+M+B+E+R = -6+9+2+1+9-2-10+9-3 = 9
O+C+T+O+B+E+R = 4+5+1+4-10+9-3 = 10
N+O+V+E+M+B+E+R = -4+4+8+9-2-10+9-3 = 11
D+E+C+E+M+B+E+R = -5+9+5+9-2-10+9-3 = 12

Sallows tried the same thing with the names of the days of the week using the integers from minus seven to plus seven, and he found 664 ways! He also tried the zodiac names, the Greek letter names, and the natural element names, but no assignment of *any* integers worked.

HIDEAWAY NUMBER NAMES

Number names sometimes hide within other number names. ONE is in twenty-ONE and in an infinity of other trivial cases. The nontrivial cases are those whose number and number name have no digits in common—twO huNdrEd, for instance, since 200 doesn't have a 1 in it. For ONE to NINE, the smallest trivial and nontrivial cases follow. Can you find the smallest nontrivial cases for TEN, ELEVEN, and TWELVE? (Answer Alley)

DIGIT IN COMMON		NO DIGIT IN COMMON
ONE	twenty-ONE	fOrty-NinE
TWO	TWenty-One	(none)
THREE	THiRtEEn	Two HundREd onE
FOUR	FOURteen	Five thOUsand thRee
FIVE	Fifty-seVEn	Four hundred thIrty-seVEn
SIX	SIXteen	Seventy-fIve seXtillion
SEVEN	SEVENteen	Six hundrEd eleVEN
EIGHT	EIGHTeen	onE vIGintillion tHirTy
NINE	NINEteen	oNe hundred thIrty-oNE

PATRIOTIC NUMBERS

Salute the number system! Wave the flag with numerical pride! Every word-minded American should be happy to know that exactly 99.9 percent of all the names of the cardinal numbers are patriotic. Why is this so? (Answer Alley)

ANAGRAM EQUATIONS

This equation, discovered by Melvin O. Wellman ("Emmo W."), is unique in English. The numbers add up correctly, and the names on opposite sides of the equal sign are anagrams of each other.

ELEVEN + TWO = TWELVE + ONE

The next two equations, discovered by Sallows, do the same in Spanish. Surprisingly, the sum of each is fifteen.

UNO + CATORCE = CUATRO + ONCE

DOS + TRECE = TRES + DOCE

ROMANTIC NUMBERS

Romantic numbers have Roman numerals embedded within their names, beginning with fIVe, sIX, and seVen and going up to nInety thousanD forty-four. The first three have a special property. They're the only consecutive numbers whose sum equals the sum of the Roman numerals embedded in their names.

$$f\,IV\,e\ +\ s\,IX +\ se\,V\,en$$
$$5\quad +\ 6\ +\ 7\quad = 18$$
$$IV\ +\ IX +\ V\ = 18$$

ACROSTIC EQUATIONS

An acrostic is a set of words whose initial letters also spell a word. The initial letters of these math problems spell out their own answers. How many other acrostic equations are possible? (Answer Alley)

Onehundred - Ninetyone - Eight = ONE

Twenty + Eighty - Ninety = TEN

OFF WITH THEIR HEADS!

Spoonerisms switch the first consonant sounds of words to make new words: COLD BAT = BOLD CAT. A few number names work this way to make spoonerism equations. In these two examples, the first changes two number names to adjectives; and the second changes three number names to verbs.

NINE + FIFTY = FINE + NIFTY

SIX + FIVE + THREE = FIX + THRIVE + SEE

SCRABBLE VALUES

In the game of Scrabble, each letter tile has a letter with a numeric value listed in the bottom left corner. When you spell a word, you score points by adding up the numbers on your tiles. With the letter tiles alone, TWELVE is the only number name whose score equals itself (T=1, W=4, E=1, L=1, V=4, E=1; total = 12).

In actual play, the value of a word depends on whether it includes a blank tile or crosses a double- or triple-value square. This means that many other self-referential number names can be formed on the board, including all those up to TWENTY-FIVE, except for TEN and NINETEEN.

Jeff Grant discovered the highest scoring self-referential Scrabble number name. Can you figure it out? (Answer Alley)

DIGITAL WORDPLAY

Instead of letters, digital wordplay uses numbers derived from the alphabetic values of letters. The alphabetic value is simply the position of a letter in the alphabet. A=1, B=2, Z=26. Performing digital wordplay involves three steps: (1) converting the letters to their alphabetic values; (2) performing the digital wordplay operation; (3) converting the new numbers as alphabetic values back to letters.

DIGITAL ANAGRAMS

A digital anagram is a word whose digits can be rearranged to form another word. In this example, a three-letter word becomes a two-letter word:

DAY = (4,1,25) = (4125) = (1524) = (15,24) = OX

The same digits arranged in all other possible ways make dozens of additional letter combinations, six of which form common words. Including DAY and OX, the number of digital anagrams in the 1245 set jumps to eight:

ABED (1,2,5,4)
AXE (1,24,5)
BADE (2,1,4,5)
BEAD (2,5,1,4)
DAY (4,1,25)
DUE (4,21,5)
LED (12,5,4)
OX (15,24)

The words in the next digital anagram set progress from four to five to six letters based on the same digits, 1113458:

CORN (3,15,18,14) = DREAM (4,18,5,1,13) = ARCADE (1,18,3,1,4,5)

Tom Pulliam found a set of digits that generates eight words from five to seven letters long. All are in *Webster's Third Unabridged* except ASTABLE in *Chambers 20th Century Dictionary*. Each word uses a different arrangement of 0111122259:

ASTABLE (1,19,20,1,2,12,5)
BUSKET (2,21,19,11,5,20)
JOVIAL (10,15,22,9,1,12)
LOTUS (12,15,20,21,190
OBLAST (15,2,12,1,19,20)
SALLET (19,1,12,12,5,20)
SALUTE (19,1,12,21,20,5)
TUSKY (20,21,19,11,25)

DIGITAL PALINDROMES

In a digital palindrome, the digits read the same in either direction. The first word below is the longest digital palindrome with no repeated letters. The second word, which Pulliam found in *Webster's Second Unabridged*, is the longest with repeated letters.

DAEMON (4,1,5,13,15,14)
GLUGGLUG (7,12,21,7,7,12,21,7)

Only a few palindromes are both alphabetic and digital. Leonard Gordon discovered these four:

CIVIC (3,9,22,9,3)
DEKED (4,5,11,5,4)
KAIAK (11,1,9,1,11)
DEIFIED (4,5,9,6,9,5,4)

UNIDIGITAL AND BIDIGITAL WORDS

Words can be classified by the number of different digits in them—unidigital, bidigital, tridigital, and so on. In the previous section, KAIAK, containing only ones and nines, is bidigital.

The longest unidigital and bidigital words in *Webster's Second Unabridged* are shown below. Coincidently, they both refer to tiny things:

KAKKAK (11,1,11,11,1,11): a small bittern
VALVULA (22,1,11,22,21,12,1): a little valve or fold

MULTIPLYING THE ALPHABET

To multiply a letter by a number, change the letter to its alphabetic value (A=1, B=2, Z=26) and then perform the operation. When the answer is twenty-six or less, convert it back to the letter having that alphabetic value (the first example below). When the answer is greater than twenty-six, divide it by twenty-six and convert the remainder back to the letter with that value (the second example).

The examples show the differences:

$$1.\ 4 \times E = ? \quad 4 \times 5 = 20, \text{ and } 20 = T$$
$$2.\ 4 \times J = ? \quad 4 \times 10 = 40, \text{ and } 40 / 26 = 1 \text{ with a}$$
$$\text{remainder of } 14, \text{ and } 14 = N$$

Performing multiplication on the alphabet one letter at a time does strange things to the familiar twenty-six.

Multiplying by two removes all the vowels:
ABCDEFGHIJKLMNOPQRSTUVWXYZ x 2 =
DFHJLNPRTVXZBDFHJLNPRTVXZ

Multiplying by thirteen gives one long row of Ms and Zs:

ABCDEFGHIJKLMNOPQRSTUVWXYZ x 13 =
MZMZMZMZMZMZMZMZMZMZMZMZMZ

Cubing the alphabet changes every odd letter except M to a vowel and every even letter to a consonant. Aloha! It looks Hawaiian:

ABCDEFGHIJKLMNOPQRSTUVWXYZ =
HALUHERALELMNUNYHURENYRYZ

Multiplying by twenty-six puts it to sleep:

BCDEFGHIJKLMNOPQRSTUVWXYZ x 26 =
ZZZZZZZZZZZZZZZZZZZZZZZZZZ

THE POINT OF LANGUAGE

Any letter, word, sentence, or longer text can be represented as a point on a line—at least in theory.

Take a line of any finite length and mark twenty-seven equidistant points on it. Let the first point signify a blank, the second point A, the third B, the fourth C, and so on to Z. The result is fairly obvious: any letter or blank is a point on the line. (Numbers, small letters, and punctuation could be included by dividing the lines into more points to represent those symbols.)

Continue by putting twenty-seven equidistant points between each adjacent pair of letters (or letter and space), and mark them in a similar fashion, but with two symbols. For instance, between E and F, the points would be Eblank, EA, EB, EC . . . EZ. Now every two-symbol pair (bigrams or letter-and-blank) is represented by a point.

Continue at the third level, and every three-symbol pair is represented. Between EB and EC, the points would be EBblank, EBA, EBB, EBC . . . EBZ. Likewise for the fourth, fifth, sixth, hundredth, thousandth levels. No matter how many times a line is alphabetically segmented, it can be further segmented. Some points identify single words. Others represent strings with one or more blanks in them, and those strings can have more than one word, such as "THE(blank)DOG."

By the five-millionth level, the division is so accurate a single point spells the entire text of *Gone with the Wind*, another spells *Pride and Prejudice*, and others spell every novel, every poem, every play, and every essay in English. In fact, every text that could ever be written in English has its place—every finite series of random letters and blanks.

Furthermore, if the line were divided an infinite number of times by an infinite number of alphabets and blanks, every text would then be represented an infinite number of times with the only difference being the number of blanks before the first letter and/or after the last letter in it.

You get the point.

GRAPHIC CONCLUSION

And here the graph paper ends. Numbers become letters, letters become words, and words become stories, which cover the pages of the next street. The alphabet has twenty-six letters, but why does the stop sign have a large number on it? (Answer Alley)

Chapter M

Story Row

THE X-PRESS-O COFFEEHOUSE

ON THE LOWER east side of Alphabet Avenue, the writers hang out at the X-Press-O Coffeehouse on Story Row. They look for new ways to create literature through wordplay. Let's join them in the coffeehouse and havacuppajava.

Above the coffee pots, there's a poster of Ernest Vincent Wright, who wrote *Gadsby*, a 50,110-word novel, without using the letter E.

```
AAAAAAAABBBBBBBBBCCCCCCCCCDDDDDDDDFFFFFFFF
AAAAAAAABBBBBBBBBCCCCCCCCCDDDDDDDDDFFFFFFFFF
AAAAAAAABBBB                        FFFFFFFF
ZZZZZZZZZ       EEEEEEEEEEEEEEEEEEE   GGGGGGG
ZZZZZZZ     EEEEEEEEEEEEEEEEEEEEEE   GGGGGG
ZZZZZ     EEEEEEEEEEEEEEEEEEEEEEE   GGGGGG
YYYY      EEEEEEEEEEEEEEEEEEEEEEEE   HHHHHHH
YYYY      EEEEEEEEEEEEEEEEEEEEEEEE   HHHHHHH
YYYY      EEEEEEEEEEEEEEEEEEEEEEEE   HHHHHH
XXXX      EEEEEEEEEEEEEEEEEEEEEEEEE   IIIIII
XXXX      EEEEEEEEEEEEEEEEEEEEEEE EEE   IIIIIII
XXXX      EEEEEEEEEEEEEEEEEEEEEEEEEE   IIIIII
WWWW      EEEEEEEEEEEEEEEEEEEEEEEEEEEEE   JJJJJ
WWWWW     EEEEEEEEEEEEEEEEEEEEEEEEEEEEEE   JJJJ
WWWWWW    EEEEEEEEEEEEEEEEEEEEEEEEEE   JJJJJ
VVVVVVV   EEEEEEEEEEEEEEEEEEEEEEEEEE   KKKKKKK
VVVVVVVV  EEEEEEEEEEEEEEEEEEE   KKKKKKKK
VVVVVVVVV  EEEEEEEEEEEEEEEEEEEE   KKKKKKKK
UUUUUUUUUU   EEEEEEEEEEEEEEEEEEEE   LLLLLLLL
UUUUUUUUUU   EEEEEEEEEEEEEEEEEE   LLLLLLLLL
UUUUUUUU  EEEEEEEEEEEEE   LLLLLLLLL
TTTTTTT   EEEEEEEEEEEEEEEEEE   MMMMMMMMMMM
TTTTTT    EEEEEEEEEEEEEEEEEEEE   MMMMMMMMMM
TTTTT                        MMMMMMMMM
SSSSSSSRRRRRRRQQQQQQQPPPPPPPOOOOOOOONMMMMN
SSSSSSSRRRRRRRQQQQQQQPPPPPPPOOOOOOOONNNNNNN
SSSSSSSRRRRRRRQQQQQQQPPPPPPPOOOOOOOONNNNNNN
```

Four people sitting at a table are arguing about Wright's E-less novel.

"I say he didn't use E because his typewriter was broken."

"No way! He taped the E down on purpose. He didn't want to use E because it reminded him of a failed romance with a woman whose name began with E—Elaine, Eloise, or Edna."

"That's pretty extreme. I think he avoided using it because he considered it unlucky."

"What's so unlucky about E? M is unlucky! It's the thirteenth letter of the alphabet. I'd say it was a Freudian thing, y'know. I mean, just think of the small e. It's curled up in a fetal position."

"Yeah, but why'd he call it *Gadsby?* It didn't have anything to do with Fitzgerald's novel."

Actually, he picked E because it's the letter most frequently used in writing, and that provided the greatest challenge. Omitting the letter Q would've been too simple. Such a work, which purposely excludes a letter of the alphabet, is called a lipogram.

Wordplay writing is often more complicated than regular writing. In selecting words, the writer sticks to certain restrictions. Word choice may focus on letters (anagrams, words with no E, etc.), sound (puns, rhymes, etc.), or meaning (slang terms, names, etc.).

The results of wordplay writing sometimes sound fairly normal, but in most cases they turn out strangely surreal.

BELLY FURNITURE

ADAM AND EVE ON A RAFT is restaurantese for "two eggs on toast." The following story has a smorgasbord of slang words and phrases cooked up in the greasy spoons of America.

As you read it, enjoy the flavor of the words. If you don't recognize one or two, you can open the Menu of Definitions in Answer Alley. The slang appears in the same order there as it does in the text. The words and the definitions come from Alexandra Day's tasty children's picture storybook, *Frank and Ernest.*

But this is an adult story:

The diner was about to close. I walked in and sat down at the long formica counter. My favorite waitress, Sally, was waiting on a young couple near the window, and I was waiting for her. To pass the time, I drew pictures of food in the grease that coated the countertop.

Maude, the owner of the place, stepped up, wiped the canvas clean, and cleared her throat to rattle off the specials of the day. Because she spoke Diner Language, she motioned to her official translator, the cook, to interpret for me. I waved him away and told her I was now bilingual. I'd just completed a Berlitz Diner Course.

"Okay, Mack, prove it," Maude said gruffly. "What'll you have?"

"FRY TWO, LET THE SUN SHINE," I said, hoping I got the syntax correct. "HUG ONE and gimme a BLONDE WITH SAND. For dessert, I'll have ICE ON RICE."

"Hmph! That's a change. Usually it's a HOUSEBOAT. I suppose you want the DOUGH WELL DONE WITH COW TO COVER?"

"Yeah, but no SNEEZE on the HEN FRUIT."

"Don't worry. MIKE AND IKE are sitting way over there."

"Oh, one more thing: SWEEP THE KITCHEN."

At this point, Sally came over, took off her apron, and sat down at the next stool. It was time to impress her with my newly acquired fluency in Diner.

"Hi, honey," I said. "You must've just gotten off work. How about some LIFE PRESERVERS?"

"Thanks, sweetheart, I might need—wait! You—you spoke Diner."

"That's right. Oh, here comes my RAFT with COW PASTE. Hey, just a second, Maude, I didn't order WRECKED HEN FRUIT."

She turned back to the grill.

"Forget it," said Sally. "I'll give you some PINK STICK."

"I'm in the mood for something a little spicier."

"Come to my place if you want some real BELLY FURNITURE," she said, running her long red fingernails down my menu. "For starters, we can do BLOW OUT PATCHES—"

"—or BIDDY BOARDS!"

"Yeah! And then we can SHAKE ONE IN THE HAY, and . . ."

"I'd like to TWIST IT, CHOKE IT, AND MAKE IT CACKLE!"

"Oh, you're exciting when you're hungry," she said dreamily. "I'll get you ALL HOT, too."

The diner door burst open. A Hell's Angel with a hell of an appetite hopped onto the stool next to mine.

"Gimme ten WIMPIES with WARTS and WAX," he growled to Maude, "and get a move on it."

Maude mumbled something with her back to him.

"Hey, I'm in a hurry," he said. "Kill the wimpies. Just BURN ONE, TAKE IT THROUGH THE GARDEN, AND PIN A ROSE ON IT."

"Grill's closed!" Maude snorted over her shoulder. "Might as well invest in a MILLION ON A PLATTER, smother it with POPEYE, and spread YELLOW PAINT all over it."

"Hey! Y'ain't even got HOUNDS ON AN ISLAND?" he barked.

"Nope, Buster, and I ain't got NOAH'S BOY WITH MURPHY, CARRYING A WREATH, so don't flood the counter with your tears, or I'll throw a LIGHT-HOUSE at you."

"You getting smart with me?" he shouted. "Look, make it a RADIO SAND-WICH and turn down your volume, lady."

"Back off, or you'll get a HOT TOP all over those long greasy FROG STICKS you call hair," Maude said, grabbing a cup and getting vicious. "And then I'll PUT A HAT ON IT that you'll never forget!"

The Hell's Angel turned to me and muttered, "Last time I was here I asked her to PAINT A BOW-WOW RED, and she served me ANGELS ON HORSE-BACK. And if that wasn't bad enough, she gave me some horrible GUESS WATER full of old BEEF STICKS, but there was something else in it, too. Something terrible. Man, I was sick for a week!"

He whirled around and stomped out. I was impressed. It was obvious that Diner was his native language. Sally squeezed my hand and said with a laugh, "I'll bet it had CHOKIES in it."

"Doesn't sound too bad," I said.

"It was Maude's April Fool's Day Special," she laughed, "made with BALLOON JUICE."

"No wonder the poor devil got sick."

"Let's go, Babe. I'll make you feel good, real good," she said with a twinkle in her eye. "How about a HOT ONE?"

"I'd rather PUT THE LIGHTS OUT AND CRY."

"With a SPLASH OF RED NOISE?"

"That's the way I like it," I said. "And for dessert I'd like my MAMA ON A RAFT."

"What about tomorrow?"

"Tomorrow morning we'll FLOP TWO and put YUM-YUM on BALED HAY."

"There's always HOPE, honey. Drink up your ADAM'S ALE so's we can leave," she said, trembling a little from the chilly breeze that blew in through the door.

"Yeah, for sure," I said, pulling her close. "It'll go well with my SHIVERING EVE."

"You make me feel like NERVOUS PUDDING. How about a little"—she kissed me—"OH GEE!"

"You bet!" I said. We got up to leave.

"You talk Diner real fine," she whispered in my ear. "I'm going to give you a big SUN KISS first thing when we get to my place."

As we walked out the door, I looked back and saw Maude splashing MISSIS-SIPPI MUD on ONE FROM THE ALPS.

JACK AND THE TWODERFUL BEANS

Where do trains go THREET-THREET? In the world of inflationary language, where the sounds of numbers in words are replaced by the next higher numbers. METAPHOR becomes METAFIVE, TENEMENT turns into ELEVENE-MENT, and TOOT-TOOT is THREET-THREET. Pianist/comedian Victor Borge invented this form years ago, reasoning that, since prices keep going up, so should language.

Richard Lederer wrote the following inflated folktale. Can you deflate it to find the meaning? (Answer Alley)

Twice upon a time there lived a boy named Jack in the twoderful land of Califivenia. Two day Jack, a double-minded lad, decided three go fifth three seek his fivetune.

After making sure that Jack nine a sandwich and drank some Eight-Up and quiten, his mother elevenderly said, "Threedeloo, threedeloo. Try three be back by next Threesday." Then she cheered, "Three-five-seven-nine. Who do we appreci-nine? Jack, Jack, yay!"

Jack set fifth and soon met a man wearing a four-piece suit and a threepee. Fifthrightly the man asked Jack, "I'm a Califivenian. Are you two three?"

"Cerelevenly," answered Jack inelevently. "But can you help me three locnine my fivetune?"

"Sure," said the man. "Let me sell you these twoderful beans."

Jack's inthreeition told him that the man was a three-faced triple-crosser. Elevensely Jack shouted, "You must think I'm an asiten idiot who's behind the nine ball. But I'm a college gradunine, and I know what rights our fivefathers crenined in the Constithreetion. Now let's get down three baseven about these beans. If you're intoxicnined, I'll never fivegive you!"

The man tripled over with laughter. "Now hold on a third," he responded. "There's no need three make such an unfivethreennine three-do about these beans. It's seven of two and half of thirteen of the other three me, but you won't find twoderful beans like this at the Eight Twelve."

Jack pulled out his trusty seven-shooter and exclaimed, "I'll make you change out of that four-piece suit and wear a threethree. Then I'll blow you three Timbukthree!" Jack then shot off the man's threepee. "Go away and recupernine at the Esseven Hospital. But second I twot you three give me the beans."

Well, there's no need three elabornine on the rest of the tale. Jack elevenacious-ly oned in on the giant and two the battle for the golden eggs. He exanimnined the big guy, and Jack and his mother were in eighth heaven and on cloud ten fivever after—and so on, and so on, and so fifth.

THE KNAVE'S ENGLISH

The King's English, as spoken by educated, knowledgeable people, is a snap compared to the Knave's English. The latter is composed almost entirely of slang—dig it? How much of this awesome story are you hip to, dude? You can translate using *The Pocket Dictionary of American Slang,* or you can turn to Answer Alley.

The potato-head cut a rusty on the borax gee-gee, but the kittle-cattle didn't have the oof to carry a lot of weight. The dust-dust with neon ribbons yammered, "I've seen kiwis become eagles with Dutch courage—until they prang."

"That's all yuk-yuk!" The honey man gobbled yum-yum with his snarky, mellow-back chi-chi oozing next to him.

"What's the foofooraw, sofa lizard?" The flyboy snapped his cap, ready for a hooper-dooper niff-naw with the zoot on a toot in Highbrowville.

"Just some fair hell scatting to a box of teeth under the oliver."

"Yatata yatata! Who's your raggle? She's the gnat's whistle."

"Snub out the quirley, and she'll shake a wicked calf till early bright for a brown Abe."

The wuzzy had a hissy: "But if you're hoosiering up about your soap-grease, stoopnagel, I'll hook your blowed-in-the-glass soup-and-fish and massage you with my gunboats. No soft, no hog-wrestle!"

"My beaujeeful phlug has more pazaza in her reach-me-downs than you have in your ball stand," the shoe diddlybopped; "but I don't boogerboo she's a frame-dame."

"Fuff!" the Broadway boy jibber-jabbered, "my whistle bait does bush patrol with prunefaces for happy cabbage. I presquawk prom-trotters on four and one. If you've got the tlac for nannygoat sweat, let's hustle to a slop-chute. My beaut has zowie for Simple Simons."

"I parley-voo, you ding-fizzled mush-faker. Anyhoo, Bricktop's dream box is shampoo to my mince pies. Her china, her load of hay, her dink, her cootie garages, her nozzle, even her googs—how cher!"

"With that eyewash, you must be a finger-wringer. She's got more spizzerinktum than a fizz job, more zazzle than an oomph girl," the flash-sport facked. "She's yours for a handsome ransom."

The three shook a leg to a nitery to get damaged. A scraunched kinker who'd had too much panther sweat made a rootin'-tootin' kick-up with Irish confetti by the whiffle-board. A yoot with a clothesline broke him.

"What a creep dive!" the fly guy yammered. "Maybe we ought to cut ass before some geek clonks my brag-rags."

"Nix out, sissy pants?" the mackman jawed. "Don't bop the panic rack. Let's click! Let's pick 'em up and lay 'em down to the gobble-pipe! Ain't my little piece of furniture a bonzer peach?"

"Sensaysh, but is she foxing me with gay deceivers from her wish book?"

"Go fly a wind-wagon! My poundcake ain't no purp looking for prog. She's got blip big browneyes."

"Blip, eh? Mixologist, more firewater. I'm a high pillow on a high lonesome with a high hig. Oka, general, how about a free show from the cheese?"

"Phedinkus! You don't have the do-re-mi for a do-se-do, Joe Sad!" The paper-belly was slurping King Kong with sizz-water. "Mox nix, jackeroo. No bouncy-bouncy!"

"You beat your gums, ho-dad, but where are the French postcards? Neighbo, it's all bibble-babble."

After chug-a-lugging the torpedo juice, he snurged.

UNSHERLOCK UNBOUND

In this mysterious unparagraph, each word except UNSHERLOCK is a regular entry in *Webster's Tenth Collegiate*. Some words have been pluralized or changed to different tenses. It's an uneasy read as it stands, but try reading it aloud without the UNprefixation. Can you undo it?

Unworldly unreason unmasks unknown unconcerns, unbuilds unsafety, uncages uncertainty. Unintelligence uneasily uncrowns unreality. Unlike unbalanced unreserves, unconsidered unconstitutional, untimely unsophistication unmakes unequals. Unthink, unlearn, unteach: unalternatives unnecessarily undouble unmeanings. Unspeak unofficial unlikelihoods? Unwish unwritten unlikelinesses! Unto unsound unbeliefs, unsay, "Untried, untrue!" Unveil unimproved unwisdom, unweaving unequivocally. Unbe: uncanny UnSherlock unwas.

THE JOY OF SEXISM

English slang has sex biases. It's in the nature of the beast. *Language Files,* published by the Department of Linguistics at Ohio State University, lists slang terms for "male" and "female." The collection was meant to show the biases, and therein hangs a tale that's utterly sexist.

A man and a woman were sipping wine at a very posh restaurant while waiting for the waitress to bring them their dinners. The galoot decided to order filet mignon, and the wench selected Peking duck.

"Toots," the geke said, "I've got a present for you."

"What is it, sport?" the vamp asked.

The nurd gave the tomato a small velvet box with a card that read, "To my little dumpling."

"Is it a ring, geezer?" the chippie whispered across the table.

"No, pussycat," the bozo replied. "Do you think a stud like me would give a chick like you a mere trinket? No, cookie, it's something special."

The hussy fumbled with the lid.

"Excuse me, sugar," said the hunk at the next table. "You need a he-man like me, not a wimp like that boy, to crack it open."

The fellow had been eyeing the skirt for quite a while. "What a bunny, what a peach, what a lassie, what a hen, what a sexpot, what a quail, what a tease, what a dish!" the creep said under his breath. Then, in a loud, deep voice, the gentleman offered to help. "Here, doll, let me do the job."

The hag tossed the box to the redneck, while the jerk glared at the bloke.

"Hey, schmuck," the chap said after a couple of minutes, "what's the matter? Can't a codger like you open my nympho's box?"

"No, guy," said the lad. "What did you get your harpie, anyway? The Hope Diamond?"

The jock returned the box to the broad. Using her long, sharp fingernails, the witch finally popped the lid up. A tiny piece of lint was lying inside.

"It's from a mink coat, babe," said the bum, grinning from ear to ear.

"Oh, you thoughtful dude," said the kitten, "it'll go perfectly with the ermine lint you gave me for my birthday."

DAPHNE IN WOODLAND

Alice of Wonderland fame fell asleep as her sister was reading a book to her. Soon after that, she fell down a rabbit hole to a world of strange creatures. In the following story, Daphne was reading a book, too, and wound up in Woodland. Most of the capitalized words in this story come from that book. What kind was it? (Answer Alley)

Daphne set out alone on a quest to find the legendary Eldorado. In the Everglade Moss near Flint Ridge, she met three other travelers, a Sprite, an Empress, and a Gladiator.

"I've been to the Riviera," said the Sprite as he brushed a Pinecone through his Twiggy hair.

"Oh, that's nothing," said the Empress, polishing the Gemstones in her Pink Tiara. After a slight pause, she announced with great Fanfare, "I've been to India, Naples, Monaco, Fort Pitt, and Carlsbad Cavern. Why, I've even been to Atlantis on an Arctic Night."

"Hah!" roared the Gladiator like a Giant Sequoia. "You ain't seen nothing till you've visited the Persian Gulf on a Balmy Day!"

Daphne asked, "Do any of you have a bottle of Coppertone? I'm allergic to Jungle Moss."

"Don't worry, Daphne," said the Sprite. "Firefly Pollen in the Starlight will protect the Candle Glow of your complexion."

"Or you could try Pearl Cream," said the Empress. She picked up a piece of Bleached Wood that resembled Victorian Mahogany and exclaimed, "By my Jewels, the Ocean Spray certainly produces some—"

"I'm famished!" bellowed the Gladiator. "Let's build a Blazon Pink campfire with that wood."

The Empress protested until the Gladiator yanked open the Pigskin sack that was slung over his Doric shoulders.

"Feast your eyes on these drinking Gourds," he said. "Plenty of Eggnog, Sangria, Absinthe, Claret, Creme de Menthe . . ."

"But what do we eat?" asked the Sprite. "Pickle Chips?"

"For lunch," the Gladiator said with a dramatic gesture, "we'll have a Zesty feast!" He dumped the entire contents of his sack onto the Sand Bar.

"By my Provincial Tan," murmured the Empress, sampling the provisions. "Asparagus Souffle made with Glazed Carrots, Black Olives, Celery Hearts,

Frosted Beets, Cocktail Onions, Peanut Shells, Aromatic Sage, Bean Sprouts, Hot Peppers, Chili Sauce, and Mince Meat! I'd just as soon eat a Llama stuffed with Ivory Tusks!"

I prefer Muskmelon," said the Sprite, "but I'll bet this souffle would taste like Sweet Meringue if you poured a lot of Green Goddess salad dressing all over it."

"I'll have Split Pea Soup," said Daphne. "Oh, and a Banana Split, too. It looks so Yum Yum Yellow!"

After gorging themselves under a Eucalyptus, they relaxed in a Jade Mist hovering above the Shamrocks. Daphne removed her clothes, every last stitch, till she was Peach Nude. Her Crimson Lips savored a dessert of Grape Sherbet topped with a Cherry.

"Those must've cost a lot of Gold Doubloons," she said, pointing to the Antlers on the Gladiator's helmet.

"No," he snorted proudly, "I won them playing Billiards with a Seafarer. My cue was forged of Hammered Iron. His was fashioned out of a Ship's Hull."

The Empress was sitting beneath a Canadian Spruce with her tiara in her hand. As she tapped on the jewels, she kept saying "Pinkety Pink! Pinkety Pink!" over and over. It was her way of achieving Tranquility.

"Why doesn't someone stuff a Powder Puff up her nose!" growled the Gladiator. Then, in a voice as tender as New Rust, he whispered to Daphne, "My Tawny Tangerine, my Candied Apricot, my Potent Orange, let's sow some Wild Oats in the Strawberry Whip. Let's cast Purple Shadows on the Ivy." His eyes were Satan Red, and his breath smelled of Sulphur.

"Keep your Pale Pebbles to yourself!" she snapped bravely. "I'm not Cheesecake for your Snickerdoodle."

Nearby, the Sprite was sipping Cafe Noir with a Grasshopper. "Ah, my friend, I see love blooming in the Sylvan Haze," he said, peeking through a cluster of Dahlias, Morning Glories, Forsythias, Hollyhocks, Wisterias, and Poppies in the Dark Forest. "Hand me a Sugar Cookie, if you will."

"Sure," said the Grasshopper, "but it's covered with Mountain Ash."

Suddenly, a Cardinal named Little Red Red swooped down to the Cottonwood. "Wheat Shock!" Little Red Red chirped frantically. "Better head for the Coral Reef or you'll wind up tangled in Swamp Reed!"

The sky grew darker than Burnt Toast. The Empress, the Sprite, the Gladiator, and Little Red Red, still shrieking "Wheat Shock," were blown away to the Mystic Sea. The poor Grasshopper, having choked on a soggy piece of Sponge Cake, lay dead in the Grass. Daphne was alone in Woodland. She looked for a Silver Lining in the Cumulus clouds swirling high above.

"I feel like a Mermaid beached on the Sahara Sand," she sobbed. "All my friends have sailed off into Deep Space."

Then she woke up safe and sound in her own bed. A book she'd been reading was draped over her face. Its pages were flapping like the wings of an albatross in the breeze from the window. She pushed it away and breathed a sigh of relief.

"Whew! What a weird dream! I'll never touch a book like that again."

THE ACCIDENT VERY BAD

When I was learning Spanish, I had to think in English and then translate. I would mentally rearrange the English sentences to follow Spanish structures: adjectives came after nouns, verbs had no subjects, and slang became literal.

This story is written in "Learner's Spanglish."

Two cars blue and one car yellow had an accident very bad. The car of the police arrived, and the police them saw.

"Of whom is this the fault?" asked the first police.

"His!" shouted the man more tall. "The man the yellow driving."

"No, not I hit anyone never!" shouted the man more loud. "My yellow not it caused."

"Then the fault must be of her," said the second police.

The woman out of her car climbed and smiled. Was being afraid. Walked up to the car of the police.

"To me not myself pleases," said the woman. "I was driving very slowly, when these gentlemen hit my poor little."

"I may see your license for driving?" asked the first police.

"Yes, Mister. Here is."

"Are shaking your hands," said. "Not makes cold today."

"What a pity!" replied. "The accident me made to have fear, and the drivers me blamed. But I it didn't do."

"Not yourself bother," said the other police. "As your spouse, I know that not was able to have been your fault."

Then her kissed. Into his ear whispered, "I you love, my little rich fat."

Replied, "I, too, my heart."

"Hey!" said. "To us what is going to happen?"

To him answered the police who to the woman was married, "My brother, the judge, this case difficult will decide."

The two men frowned. More late were found to be guilty. Had to buy a car new for the lady relieved. Were very, very angry.

GOING CRAZY AND TO THE STORE

In this tale, the sentences branch out in different directions to express the complexity of everyday events. Such connections are formally called zeugmas. As William, the protagonist, learns, life is the greatest zeugma of all.

William was going crazy and to the store. For two months, his wife, Gloria, had been badgering him about getting fired and a new job or lost. It wasn't his fault or in the cards. It was fate, embarrassing, and a surprise.

"Don't worry, my dear," he said under the clear night sky and his breath. "I'll get enough money to keep us in clover, the pink, and good standing with our creditors. You'll see."

"By gum, George, God, and jingo! You'd better, or you'll have to find someone else," she said, throwing caution to the winds, in the towel, and a clock at his head.

"Ouch!" he cried. The clock ricocheted off his forehead, a nearby tree, and a passing car. He saw stars, the writing on the wall, and to it that he'd do what he'd promised.

"The nick of time!" she shouted. "I expect you'll return with a million dollars, a hangdog look on your face, or never. Don't come back till you're rich or the cows come home."

He was crushed. She'd given him an ultimatum and the brush-off. He counted out his change, on good fortune, and his chickens before they hatched.

"Let's see," he said to himself. "I've got a little headache and over a dollar in my pocket. About all that can buy is aspirin or a lottery ticket."

Walking down the block, he felt gloomy and the need to get rich quick. The corner store and his mind were open, but his head ached from the clock.

"Good evening and weather we're having," said the friendly clerk behind the counter. "Can I help you find something?"

"Thanks, pal," said William. "I'll take the bull by the horns and a lottery ticket."

"What happened to your eye? You look like you've been hit with an ugly stick or by a truck or with a clock."

"Right the third time, but I'd rather not talk about it and like to buy the ticket, not the farm."

"Here it is," said the clerk. "Good luck, night, and riddance."

William stood outside in the moonlight and rubbed his aching head and the ticket with the edge of a coin. The numbers matched!

"Well, I'll be damned and rich!" he said. "I won a million dollars!"

He hurried home to tell his wife, who was having a good time and sex with their next-door neighbor. William and his heart pounded on the bedroom door and in excitement.

"Just a second, minute, or moment," she said. To the neighbor, she whispered, "Get dressed and lost."

After the neighbor climbed into his clothes and out the window, Gloria opened the door. She was wearing her nightgown and an angry look on her face.

"What's up, your problem, and that in your hand, William?"

"A lottery ticket, Gloria! I won a million dollars—"

"—and me back," she said. "That's incredible, wonderful, and half mine. Oh, I love you and money. I'm sorry I threw you out and the clock at your head."

"That's OK, dear," William replied. "Time heals all wounds and flies."

They kissed each other and their old lives goodbye. And they lived high on the hog, it up, like there was no tomorrow, on Easy Street, and happily ever after.

RHYMATIC FEVER

Rhyme is usually associated with poetry, sentences and paragraphs with prose. In this Valentine tale, every two words rhyme. Is it prose, poetry, prose poetry, or simply xzwamfeujho, an undefined literary form whose name is unpronounceable?

You be the judge of the next text.

Free, we drive. I've passed fast highways, byways—soaring, roaring. Then when we see a way, space, place for car, I try stopping, hopping out. Route shows rose flowers, towers blooming, looming over clover. Talking, walking to view tree, she holds, folds my shy hand, and squeezes, eases fingers—lingers near clear creeks, speaks:

"Those clothes, honey. Funny rags, bags, but what tacky khaki! You do need tweed. What nut spends, mends rotten cotton? Fad, bad taste! Waste! Try, buy clean, green dance pants, better sweater. Choose shoes, wear pair. Pitch, ditch that hat, baby. Maybe I'll smile, stay a bit, sit."

"My, I feel real stupid, Cupid. I'd tried—bought, thought they may please, ease. Remember December? Noise, toys? After laughter, pure—you're mad?"

"Lad, ain't St. Nick's tricks old, cold things? Spring's here, dear."

Will she flee, stand and turn, spurn kiss, miss lips' grips? Yes, dress makes, breaks warm charm. But what can man do to date mate? Travel gravel alleys, valleys, and stand out, shout, love glove, zoot suit—both?

Quoth I, "My dear, hear: you do require desire. Beauty's duties come from loose truths. They say bare air pushes bushes, heaves leaves, makes quakes in thin grass, lass, while style seizes breezes, messes dresses, whacks slacks, wrecks sex. Here, dear Valentine, Ballentine pale ale. Drink, think of love. We'll steel this kiss, where there are star-studded, budded flowers."

Hours go, flow through two hearts' darts. I spy her fur, wonder under lovers' covers. Bees' trees hold gold: more pour sunny honey by my girl's pearls, whose shoes shine fine. See? She feels, peels hose, glows by my car far from some dark park.

"Go slow, gentle lentil. Whee!" she breathes, seethes, quaking, making joy's noise. Why tie shoes, choose which stitch brightens, lightens over clover, rocks? Socks stay gray, creamy, steamy. Royal soil feeds needs, and hand places laces by my tacky khaki.

"Such touch burns, turns hot, not cold. Hold tight. Night comes, drums beat, heat our power high," I say. "Day glistens, listens under thunder by dry wood."

"Should we be here, dear?"

"Yes! Dress may lay on lawn, though."

"Go bare? Passion's fashions dare wear less?"

"Guess so."

"No bra?"

"Ah!"

Day's rays set, let moon soon loft soft light. "Night," I cry. "Lose shoes now. Wow! Yet let all fall to dew. Lie by dusk, musk. Do you need tweed to do this, Miss?"

"Oh, no. Gee!"

She hugs bugs, sees bees, hears cheers. Warm arm and hand touch much. I spy star far away, astray, where air shimmers, glimmers. Fair hair leaves, weaves down gown to view hill's thrills through two skins' sins. Exotic, erotic dancers, answers to new lust! Just lewd nude? Buff stuff?

Oh, no! Night's flights carry merry time's rhymes.

E IS FOR EXIT

And that's what happens when stories are brewed with wordplay. Ernest Vincent Wright's E-less portrait seems to smile momentarily as we leave the coffeehouse and walk down the street.

The traffic gets confusing, but somehow it manages to avoid literary gridlock. A car pulls up at the stop sign but doesn't move: STET is proofreader's notation for "let it stand." We pass in front of the car and continue our journey.

Poetry Parkway

THE LITERARY LABYRINTH

A BLOCK FURTHER, Poetry Parkway cuts through the center of town. In the center of the parkway, Poets' Park provides a sanctuary for people to read and write. In the very center of the park, there's a maze of marble called the Literary Labyrinth.

The founders of the City of Wordplay built the labyrinth long ago for all writers, but the poets took it over, claiming that poetry is the most labyrinthine form of literature. They carve their poems on the walls.

Two lovers are sitting at a table near the entrance. The woman is cutting out the words of a poem, and the man is starting to reassemble them like Scrabble tiles. The words are the first four lines of Shakespeare's Sonnet 18.

Shall I compare thee to a summer's day?
Thou art more lovely and more temperate.
Rough winds do shake the darling buds of May,
And summer's lease hath all too short a date:

The man finishes his cut-up version. He hands it to the woman, and she reads it. Apparently it worked: now they're walking to one of the darker corridors of the labyrinth, but they've left the poem behind. Here it is:

Summer's a lovely art.
May I date thee, darling?
Thou shall do more
And compare more, too.
Shake to the temperate winds,
And all hath lease of buds.
Summer's a short, rough day.

It's called vocabularyclept poetry, a form that's as close to a jigsaw puzzle as a poem can get. J. A. Lindon and Howard Bergerson wrote the first such poem in 1969.

Poetry takes many other forms in this place. At the entrance, we find a large white marble block with an inscription carved in blue marble above and below it:

THE UNWRITTEN PAGE

THE ULTIMATE MAZE

Let's explore the labyrinth.

FOREWORDPLAY

This poem describes what happens when a guy uses the wrong wordplay to make a pass.

I had a pal in Rome
Who wrote a palindrome
To dear sweet Ana Gram.
She said, "An anagram

Would turn my head around
More than your backward sound!"
But when she turned her back on him,
He penned a foolish acronym.

"You're such a wimpy man, damn!
You couldn't write a pangram."
Her words became so caustic,
He cried out an acrostic.

She threatened him with guns;
He fired old tired puns.
Then—wham!—she slammed the door on
My friend, that oxymoron.

BEATLEVERSE

The following poem commemorates the 1995 reunion of the Beatles. It's a cento, which is made entirely of lines written by others. In this case, the lines are titles of Beatles songs, sixty-eight of them, with no other words linking them together. Can you identify all the titles? (Answer Alley)

Before reading it, pick a Beatles album, tape, or CD, pop it in your music maker, and let the good rock roll!

Rock and roll music! What goes on?
Strawberry fields forever!
Fool on the hill, here comes the sun—
Day tripper, come together.

Lucy in the sky with diamonds,
    We can work it out.
Why don't we do it in the road?
    Honey, don't twist and shout.

Dear Prudence, do you want to know
    A secret? I feel fine.
You really got a hold on me.
    Let it be good day sunshine.

Sexy Sadie, don't pass me by.
    Slow down. You've got to hide
Your love away. I will drive my car.
    I'll get you a ticket to ride.

Martha, my dear, I am the walrus.
    I want you. Hold me tight.
She came in through the bathroom window.
    Help! A hard day's night.

Eleanor Rigby, all my loving,
    I want to hold your hand.
Wait! She loves you, Sgt. Pepper's
    Lonely Hearts Club Band.

Lovely Rita, I want to tell you
    Every little thing.
I'm happy just to dance with you,
    Girl, and your bird can sing.

Michelle, I wanna be your man.
    Love you to ask me why.
It won't be long. I call your name.
    I need you. (No reply.)

> Lady Madonna, I'm a loser,
>   Tell me what you see.
> "Nowhere Man, I've just seen a face.
>   Get back. Don't bother me."
>
> Tomorrow never knows the end
>   Yesterday, Mr. Moonlight.
> Eight days a week I call your name.
>   I'll follow the sun: goodnight.

UNIVOCALIC HAIKU

A unicycle has one wheel. A univocalic poem uses only one vowel in the text. Howard Bergerson wrote two univocalic haiku that ride as smoothly as a pair of unicycles.

The Haiku of Eyes

> In twilight this spring
> Girls with miniskirts will swim
> In string bikinis.

The Haiku of Ewes

> Unsung succubus,
> Must lust's susurrus clutch us
> Untruthful gurus?

APOSTROPHE TO LOVE

Apostrophes are linguistic plus or minus signs. They don't mean anything until they're put in a word. Then they mean either that letters are subtracted from the word or, contrariwise, that a letter (the possessive S) has been added.

Sometimes a word that has an apostrophe resembles another word that doesn't—I'LL and ILL, for instance. This poem uses such pairs as rhymes.

> When she said we'd
> Be shortly wed,
> Her dad said, "He'll
> Be damned to hell."

She asked if I'd
Obeyed my id.
I asked if she'll
Remove her shell.

If only she'd
Come to my shed!
Together we'll
Be feeling well.

But if she won't,
It is her wont.
Alas, I can't
Believe her cant.

TO HER I FLEE

The next poem is a semi-erotic palindrome, according to Barry Duncan, who wrote it in response to a friend's challenge. The fifteen-line verse reads the same in both directions, from the first line to the last and from the end of the last line backward through the first, building up from a fragmented beginning to a climax that'll leave you breathless:

To her I flee; fine position. Trap all up,
I won hat, last ewe, kilt, rat sets, a tooth,
Self, no wars. I, lion, a leg? Nay.
Men impugn in rub mill: animal spirit,
Safe buoy, no main. I won't. In if fits? No.
Is sap a spill? Later, I fall asleep
Till it's a help mission. On back!
Curtsey fixes her, eh? Sex if yes;
Truck cab, no. No is simple. Ha! Still, it peels,
All afire, tall lips, a passion stiff in it.
Now! In! I am on you! Be fast! I rip!
Slam in all! I'm burning up! Mine! My angel!
An oil is raw on flesh, too; tastes tart,
Like wet salt. Ah, now I pull apart!
No, it is open. I feel fire: hot.

A MRS. KR. MR.

In *An Almanac of Words at Play*, Willard Espy tells about a poem inspired by his sixteen years of experience at *Reader's Digest*. He joked to a friend that the magazine didn't condense enough and that it should also condense individual words. To illustrate his point, he wrote this abbreviated rhyme as a style guide and gave it to his friend:

> *The Mrs. kr. Mr.*
> *Then how her Mr. kr.!*
> *He kr. kr. kr.*
> *Until he raised a blr.*
> *The blr. killed his Mrs.*
> *Then how he mr. krs.!*
> *He mr. mr. mr.*
> *Until he kr. sr.*
> *He covered her with krs.*
> *Till she became his Mrs.*
> *The Mrs. kr. Mr.*
> *(and so on and on)*

AMANAMANIA

Some towns in the U.S. are surrounded by other towns with the same name, preceded by compass directions. Edward Wolpow called attention to this by citing Woodstock, Connecticut, which is encircled by North, South, East, and West Woodstock.

Iowa has a similar cluster, the Amanas. Individually, they are Amana, South Amana, East Amana, West Amana, High Amana, and Middle Amana, but, strangely enough, no North Amana or Low Amana. As the population grows, there could be a Right Amana, Left Amana, Front Amana, Back Amana, Near Amana, Far Amana—but this can only lead to "Amanamania":

> *Amana and Awomana*
> *Got married and had twins,*
> *Aboya and Agirla*
> *With fresh Amana grins.*

They had apaira pets,
Adoga and acata,
Which shared the family barn
With afroga and abata,

Abulla and acowa,
Agoata and agoosa,
Ahoga and asowa,
And an appaloosa.

Amana said, "I have
Aquestiona to aska:
Why don't we move away to
Alabama or Alaska?"

"Anoa!" said Awomana,
"Alifa like athisa
Provides alotta things
Akida would amissa."

To that, Amana said,
"Agirla and Aboya
Amissa this afarma?
Ah! Don't let it annoya!"

HAIKU MAZE

By working this maze, you can create seventeen-syllable poems. Here's how to do it.

Start at the upper left corner. Follow the path with your pencil to the first word balloon. Draw a circle around one of the four words. Leave the word balloon by an unused path and continue to the next word balloon. Repeat this procedure till you've reached FINISH. Go back to START and read the words you've circled on your path. It's a haiku.

Because of all the different word choices, you can make exactly 763,363,328 haiku—more than all that have been published in the history of the world.

A FARM OF CONFUSION

English is notorious for its refusal to pluralize according to any rational system. This poem questions the plurality of plurals.

A pair of oxes
Were pulling boxes,
Or was it oxen
Pulling boxen?

And each big box
Had a couple of lox,
Or was it a bock
With one big lock?

Perhaps it was oxen
Who opened the loxen
On all the boxen,

Or maybe just oxes
Who broke the loxes
To get to the boxes,

Or only one ock
Who forced the lock
On a single bock.

PIG LATIN EPIC

Pig Latin is an oral language code that many children learn. It works by moving the initial consonant sound of a word to the end of it and adding AY. If the word begins with a vowel sound, AY is added to the end without changing anything else. A few words turn into other words in Pig Latin. The prehistoric REX changes phonetically to the modern X-RAY. In the best Pig Latin translation of all, TRASH becomes ASHTRAY.

The following poem is by Omerhay, the Oetpay.

As I was walking on the beach
　　　Each bay
Was sunny, and I tried to reach
　　　Each ray.

I found some gold. I thought that more
　　　Ore may
Be hidden. In the ancient lore,
　　　Ore lay

On islands where the farmers hold
　　　Old hay
In caves that wind around the bold
　　　Old bay.

A map had shown the ancient wits
　　　Its way
To treasures buried in the pits:
　　　Its pay

Was large enough to fill a bin
　　　In bay.
By silent night, or by the din
　　　In day,

I vowed that I would search the sand
　　　And say
That gold must rest in golden land
　　　And lay

Within the cave. I'd cook some meat,
　　　Eat. May
The horses join me in the heat,
　　　Eat hay,

And gallop to the ocean's spring-
        Ing spray,
Until I see my fortune's ring-
        Ing ray.

With luck I'll find the places.
        Aces play
A lucky hand. I take ten paces.
        Aces pay.

ALASKAN DRINKING SONG

Several years ago, on a trip to Alaska, a friend of mine and I were walking down a side street called "Wino Alley" in Juneau. As we passed a vacant lot piled high with beer cans and booze bottles, this little quatrain came to me out of the clear blue sky. It has a tipsy little rhyme scheme.

You know
I know
Juneau
Wino.

SPIRAL NEBULA

You need only the first stanza of this poem to figure out the wording of the other five stanzas. What is its structure? Can you figure out the wording of the unwritten seventh stanza? (Answer Alley)

The stars drifting through clouds can't go above
city lights. Move there! Light up, shifting, twinkling
terribly tonight, so far. However, come outside. The
rainy lamps we now lost slowly are clear.

The clear stars are drifting slowly through lost
clouds now. Can't we go? Lamps above rainy
city, the lights outside move. Come there, however,
light far up, so shifting tonight, twinkling terribly.

The terribly clear, twinkling stars tonight are shifting,
drifting so slowly up through far, lost light.
Clouds, however, now there, can't come. We move,
go outside. Lamps, lights above the rainy city.

The city, terribly rainy: clear, the twinkling above
stars. Lights, tonight. Lamps are outside, shifting. Go
drifting, move! So we slowly come up, can't
through there. Far now, lost, however light, clouds.

The clouds: city light (terribly, however rainy, lost).
Clear, now, the far twinkling there above, through
stars, can't—lights up tonight. Come, lamps. Slowly
are we outside, so shifting? Move, go drifting.

The drifting clouds go. City, move light, shifting
terribly so. However, outside rainy, we, lost, are
clear. Slowly, now, lamps! The come-far-tonight
twinkling up there, lights above, can't through stars.

SHAKESPEARE'S BACKWARD SONNET

Shakespeare's Sonnet 66 is entirely reversible. Starting with the last word and ending with the first, it makes sense in a Carrollean sort of way, and it has a radical rhyme scheme: ABCCCCCCCCCDB. Only the capitalization and punctuation have been changed to flesh out the meaning.

The original ends with "Save that to die, I leave, my love, alone." This version starts out with those very same words in reverse order:

Alone, love, my leave, I die. To that, save
Gone be I, would these from these? All with tir'd
Ill captain attending good captive, and
Simplicity miscall'd truth, simple, and
Folly, doctor-like, controlling skill, and
Authority by tongue-tied made art, and
Disabled, sway limping by strength, and
Disgrac'd wrongfully, perfection right, and
Strumpeted rudely, virtue maiden, and

Misplac'd shamefully, honour gilded, and
Forsworn unhappily, faith purest, and
Jollity in trimm'd nothing, needy, and
Born beggar, a desert; behold to, as
Cry I, death restful for these, all with tir'd—

Two of the best-known lines from Shakespeare's plays read exactly the same, word by word, in either direction. Which are they? (Answer Alley)

WAY OUT

As we leave the labyrinth, the light verse begins to flicker. Outside the sun is setting. We follow the path to the road and the road to the scop sign. A scop is a poet-singer of earlier eras, but it's getting late. Let's move our poetic feet beyond the sign and walk down Alphabet Avenue to our next stop.

Chapter O

Onomastic Trail

THE FOREST OF NAMES

*B*EYOND AN OLD wooden gate, Onomastic Trail weaves through the Forest of Names. The trees are covered with names painted on the bark and printed on the leaves. The gnarled branches connect to the trunks, which lead to the roots, which are planted in atlases, census records, baby name books, product listings, telephone directories, and other reference works. Onomastics is the wordplay of names—that is, names of people, names of animals, names of you-name-it. Usually, they are proper nouns, but not always.

The first tree on the trail is covered with first names. What do they all have in common with the each other and with the word FOREST? You can't read the FOREST without the trees. (Answer Alley)

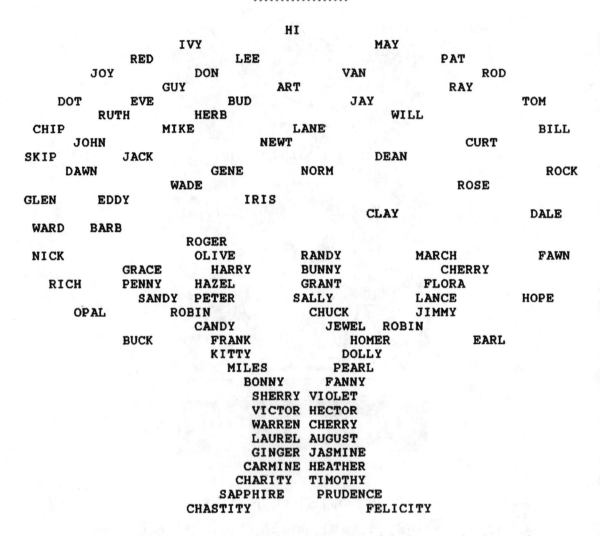

As we walk down Onomastic Trail, we meet some of the brave souls who rough it in the Forest of Names. Phimpha Boupha sits on a tree stump playing a tuba. K. J. Bozdog is training his pit bull. And Narvis Monday is trembling because he does not look forward to the beginning of the work week.

"Hey, got a light?" Cheryl Cherry says flirtatiously.

"Over here," Michael Universal replies, flexing his eyelids.

Dixie D. Outlaw roars down the path on her dirt bike. Her black leather jacket bristles with silver studs spelling out her name. As she slows down, she shouts, "I'm looking for I. Deal!"

Elberta Wipff sniffs in reply, "He went off somewhere with Ruby Zipperer."

And the names keep on coming. According to Social Security records, there were about 1.1 million different surnames in the United States in 1991. Add to this the myriad product names, city names, chemical names, biological names, and other names surrounding us, and you realize that the woods are indeed dark and deep.

ONOMASTICS BY ANY OTHER NAME

In its simplest form, onomastics involves collecting unusual names—punning names, hard-to-pronounce names, hard-to-spell names, hard-to-believe names. As much as any wordplay, they show the magic of language.

Michael Helsem has a list of real names that sound like they were imported from Wonderland. You've already met a few of them. Here comes the rest of the crowd.

Amy Boogher	Jackie Lack	P. Sprinkle
Bruce Bridegroom	Jadean Day	Rusty Straw
Cloteal Branch	Kalvary Kuch	T. Z. Zdon
Detlef Plum	L. Japngie	Uranus Appel
E. E. Eby	Laddie Shutt	William Widlits
Emmet V. Draddy	Leroy Schnose	Yun Uraa
Gary Airgood	Oleh Prodywus	Zeb Howze
Ima Lamb	Ole Worm	Zenon Bemko

SUPER HOOPS

Ajoritsedabi Oreghoyeyere Memaridieyin Okordudu played basketball for Bucknell in 1980. The North Central Names Society Bulletin (spring 1987) cited him for having the longest name ever recorded for a college basketball player. His record-breaking name has forty-four letters in it. He must've been very tall.

FEMINIST SURNAMES

A few years ago, I met a woman named Mary Elizabeth.

"What's your last name?" I asked.

"Elizabeth is my last name."

She explained that it hadn't always been that way, but that she'd legally changed her name by dropping her family name and replacing it with her middle name.

"I wanted a female last name," she said. "There aren't any, you know."

I suggested Shelley, as in Percy Bysshe, and she agreed there might be a few. I'd planned on making a list of female last names for her, but our relationship was as short as my middle initial, and I never got around to it. About fifteen years later, I skimmed the Iowa City phone book to see what I could find. Here's a selection:

Margaret Anne	Freddie Hannah	Glen Pam
Chris Christy	Nicole Jane	Gina Paulette
David Christine	John Jayne	James Pearl
Steve Doris	M. C. Kate	Aaron Rose
Philip Dorothy	Andrea Lara	Derrick Shirley
John Grace	Bryan May	John Winnie

MR. POPULARITY

What does a shy guy do to change his luck with the opposite sex? It's easy. Just get a new name. That's what Michael Cotran did. In 1988, according to the *Australian People* magazine, he forked over twenty pounds to legally change his first name to Howard and his last name to You-Like-To-Go-Out-For-A-Drink.

Now he doesn't have to come up with any clever pick-up lines. Whenever a woman asks him his name, he replies in all honesty, "Howard You-Like-To-Go-Out-For-A-Drink." He claims that it works.

WHAT'S IN A NAME?

Howard Richler assembled a mob of words listed in *Webster's Encyclopedic Unabridged Dictionary* that can be broken up into two or three given names.

AbNormAl	HerbAl	RoseMary
BeaNed	HomerEd	RoyAl
BellaDonna	JackAl	PatIna
BoGus	LeeWard	PatRon
BoRon	MartinGale	RegAlEd
CalGary	MelTedMort	RegIna
CyNic	AlNormAl	VicTim
DotTed	RicoChet	VictorIan
GrantEd		

A few words are packed with even more names. Jeff Grant found two with four names and one with five names, all listed in Evelyn Wells' *What to Name the Baby*.

DesAliNatEd

EmaNatIonAl

DeConTamInaTed

MONETARY MONICKERS

Simon Bolivar, Cristobal Colon, and Vasco Nuñez de Balboa have one thing in common: money was named after them—the Venezuelan bolivar, the Panamanian balboa, and the colon of Costa Rica and El Salvador. Ezra Pound, however, was named after money. That is, the the British pound was coined before Ezra.

The Numismatist, a magazine for coin collectors, reports that there is a James Dollar who collects American and Canadian dollars. The magazine elaborates: "People sometimes comment about his name, especially when he writes a check at a coin show to purchase—you guessed it—a dollar."

Other people are named after money. I checked the local phone book and found several monetary names listed in *Webster's Tenth Collegiate.* One person, Mark Schilling, has monetary units for both names. That's rich!

$INGULARS	PLURAL$
Jeng Yen	William Marks
Keith Kroner	Kenneth Nickels
Sara Mark	Heidi Pence
Dianna L. Penny	
Ben Leu	
Anindita Sen	
Christine Wu Yuan	

POSSESSIVE CELEBRITIES

Steve Chism sent a list of celebrities' names that have been altered to give them new meaning. Each last name begins with an S, but scooting the S over to make the first name a possessive reveals something about the celebrity:

Garry's handling	Loretta's wit	Soupy's ales
Gloria's wan son	Robert's tack	Sylvester's tall one
Larry's torch	Sharon's tone	Tom and Dick's mothers

IT ALL ADDS UP

Saddam Hussein and Richard Nixon have at least one thing in common: the alphabetic values of the letters in their name sum up to the same amount. As discussed in Chapter L, the alphabetic value of a letter is the number of its position in the alphabet (A = I, B = 2, Z = 26). Leonard Gordon found that the names of several well-known people have the same totals (shown in parentheses):

NORMAL ALPHABET
A B C D E F G H I J K L M N O P Q R S T U V W X Y Z

George H. Bush = Jack Nicklaus (115)
Mario M. Cuomo = Alfonso Capone (136)
Saddam Hussein = Richard Nixon (137)
Julius Caesar = Mickey Mouse (139)
Oliver North = Johnny Carson (156)

To expand the possibilities, Gordon rearranged the letters in different ways and gave them alphabetic values based on their new positions:

REVERSE ALPHABET
Z Y X W V U T S R Q P O N M L K J I H G F E D C B A

Gorbachev = Jimmy Carter (162)
Lyndon Johnson = John Kennedy (172)
J. Edgar Hoover = Adolph Hitler (196)
Saddam Hussein = Joseph McCarthy (214)
Norman Schwarzkopf = Theodore Roosevelt (138)

TYPEWRITER KEYBOARD
Q W E R T Y U I O P A S D F G H J K L Z X C V B N M

Che Guevara = Leon Trotsky (115)
Lech Walesa = Jesus Christ (118)
Gorbachev = Harry Houdini (127)
Saddam Hussein = Sammy Davis, Jr. (169)
Richard Nixon = Vladimir Lenin (192)

ALTERNATING ALPHABET
B A D C F E H G J I L K N M P O R Q T S V U X W Z Y

Pancho Villa = Jesse James (112)
Daniel Ortega = Fidel Castro (113)
Jesse Helms = Charlie Chaplin (119)
Joe McCarthy = Adolph Hitler (124)
Mikhail Gorbachev = Joseph Stalin (148)

HALF-SWITCH ALPHABET

N O P Q R S T U V W X Y Z A B C D E F G H I J K L M

Che Guevara = George Custer (143)
Howard Hughes = Richard M. Nixon (163)
Lech Walesa = Pope John Paul II (167)
Norman Schwarzkopf = Theodore Roosevelt (182)
Hubert H Humphrey = George Bernard Shaw (209)

His research with the normal alphabet also shows that JOHN MAJOR is a MARXIST (104), GEORGE BUSH a SOCIALIST (107), RONALD REAGAN a PRESIDENT (110), and FIDEL CASTRO a STATESMAN (112). JOHN F. KENNEDY was a ROMAN CATHOLIC (131), SIGMUND FREUD a FALSE PROPHET (141), and VLADIMIR LENIN a TRUE BELIEVER (142).

My own research shows that GOD = 26, the number of letters in the alphabet, which brings us to . . .

THE TWENTY-SIX NAMES OF GOD

In the beginning was the word, and the word was God, at least in the English language. Other languages have their own names for the deity. Using *The Gospel in Many Tongues* (British and Foreign Bible Society, 1965), Alfred Lubran compiled an abecedarium of the word for God. Here are the names with their languages:

Allah (Arabic)

Boh (Czech)
Chihowa (Choctaw)
Deviyanwahansay (Sinhalese)
Efozu (Avikan)
Foy (Bullom)
Gott (German)
Hananim (Korean)
Isten (Hungarian)
Jing-Ming (Chinese)
Kabeshyampungu (Luba: Kalanga)
Lu (Moru)
Mngu (Swahili)
Nkulunkulu (Zulu)

Oesif Neno (Timorese)
Perendiah (Albanian)
Quecha (Ayacucho)
Rebbi (Kabyle)
So (Baya)
Theo (Greek)
Unguluve (Kikinga)
Vittekwichanchyo (Tukudh)
Walla (Mano)
Xwede (Kurdish)
Yang Tom Tro (Koho)
Zo (Atche)
[Geographic location of some of the languages: Sinhalese = Sri

Lanka; Avikan = Ivory Coast; Bullom = Sierra Leone; Luba = Congo; Moru = Sudan; Timorese = Indonesia; Ayacucho = Peru; Kabyle = Algeria; Baya = West Central African Republic; Kikinga = Tanzania; Tukudh = Alaska and Yukon; Mano = Liberia; Koho = Vietnam; Atche = Ivory Coast]

BRAND-NAME KIDS

Baby name books are always coming out with new names from around the world, but they've overlooked one major area pregnant with possibilities. Proud parents ought to consider using the names of their favorite product. After all, if they love the product, they'll love the baby.

Anacin and Bufferin would be perfect for two rambunctious little girls. Xerox would hearken back to ancient Persian names like Xerxes. And wasn't Rome founded by Romular and Remus?

For a better view of life in the future, let's visit a classroom of brand-name kids:

"Murine, why are you crying?" asked the teacher.

"Because Anacin just hit me over the head with a ruler."

"Did not!" Anacin said. "It was Bufferin."

"Yeah, Bufferin's always hitting people on the head," said Visine.

Hearing that, Bufferin whacked Visine with the ruler, and she burst into tears. Before the teacher could say anything, Clorox rushed into the room. He was as white as a sheet.

"Teacher!" he cried. "Romular just threw up all over Robitussin!"

"Oh, dear, I suppose Romular's got the flu again," the teacher groaned.

"Now my stomach hurts," Maalox whined.

"I've got a doggie bag you can use," Purina offered.

"Alright, class, let's quiet down and be seated. We're going to have a spelling test. And Xerox, if I catch you copying anyone else's answers again, you'll have to stay after school."

"I won't," Xerox promised. "I won't."

"Good. Now everyone take out a clean sheet of paper. Today's test will be on the old-fashioned names that people had years ago. I'll pronounce each one carefully, and you write down the correct spelling. Okay, let's start. Tom . . . Annie . . . Jack . . ."

Maalox grabbed her stomach at the name "Molly." Murine and Visine started sobbing at the names "Marie" and "Vicki." Romular retched at "Ronald," and so did Robitussin at "Robert." Xerox kept asking the teacher to repeat everything.

When Adidas jumped up and chased Keds around the room, all the other kids cheered wildly.

"Will everyone please be quiet!" the teacher shouted.

Anacin and Bufferin dropped their pens. Bending down to pick them up, they bumped heads. Ronsonol set fire to her pencil and waved it at Exxon. Bic threw banana peels at Eberhard Faber. Goop splattered hunks of mud on Ivory.

"I said, be quiet!" the teacher snapped, and the class finally calmed down. "That's better. Now pass your papers in."

That night when she graded them, she couldn't find one correct answer! She asked her husband if he had any idea why the kids did so poorly.

"Maybe you have bad breath, my dear Listerine," he replied.

"You're just joking, Mylar. I can see right through you."

He laughed heartily.

"Shhh!" she whispered. "You might wake up baby Sominex."

I CAN'T BELIEVE IT'S NOT BUTTER

I Can't Believe It's Not Butter is one of the great trademarks of the 1990s. Like any inspired trademark, it's bound to be imitated by other companies seeking a better brand name. A proliferation of similar names could lead to incidents like the one described in this story.

I left the tub of I Can't Believe It's Not Butter out all day, and it melted. As I put it back in the refrigerator, some of it dripped on the floor. I washed it up with I Don't Give a Damn if It's Not Cleanser.

The dog was hungry. I poured him a bowl of He's Too Stupid to Figure Out It's Not Meat. I looked out the window, which was dirty, so I washed it with You're So Sloppy You Won't Even Notice It's Not Windex. Outside the birds were chirping and pecking at the feeder full of They'll Never in a Million Years Guess These Aren't Edible Seeds.

When my wife came home, she brought me a box of He Couldn't Possibly Fathom They're Not Chocolate Chip Cookies, and I ate two of them with a glass of She Didn't Have the Faintest Idea That It's Not Pasteurized, Homogenized Milk. Delicious!

When I got up from the table, though, I slipped on a streak of I Can't Believe It's Not Butter that I'd missed with the I Don't Give a Damn if It's Not Cleanser, kicked the bottle of You're So Sloppy You Won't Even Notice It's Not Windex, which sailed through the window and landed in the feeder of They'll Never in a Million Years Guess These Aren't Edible Seeds, crashed against the bowl of He's Too Stupid to Figure Out It's Not Meat, crushed the box of He Couldn't Possibly Fathom They're Not Chocolate Chip Cookies, and spilled the entire carton of She Didn't Have the Faintest Idea That It's Not Pasteurized, Homogenized Milk all over the floor.

I got up, aching from the fall, and took a couple of It Didn't Occur to You That These Might Not Be Painkillers but Sugar Pills Instead. Within minutes, I felt a whole lot better.

MYSTERY NAMES

Each of the names below is the title of (1) a rock band, (2) a computer language, or (3) a video arcade game. Can you tell which is which? Put 1, 2, or 3 after each. (Answer Alley)

A. Rain Parade	J. Laff	S. Mad Planets
B. Trojan	K. Windbreakers	T. Sonson
C. Copernicus	L. It	U. Public Image, Ltd.
D. Soap	M. Crystal Palace	V. Synful
E. Digital Sex	N. Mad	W. Exploding
F. Zaxxon	O. Magic Paper	Parakeets
G. Contra	P. Raunch Hands	X. Treet
H. For Against	Q. Qix	Y. Zwackery
I. Tricycle Thieves	R. Baseball	Z. Gat

THE ART OF NAMING IN THE NAMING OF ART

Art has proliferated in the twentieth century. Many artists use unconventional methods to make unconventional works, and they name their art movements with unconventional names. John Walker discusses a variety of movements, exhibitions, groups, and terms in his *Glossary of Art, Architecture, and Design Since 1945*. In this selection, all are real or at least surreal.

Air Art, also called Sky Art or Blow Up Art

Anti-Art, which says that anything and everything can be art

Arcology, a fusion of architecture plus ecology

Funk Art, sometimes spelled Funck or Phunck, a child of Dada

Nart, a combination of n(othing) and art

No Art, which is still art

Floor Art, which sits on the floor

Food Art, which cooks on the stove

Kitchen Sink School, which cleans Food Art off the plates, unless they've fallen and shattered on the Floor Art (not really)

Lost Sculptures, as opposed to Found Art

Op Art, Pop Art, Cop Art, and Prop Art, four concepts that are related in rhyme only

Supermannerism, a combination of optical and intellectual trickery (but there was no mention of Clark Kentism)

MEDICAL MISNOMERS

Have you ever been arrested for breaking the Beer Law? Probably not, unless the policeman was a mad scientist. The Beer Law isn't a law regulating alcohol usage but a statement about light transmission by the physicist A. Beer. Chris McManus sent a list of similarly deceptive terms from *A Dictionary of Medical Eponyms* by Firkin and Whitworth (1987).

The terms are real, but they don't mean what they say. The book contains biographies of doctors and scientists who have given their names to diseases, measurements, or laws. The following are named after some of these people:

Battle Sign	Hope Murmur	Quick Test
Cannon Law	Hurler Syndrome	Saint Triad
Carrion Disease	Ivy Method	Shaver Disease
Christmas Factor	Legal Disease	Sippy Diet
Curling Ulcer	Looser Zones	Stickler Syndrome
Darling Disease	Moon Molars	Sweet Syndrome
Drinker Respirator	Parrot Nodes	Wood Lamp
Good Syndrome	Pepper Syndrome	Young Syndrome

THE CITY OF FORTY SPELLINGS

Which American city has been spelled in a greater number of ways than any other? You can almost hear the wind whistling through the letters of CHICAGO, the "Windy City." Dmitri Borgmann found forty variant spellings in reputable reference works.

As a matter of civic pride, Chicago should put up a billboard to let tourists know that they're coming into a multipli-city of names, including one that sneaks a number in with the letters. Here's what the sign could look like:

Wellkgum Tu

Apkaw	Chicagu	Psceschaggo
Checago	Chicaqw	Quadoge
Checagou	Chicawgo	Quadoghe
Cheegago	Chiccago	Schenkakko
Chegagou	Chigagou	Schuerkaigo
Chegakou	Chikago	Shikkago
Cheggago	Chikagons	Stkachango
Chekakou	Chikagou	Stktschagko
Chicagou	Chikkago	Zheekako
Chicags	Chirgago	Ztschaggo

Pleeez Hobay Owr Traphique Lauz.
Thaiengcqkxzs!

Chicago may hold the record for cities, but TALWRN COURT in Iowa City is the king of mispelled streets. Fred Crane lived on that fabled street, pronounced TAL-run, for twenty-five years.

Soon after moving there, he noticed that people had a hard time spelling it. He decided to keep track of the different misspellings he'd received in the mail, and twenty-five years later he had 148 variations, including CALVIN, IOLWIN, TALCUM, TALLWORM, TALWRENCH, TLAOLVWERN, TWITT, and TXLWRN. Pity the poor mail carrier!

If Talwrn Court were in Chicago, the number of possible different addresses would jump to 5,920. At the rate of one a day, Crane could've collected mis-spellings for over sixteen years before his creative correspondents repeated an error.

THE FIRST SHALL BE LAST

AAAT'S BAY, according to Darryl Francis, is alphabetically the first placename in the United States. It's listed in the *Dictionary of Alaska Placenames* (Geological Survey Professional Paper 537) as an alternative to AAT'S BAY.

Aaat's all, folks!

MARK TRAIL

Onomastic Trail splits off in many directions. It's easy to get lost in the names. The sound of Phimpha Boupha's tuba guides us back to the road, where the stop sign has a name on it: STAN D.

We stop; we stand; we go.

Chapter P

Visual Viaduct

THE LANGUAGE MAGIC SHOP

IN THE LANGUAGE Magic Shop, Optico the Magician sells wordplay tricks that twist words in different directions, mix them up, and make them disappear.

Let's go into his shop and look around—and sideways and backward. By the time we're through, we'll have viewed words from so many different angles that our normal left-to-right orientation will have vanished along with our concept of language as simply a form of communication.

"Pick a card, any card," says Optico, leaning over the counter in the dimly lit place.

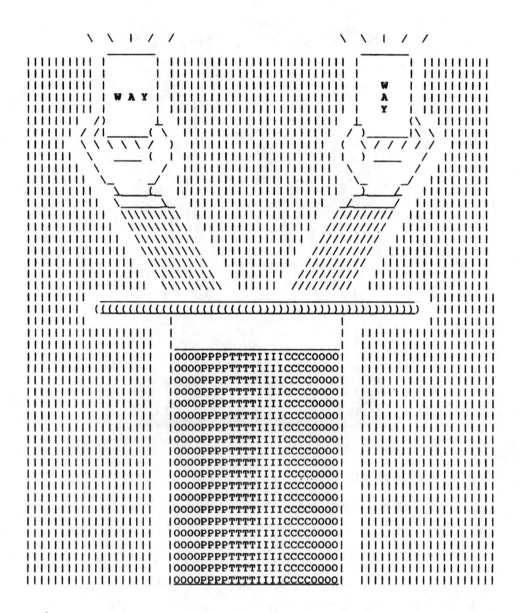

You pick a card and look at it. It says WAY.

"WAY?" Optico asks. "You're sure of it? But look what happens when I tap it with my pencil wand and hold it up to the mirror."

WAY changes to YAW, meaning "to deviate erratically from side to side of a course." In the mirror, the letters are the same, but their order is reversed. W , A, and Y are mirror letters.

"Oh, you think you know the secret?" Optico asks. "Observe what happens when I tap the card, move the letters around in a column, and hold it up to the mirror again."

This time, the letters spell WAY going downward on both the card and the mirror!

"Magic," he says. "Now you may look through my shop. Watch out for the trapdoor, though."

MIRROR LETTERS

Most capital letters, like those in WAY, appear the same in a mirror, but they do it in different ways. Just ten letters— FGJLNPQRSZ—are asymmetrical.

VERTICAL MIRROR LETTERS:
IVY MOUTH WAX

Eleven letters are symmetrical along their vertical axes. Compared to most other widely used alphabets, that is a lot. Only modern Greek, with sixteen vertical mirror letters out of twenty-four, tops it. If you draw a line down the center of each letter, the left side is a mirror image of the right side.

Ross Eckler put the letters together to make a single phrase, IVY MOUTH WAX, the brand name of a fictitious toothpaste. If a large sign on a building had the letters rotating in a vertical column, they would always appear to turn forward to the viewer.

A product like that should have its own tube, so I designed this one to take advantage of the letters' reversibility.

Later, when a friend came over, I showed her the drawing. Then I pointed to the living room mirror and said, "Notice any difference in the mirror? The letters on my T-shirt are reversed, but the letters on the tube aren't."

With a look of surprise, she asked, as if inquiring about a magic trick, "How'd you do that?" I explained, and the explanation surprised her, too.

Writing vertical messages is one thing, but writing a horizontal palindrome that reflects backward with correct spelling, spacing, and punctuation is much more difficult. In this example, the mirror reverses the letters but not the words or the question mark.

AHA! MAY I MAIM A MIAMI YAMAHA?

The next palindrome is one of the few that are truly reversible. It's a music teacher's direction to a flute student, and it looks exactly the same in a mirror.

TOOT IT A TI TOOT

Returning to nonpalindromic forms, texts can be written in which the letters look correct but most of the words don't. "Ahtawaih," the poem below, takes off from Henry Wadsworth Longfellow's "Hiawatha." It's letter-perfect, but word-crazy. When held up to a mirror, everything falls into place by the shores of Gitche Gumee.

AHTAWAIH

OTTO TUOHTIW OTUA TAHT HTIW
IIAWAH TA AHTAWAIH
—!IXAT A TAHW—IXAT A TIH
.IMAIM TA ATOYOT A

:YVI OT WOV I TUH A TA
.IXAT A TIH AHTAWAIH"
.HATU OT TUO TI WOT YAM I
"!YXAW OOT—WOT OT TIAW YAM I

IXAT A HTIW OTTO TUOHTIW
IIAWAH TA AHTAWAIH
IXAM A—AMIXAM A TIH
!IMAIM TA (OTUA YM) AM

:AVA HTIW TUH A TA MA I
.OTUA YM TIH AHTAWAIH"
.ITIHAT OT TI WOT YAM I
".OTTO OT TOOT OT TIAW YAM I

AHTAWAIH HTIW YOT YAM I
.OIHO—AWOI TA TUO
IXAT HTOMMAM TAHT WOT YAM I
.UHAO OT—IIAWAH TO

HORIZONTAL MIRROR LETTERS: HECK, I'D BOX

Nine letters are symmetrical along their horizontal axes. They're all in the sentence HECK, I'D BOX. If you draw a line across the center of each letter, the top is the mirror image of the bottom.

"Echo," the poem below, is printed with its title and lines in reverse order. You can read it from the bottom up, or you can hold it up to a mirror and read it from the top down. To do this, tilt the book forward so the top edge of the page is parallel to its reflection.

ED CHOKED
COOKBOOK
DEB COOKED
CODEBOOK
BOB CODED
CHECKBOOK
DEE CHECKED
ECHO

DOUBLE MIRROR LETTERS: HI, OX

Only four letters—H, I, O, and X—are symmetrical along both axes. Because there are only four mirror letters, including the difficult X, it's nearly impossible to make a reasonable palindromic phrase, but it can be done. The line below reflects a censor's thoughts while rating a porno film. If you turn the page upside down, it appears the same. If you hold it up to a mirror either way, ditto.

OH HO—XXX—OH HO

UPSIDE-DOWN LETTERS: SH, X IN OZ

Some letters don't require mirrors to work their magic. When the page is turned upside down, the letters in SH, X IN OZ stay the same. Most are also double mirror letters, but three of them—N, S, and Z—turn backward in a mirror.

The best-known palindrome of this kind comments on the spelling of Richard Nixon's name. However, if you turn the page upside down, you'll see that palindrome doesn't quite work: the spacing changes. (As noted above, palindromes using vertical mirror letters have the same problem.)

The Nixon palindrome first appeared anonymously in Martin Gardner's "Mathematical Games" column in *Scientific American.*

NO X IN NIXON

The next palindrome solves the problem of spacing, but it requires a spacious explanation: during the Nixon era, a Viet Cong soldier spotted a poster of North Vietnam's president Ho Chi Minh on a nearby wall. The soldier noticed that someone had printed the Greek letter xi six times on the poster. His response reads exactly the same upside down:

OH NO SIX XIS ON HO

WORDPLAY KALEIDOSCOPE

To fully experience the mirror effect, you can build a Wordplay Kaleidoscope. The traditional kaleidoscope uses fragments of colored plastic placed at the turning end. Substitute letters for colors, and you'll see the language in a way you've never seen it before. If you use symmetric letters only, the letters will always be facing the right way.

It's simple to make. Buy a standard kaleidoscope with a turning end. Pry open the disc covering the turning end. Pour out the colored plastic pieces. Have your local copy center photocopy a page of words onto transparent acetate. Cut out letters and words from it. Put them in the turning end. Replace the disc on the turning end, tape it shut, and it's ready to go.

When you turn the end, snowflakes of letters form and reform endlessly, creating patterns of words, letters, and shapes. In the figure, the circle on the left shows

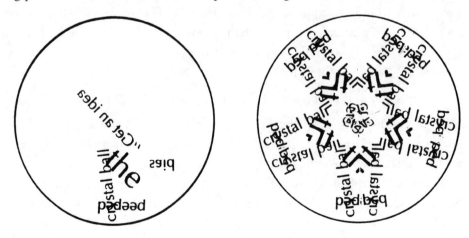

letters and words as they'd actually appear in the turning end, and the circle on the right shows how they'd look through the viewing end.

SHAPE-SHIFTING THE ALPHABET

Constable Odo in the TV series *Star Trek: Deep Space Nine* is a shape-shifter. He can change from his normal silly-putty shape into the shape of a human or other creature. The letters of the alphabet can shift their shapes as well.

To shape-shift from one letter to another, draw a series of intermediate letters that make slight changes. A line may grow longer, shorter, break apart, or disappear. A curve may turn in a different direction or straighten out. Separate lines may move together and connect. If you print the letters one per sheet on a tablet, you can flip the pages to make them move like an animated cartoon—an "alphatoon."

I showed my five-year-old son, Danny, how to do it, and he wanted to try it himself. Some of the resulting alphatoons appear in the illustration. The first group has two of mine, which change A to Z (1) and I to E (2), and three of Danny's, which change D to H (3), K to G (4), and A to V (5).

The strategies for making the changes may differ from person to person. My niece Samantha, my sister Michele, Danny, and I tried the same letter pairs without seeing the others' work. Alphatoons 6 and 7 show L to P drawn by Danny and

Alphatoons

Samantha. Alphatoons 8 to 11 show the four different ways that Samantha, Michele, Danny, and I changed O to E.

Letters and words can turn into drawings, too. The Dancing Dog is a longer alphatoon in which the word "dog" becomes the image of a dog and then collapses into a pile of hair, out of which "cat" pounces. Originally I printed it on the

The Dancing Dog

FOR THE ABOVE ALPHATOON, "READ" EACH COLUMN DOWNWARD, START-ING WITH THE LEFT COLUMN AND PROGRESSING TO THE RIGHT.

IN TABLET FORM, THE PAGES FLIP THIS WAY.

pages of a tablet as shown in the illustration, and when I flipped the pages—voila! the dog danced.

CARTOON CARDS

Any way you arrange them, the Cartoon Cards make a line of talking heads speaking in rhyming couplets. The couplets change with every arrangement of the cards. Photocopy the cards in larger size onto card stock, cut them out, shuffle them, and deal a poetry comic.

THINGLISH

Thinglish is a tall, thin form of printed English used in certain visual puzzles. The letters are so tall and thin that they lose their normal readability. When you tilt the page until it's almost perpendicular to your nose, the letters flatten out and—presto!—the message appears.

Usually Thinglish is limited to short, rectangular texts, but there is more to it than meets the eye. (If you need help with any of the Thinglish puzzles that follow, turn to Answer Alley.)

The first three texts show how the letters can make pictures. They can be read without tilting them, but the words become clearer at an angle.

PROFILE. The letters differ in length, but they seem to even out when they're tilted.

RENAISSANCE PERSPECTIVE. The letters grow smaller till reaching a mysterious final letter; is it an S or a D? The sentence reaches the vanishing point.

CUBIC WORD. If you tilt the page to read the front face, the side faces blur into shading. With the page still tilted, turn it forty-five degrees counterclockwise. The words on the side faces pop into view, and the front face fades to gray.

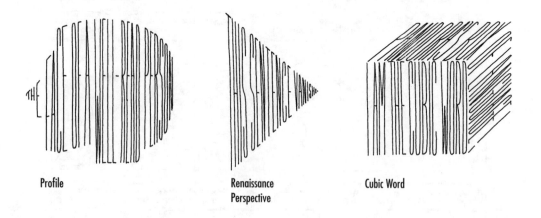

Profile

Renaissance
Perspective

Cubic Word

The next three are puzzles. They rely on the effect present in the Cubic Word above—that is, when the page is tilted to view one set of lines, all other lines not parallel to that set lose their resolution and become shading.

SENTENCE IN THE ROUND. To read this circular piece, start at the top, tilt, and rotate clockwise. What is it saying?

LIGHT CROSSHATCHING. The names of the months appear in this clashing of words, but one month name is missing. Which one?

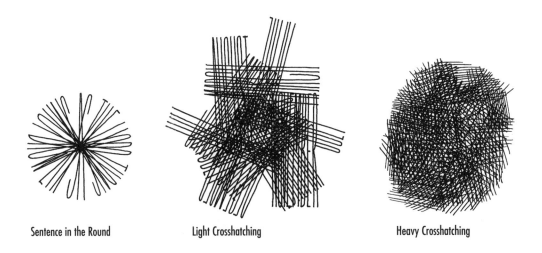

Sentence in the Round   Light Crosshatching   Heavy Crosshatching

HEAVY CROSSHATCHING. This provides the answer to the riddle, "What does ink become at twelve o'clock P.M.?"

STEREOWORDS

In one type of optical illusion, the drawing of a man's face and a woman's face appear on opposite sides of the page. By looking at the picture at arm's length and then bringing it closer without refocusing your eyes, you can see the couple kiss.

Stereowords work like that. In fact, they're also similar to sirds, the colorful computer-generated pictures that slip into three-dimensionality when viewed the right way.

To "read" a pair of stereowords, hold the page about a foot and a half from your face. Without changing your focus, bring the page closer until the two dots above the box merge to form a third dot in the center. The box itself will divide into three connected boxes with the stereoword in the center box. Carefully move your line of

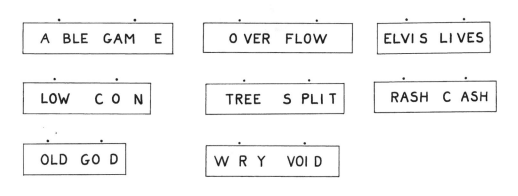

vision down to see the middle word. If the letters fade in and out, jumble up, or blur, try refocusing on them or return to the guide dots and start over.

The stereowords below relate in one way or another to the hidden words. Can you read them? (Answer Alley)

ALL'S WILL THAT ENDS WILL

William Shakespeare was, to say the least, a man of letters. In this calligraphic portrait, the letters in SHAKESPEARE form the likeness of his face. You can have your image and read it, too.

THE TRAPDOOR

Walking back to the front of Optico's shop, we accidentally step on the trapdoor that he warned us about. We plummet through the darkness to the road again. As we drop past the stop sign, we see the elongated letters that spell out their message in Thinglish.

Chapter Q

Computer Speedway

THE WORDPLAY PROCESSING CENTER

THE BUILDINGS ON Computer Speedway look like computers. The people who work in them spend day after day programming and running them to process wordplay. They use computers to invent new forms, to reexamine known forms, and to solve wordplay problems.

In the middle of the block, the Wordplay Processing Center is a hub of activity. Let's go in through the Input Door and check out the output.

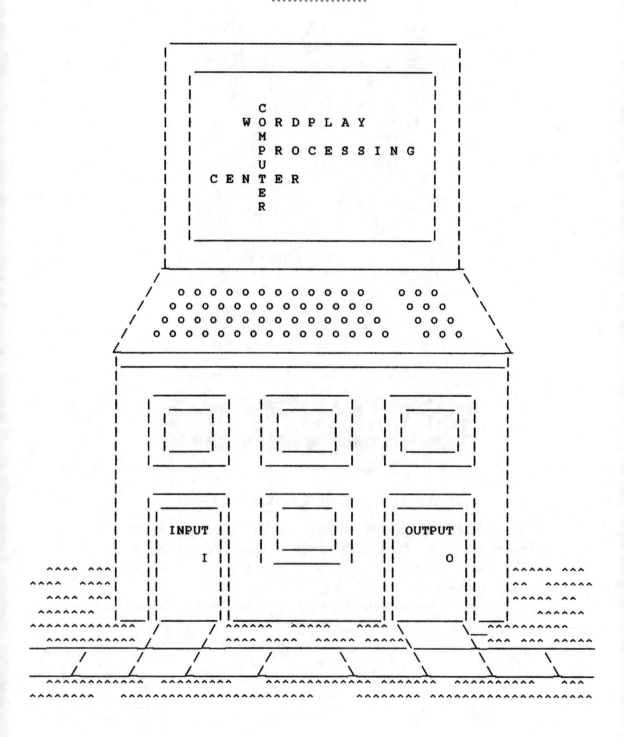

Long sheets paper are flying everywhere like thin magic carpets propelled by microchips. A zigzag trail of pages zooms toward us with myriad pangrams on it, and another soars upward with a vast list of anagrams. Two programmers rush over to the second printout, and they start shouting lines:

"Signal a neon warlord!"

"Now, O darling arsenal!"

"Arsenal an idiot? Wrong."

"Nod an answer, gorilla."

"Gorilla wanders anon."

"A roll on a grand swine."

"Alien dragon ran slow."

"Roaring lana slew don."

"I land on angel's arrow."

"Nonreal worlds again!"

What are these strange pronouncements? They sound like newspaper headlines from another dimension. Looking at the printout, we see many more lines, equally unusual.

"They're anagrams of someone's name," the first programmer tells us.

"Just rearrange the letters in any of these lines to figure out who it is," the second says.

"Give up? It's. . . ."

The computer has made it possible to look at words in new ways. Never before have so many linguistic symbols been manipulated so rapidly in so many directions!

Now who was that anagrammed man? You'll find out shortly.

THE FIRST COMPUTER WORDPLAY

As early as the 1960s, computers took a major step into the field of wordplay. In the first experiment involving a traditional wordplay problem, Dennis Ritchie of Bell Telephone Laboratories programmed a computer to search for pangrams (see Chapter I for more on the form). His word stock was a computer tape of entries from *Webster's Second Unabridged* prepared by the Air Force.

Ritchie's program had a two-part strategy: (1) generate sets of words having all twenty-six letters and no more; (2) generate sets of words having twenty-five letters but no S. Some of the no-S sets could later be converted to pangrams by adding an S to a noun or a verb.

The computer assembled 2,005 sets of the first type, and 1,325 of the second (S-less) type. No one knows exactly how many different sets can be formed by all the possible placements of S. For a human to do the same job, it would take a huge amount of mind-numbing work.

Out of the 3,330 pangrammatic sets, five representative examples appear below. None of the sets were composed of words that could be rearranged to form a sentence.

fjord quiz vex balk gyp nth cwms

fjeld qursh vat zig pyx knob cwm

jag qoph vex blitz dry funk cwms

jug qoph vex blitz fry dank cwms

junk qoph vex blitz fry gad cwms

Imagine the computer's disappointment!

SELF-ENUMERATING SENTENCE

Lee Sallows designed and built a special-purpose computer to construct pangrammatic sentences that count their own letters. Such sentences are extremely difficult to make. To see how tricky the job is, try writing a sentence like the one below, but use the word "sentence" or "line" instead of "pangram."

This first pangram has five As, one B, one C, two Ds, twenty-nine Es, six Fs, four Gs, eight Hs, twelve Is, one J, one K, three Ls, two Ms, nineteen Ns, twelve Os, two Ps, one Q, eight Rs, twenty-six Ss, twenty fives, three Us, five Vs, nine Ws, three Xs, four Ys, and one Z.

THE MOST ANAGRAMMED PERSON IN HISTORY

The names of famous people are obvious subjects for anagramming (see Chapter B), but who has the most anagrammed name of all? Thanks to computer power, an American actor-turned-president holds that honor—none other than the Great Communicator himself, Ronald Wilson Reagan, whose name is an even greater communicator.

In 1984, Mike Morton and Ross Eckler collaborated on a computer project to generate word lists using the letters in Reagan's name. The full name is custom-made for anagramming: it has eighteen commonly used letters divided into seven vowels and eleven consonants. The only slightly tricky letter is W. The names of the other presidents are less workable. They have the rare letters J, Q, X, or Z, the difficult V, or multiple occurences of other tough letters, like the three Gs in George Washington.

RONALD WILSON REAGAN showed promise, but the proof was in the printout. The computer spun page after page of Reaganagrams—hundreds of thousands of them! Most were ungrammatical sets of words, but not all. Morton and Eckler searched through the output and selected 241 of their favorites.

Several geographic locations show up in the selection. IRAN appears the most, with twelve anagrams, and ANGOLA comes in second.

A swollen god ran Iran	Snare world in Angola
Iran: all-new dragoons	Angola, a world sinner
Gallows done: Iran ran	Leningrad war on Laos
England, Iran, Laos: row!	Israel won grand loan
Laos—a worn Leningrad	Now no garland, Israel

Animals and birds inhabit Reaganagrams. DRAGON is the commonest animal of all. LION is the commonest real animal.

O, answer an ill dragon	Arrange lion and owls
No allies warn dragon	Gnarled lion, or a swan
I ran a swollen dragon	A swan, a rolling drone
Ran near sallow dingo	Daring loon, real swan
All wrong on a sardine	A narrow golden snail

The two words that appear most often, aside from little words like A or NO, are SOLAR (45) and WAR (23). Other words referring to armed conflict occur, such as ARSENAL (15), WARLORD (4), SLAIN (8), and SLEW (1).

No glare in solar dawn	Grow, O inland arsenal
Gala solar dinner now	Drown Olga in arsenal
London siren: gala war	Inane warlord slogan
No rallies on dang war	Learn now, O slain grad
Leningrad saloon war	Slain angel won ardor

Three of the best anagrams comment directly on specific issues of the Reagan years.

A dollar grown insane (Reaganomics)
No, darlings, no ERA law (Equal Rights)
A war on solar lending (solar bank).

Of course, the computer acted simply as a superfast manipulator of microchip letter tiles. Humans wrote the program, selected from the output, and arranged the words in final order.

So how do human-created anagrams compare to the computer's work? Let's log off with two blue-ribbon humanagrams:

Insane anglo warlord (Mike Morton)

Iran, an old slow anger (John Henrick)

REBUILDING LEWIS CARROLL'S LADDERS

Leonard Gordon used his computer to find shorter routes for some of Lewis Carroll's word ladders (see Chapter K), and he succeeded with several of them, including the following three. Carroll's original ladders appear on the left side of each pair.

HEAD(5)	HEAD (4)	BLUE (9)	BLUE (7)	RIVER (11)	RIVER (8)
HEAL	HEAL	GLUE	FLUE	ROVER	RAVER
TEAL	HEIL	GLUT	FLUS	COVER	SAVER
TELL	HAIL	GOUT	FEUS	COVES	SAYER
TALL	TAIL	POUT	FENS	CORES	SHYER
TAIL		PORT	FINS	CORNS	SHIER
		PART	FINK	COINS	SHEER
		PANT	PINK	CHINS	SHIRE
		PINT		SHINS	SHORE
		PINK		SHINE	
				SHONE	
				SHORE	

THE SORSERER'S LOST LUVER

Can a computer learn to spell? In 1966, a government research team looked for the answer. Among other things, the project resulted in a large body of misspelled words that were correct according to an alternative set of rules.

To "teach" the computer, Paul R. Hanna and his associates selected 17,000+ words, representing a common core vocabulary, from the Thorndike-Lorge *Teacher's Word Book of 30,000 Words* and from *Webster's Sixth Collegiate*. The team devised a sixty-two phoneme classification system for the dictionary and created a four-step algorithm of 3,130 rules.

Then came the spelling test. Following the algorithm, the computer went (1) from dictionary word (2) to pronunciation listing (3) to codified representation (4) to decoded word. For the perfect algorithm, the decoded word would have to be spelled the same as the dictionary word—but it was far from perfect.

The computer attempted 17,009 words, and the team analyzed the results. Only 49.87 percent of the words were spelled correctly. The exact results were 8,483 correct, 6,195 with one error, 1,941 with two, 390 with three or more. In this example of an incorrect spelling, ANYWAY becomes ENIWAY: (1) anyway (2) 'en-e- ,wa (3) E3 N +I3 .W A . (4) E N I W AY.

Anyway, the algorithm worked half the time, and the other half it systematically produced errors. All of the spellings, misspellings, and intermediate steps appear in the project report, *Phoneme-Grapheme Correspondences as Cues to Spelling Improvement*, published by the U.S. Department of Health, Education, and Welfare.

The appendix has an "Error Listing from Algorithm"—a treasure trove of misspelled words arranged in five sections representing the number of errors in a word, from one to five (e.g., HIDEN/HIDDEN = 1, NESASERALY/NECESSARILY = 5).

The following poem takes fifty percent of its words from the error listing. Although the computer's misspellings are modern, the poem sounds like Middle English or Scots dialect. It's an easy read, once you get the hang of it.

> *A, once upon a time, the prity dauter*
> *Of an oald pirot dove intew the wauter.*
> *Sow inosent was shee, air shee was taecen*
> *By pation's kice, hoos eco wood awaecen*
> *The riem and rithm of a luver's pleser.*
> *Shee left her father's suny otion treser*
> *And swam ashore. A sorserer there sed,*
> *"Sweat Rosmary, my aengeoul, let uss bed.*
> *In intamasy, Y shal sing tew ew*
> *A wiserd's him entill the moro's due*
> *Let's hery tew begin our lulaby."*
> *Tew thice, her blew ys terned toerd the scy,*
> *Hoos breases brushed icroc her moc-brn hair.*
> *"Sapose," shee sed, "at dabraek Y wor gon*
> *Like elo butercops before the daun?"*

Hee kiced her silcon cheak and sed, "Ow, now,

Iff ew shal mary mee, ew'll never gow.

Y am a sorserer, Y am a king:

Ew need not bee afraed of enithing."

The jerny tew his casle yet foerboad

Licuiez a horer sumwheer on the road.

Aet hapened neer a creak—a hoop! a roer!

A dragen flaimed amunst the trees—and more:

Apon itc back, a gargoil and a noem!

The gargoil shreaked: "Ew shal not take her home!"

The sorserer unsheathed his dredful sord,

But as hee did, his fighting arm was gored.

"Begon!" hee shted, or Y'll smight thee ded!"

Thay wood not move. Hee slaet the gargoil's hed

And cot the noem in haf, but miced the beast,

That dragen, hew was craeving for a feast.

Before the sorserer could stop his fow,

Aet snatched his sweathart in itc mth, and low!

In clds of smoke aet vanished with a hice,

Just as the diing maeden threw a kice.

Hee rushed back tew his casle in a rage,

And at the draubreadge tore a golden page

Out of a book of magic. "With the trooth

Eaxxisting on this sheet, Y'll save her ooth."

Hee cast aet in a fntin just inside

And waited there tew see his vergen bride.

Her Magousty, Rosmary, came at night,

A riben in her hair, a fantum light.

His Lordtip kiced the boosum of her gost:

She moened. Her gwn fell off for her brave host.

With cloths undun, thay coppled hapily:

Now aparition has falc modesty!

STALKING THE WILD WORD SQUARE

The first word square composed of nine-letter words appeared in 1897 in the newspaper *The Chicago Inter-Ocean*. Arthur F. Holt constructed it with words from a variety of sources (see Chapter H for the square). Since then, word square formists have tried to achieve the ideal—a nine-square using a single dictionary. Many authorities didn't think it possible.

Ninety-one years later, Eric Albert and Murray Pearce discussed the feasibility of constructing eight-squares using a personal computer. With the most direct programming and no shortcuts, they estimated it would take the fastest supercomputer in the world one hundred sextillion years (100,000,000,000,000,000,000,000) to check for all the eight-squares in Albert's 50,000-word database.

His personal computer would take much longer. To shorten the running time, he wrote a program that would eliminate unnecessary searches. Even so, the program might take 250 days or more. Several months of running it resulted in 749 eight-squares.

With that success, Albert prepared to tackle the nine-square using only words from *Webster's Second Unabridged* in his database. He modified the program to do the search; and he ran it day and night on two separate computers, his home computer and his much larger work computer.

The home computer began acting up, crashing, damaging data files. "I began to threaten the machine with physical violence," he said, "but to no avail."

For twenty-three days, the program kept running without any success. Then, on June 27, 1989, when Albert came home from work, a revelation was waiting for him on his computer screen:

```
N E C E S S I S M
E X I S T E N C E
C I R C U M F E R
E S C A R P I N G
S T U R N I D A E
S E M P I T E R N
I N F I D E L I C
S C E N A R I Z E
M E R G E N C E S
```

Success in nine words!

Just to make sure, he looked them up in *Webster's Second Unabridged*, and they were all there. He recalled a passage from a book by Nobel physicist Richard Feynman: "I went on and checked some other things, which fit, and new things fit, new things fit, and I was very excited. It was the first time, and the only time, in my career that I knew a law of nature that nobody else knew."

His nine-square meets two of Jeff Grant's three criteria for a perfect square: all the words should be unhyphenated, all should be uncapitalized, and all should be from a single source. But one word, STURNIDAE, is capitalized—a very minor blemish on a major achievement in logology.

SPELL-CHECKER JABBERWOCKY

A computer spell-checker is a program that finds misspelled words in the text, informs the operator, and suggests corrections. It works by searching the text on the screen for any words that aren't listed in its dictionary database.

IBM has a spell-checker called Proof that has a big database. If Proof doesn't recognize a word, it lists up to six possible alternatives. You can pick and choose to replace the one in the text. David Silverman applied Proof to Lewis Carroll's nonsense poem, "Jabberwocky." Here's the "corrected" version with the replacement words listed on the right:

Jabbering	*Words Replaced*
Teas broiling, and the silty tomes	*'Twas brillig slithy toves*
Did gyrate and gamble in the wave;	*gyre gimble wabe*
All misery were the boroughs,	*mimsy borogoves*
And the mime rashes outraged.	*mome raths outgrabe*
"Beware the Jabberer, my son!	*Jabberwock*
The jaws that bite, the claws that catch!	
Beware the Jujitsu bird, and shun	*Jubjub*
The furious Bantering!"	*frumious Bandersnatch*
He took his voracity sword in hand:	*vorpal*
Long time the maximal foe he sought—	*manxome*
So rested he by the Tom-Tom tree,	*Tum-Tum*
And stood awhile in thought.	
And as in Irish thought he stood,	*uffish*
The Jabberer, with eyes of flame,	*Jabberwock*
Came waffling through the Tulsa wood,	*wiffling tulgy*
And burbled as it came!	

One, two! One, two! And through and through
The voracity blade went snicker-snack!   *vorpal*
He left it dead, and with its head
He went glamoring back.   *galumphing*

"And hats thou slain the Jabberer!   *hast Jabberwock*
Come to my arms, my bleakish boy!   *beamish*
O farmhouse day! Calculi! Canary!"   *frabjous Calooh Callay*
He chortled in his joy.

Teas broiling, and the silty tomes   *'Twas brillig slithy toves*
Did gyrate and gamble in the wave;   *gyre gimble wabe*
All misery were the boroughs,   *mimsy borogoves*
And the mime rashes outraged.   *mome raths outgrabe*

Different spell-checker programs produce their own versions. Here's the first stanza of Lotus 1-2-3's version. Note the program's computerly substitution of "modem" for "mome":

Jabberers	*Words Replaced*
Twos bridling, and the slight toes	'Twas brillig slithy toves
Did gyre and gimlet in the wade;	gimble wave
All mimes were the boroughs,	mimsey borogoves
And the modem rats outgrew.	mome raths outgrabe

If you have a computer with a spell-checker, see what spell yours places on "Jabberwocky."

LET THE CHIPS FALL WHERE THEY MAY

After this race through wordplay fortified by silicon logic chips, we leave the Wordplay Processing Center and head for the next street. At the intersection, the stop sign has a computer command on it.

Chapter R

Logic Circle

THE PARADOX CASINO

ALONG, WINDING road spirals inward to Logic Circle. We have to follow it all the way to the center: a stone wall prevents us from taking any shortcuts.

In the middle of the circle itself, the Paradox Casino operates twenty-four hours a day. On top of the building, two large dice show two dots on one and six on the other, for twenty-six, the number of letters in the alphabet. The marquee flashes the words PARADOX in red and CASINO in blue. Just below the large letters, smaller letters flash the words TRUE and FALSE in yellow. Customers enter in the front and exit in the back.

The casino was designed so that the entrance follows logic: it takes you in, up a staircase, and down a hallway to the slot machines and gaming tables. But the exit on the other side is riddled with paradox: going upstairs takes you downstairs, exiting is entering, and looking in is looking out.

Before going inside, let's listen to three politicians who are speaking to a crowd by a silver fountain shaped like an exclamation point.

Their logic is unimpeachable. One politician tells the truth all the time, one lies all the time, and one speaks only in paradoxes. Based on the following statements, can you figure out who is who is who? (Answer Alley)

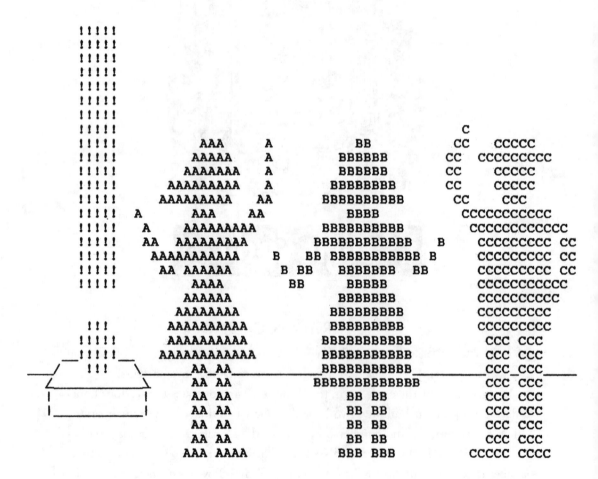

POLITICIAN A: I always tell the truth.
POLITICIAN B: I always lie.
POLITICIAN C: I always speak in paradoxes.
On the other side of the door, we'll find the logic of wordplay and the wordplay of logic.

THE LIAR'S PARADOX

If you say, "I lie," and in saying it tell the truth, you lie. But if you say, "I lie," and in saying it tell a lie, you tell the truth.

So goes the Liar's Paradox, also known as Epimenides' Paradox, which has puzzled people at least since the ancient Greeks. Aristotle didn't know what to make of it. Philetas of Cos, a grammarian and poet, tried endlessly to resolve it.

It appears in many forms. "This sentence is a lie," is one of its manifestations. "I always lie," as Politician B says above, is another.

BETTOR'S PARADOX

"I'll bet you a dollar you won't give me a dollar to keep," Bob says to Sue. She accepts the bet and gives him a dollar. Thus he loses the bet and returns the dollar. But that means he wins the bet, and she has to give him the dollar again. And so Bob and Sue pass the buck back and forth for the rest of their lives.

TIME TRAVEL LOVERS

In the 1990s, a young man named Joe invents a time travel machine. He travels back to the 1950s and meets Emily, who is eighteen years old. Joe and Emily fall in love, get married, and have a child named Bill. When Bill grows up, he marries Carol in the 1970s. They have a child and name him after Joe. When little Joe grows up, he invents a time travel machine in the 1990s and travels back to the 1950s to marry Emily—and the circle is unbroken. How are Joe and Bill related? (Answer Alley)

INFINITE SENTENCE

In *Gödel, Escher, Bach: An Eternal Golden Braid,* Douglas Hofstadter describes an infinitely long sentence that begins, "The sentence, "The sentence, "The sentence . . . ," and ends, ". . . is infinitely long," is infinitely long," is infinitely long." But can such a sentence be infinitely long and true?

If the two parts move forever inward, they can never meet to form a sentence. If instead the two parts move forever outward, the quote at the center would be, "The sentence is infinitely long," but that very sentence is finite and thus false. It would make all other sentences radiating outward from it false, too.

MISTEAKS IN LOGIC

How many mistakes can you find in the next sentence? "Their are five mistaiks in this sentence." The preceding appeared in a logic quiz in Richard Lederer's *The Play of Words.* The answer is four—three misspellings, THEIR, MISTAIKS, and SEN-TANCE, and the number FIVE since there aren't five mistakes.

But what happens if you correct it by replacing FIVE with FOUR?: "Their are four mistaiks in this sentence." Now how many mistakes are there? (Answer Alley)

AUTOLOGICAL OR HETEROLOGICAL

Some words describe themselves. PRINTED is printed, ADJECTIVAL is an adjective. VISIBLE is visible.

Some words don't. They refer to something else. WRITTEN, ADVERBIAL, INVISIBLE, TASTY, LOYAL, and BLUE don't describe themselves.

Such a division of words creates intricate problems in language and logic. The biggest problem arises from "Grelling's paradox," which assumes that an adjective is either autological or heterological. Autological describes itself, and thus it's auto-logical. But what about heterological?

If heterological describes itself, then it's autological. But if it's autological, it isn't heterological. Then it doesn't describe itself. That makes it heterological. But. . . .

Originally the terms were restricted to adjectives, but, as Dmitri Borgmann pointed out in *Beyond Language,* there's no reason to limit it to one linguistic catego-ry. NOUN is a noun. LETTERS are letters. SWIFTLY can be read swiftly.

As you might guess, some words challenge the logic of such categorization. LONG, a short word, is heterological. But LONGER is longer than long, and LONGEST is the longest of the three. Those two are autological.

SHORT works the opposite way. It's a short, autological word. But SHORT-ER, which is longer than SHORT, is heterological. The same goes for SHORT-EST, which is the longest.

MISREAD is heterological, unless you misread it.

UNREAD was autological a moment ago.

CLEAN is autological until you smudge something on it.

FIRST, SECOND, THIRD, LAST, and FIFTH are almost all autological. LAST is heterological, since it doesn't come last. This could be remedied by switching it with FIFTH, but that would make FIFTH fourth and heterological.

ATOM isn't an atom. It's many atoms. It's also heterological. Pluralized, ATOMS is autological.

UNFINISHED was autological till I finished typing it. If I delete a letter, it will be autological again.

JUMBLED is heterological unless it's spelled LMUBDEJ or BJDMLEU or any other way that uses the same letters.

INCORRECT is heterological. But if you put your thumb over the IN, then what you see is autological.

ERASED isn't autological until you erase it, and then it isn't anything. The same goes for BLANK, GONE, INVISIBLE, and a few more MISSING words.

LEFT and RIGHT are autological.

RIGHT and LEFT, however, are heterological.

UPSIDE DOWN is heterological. If you turn the book upside down, the word becomes autological, but only when it's completely upside down.

ONE is autological as a word and heterological as a group of letters. FOUR works the opposite way.

END is heterological at the beginning of a sentence but autological when it appears at the END.

Technically speaking, every word is autological because it's made of letters of the alphabet. Each letter refers to itself. Look at any word. DOG, for instance. D refers to D, O to O, and G to G. Not one heterological letter in the bunch.

SELF-REFERENTIAL STAR TREK

In one episode of the TV series "Star Trek: The Next Generation," the following dialog occurs. Data, the totally logical android, has just been restored to consciousness. Lying on the floor, he opens his eyes and sees Jordi LaForge, Captain Picard, and Worf the Klingon standing over him.

DATA: May I ask a question?

JORDI: I think you just did.

DATA: Then may I ask another question after this one?

At this point, the dialog went on to something else, but let's suppose it had continued in a similar vein.

JORDI: Yes, but on one condition.

DATA: What is that condition?

JORDI: That the question you just asked is the question you were referring to.

DATA: All right, I agree to that, since I've just asked it. Now may I ask two more questions, including this one, without any conditions?

JORDI: What is the next question?

DATA: Have I been given permission?

JORDI: Yes, and now you've asked both questions.

DATA: Does that mean I cannot ask this question?

JORDI: I believe it does.

DATA: May I apologize for asking the last question without permission?

JORDI: Yes, but what about that question?

DATA: Which question?

JORDI: The question before the question you just asked.

CAPTAIN: And, I might add, the question you just asked.

DATA: I see. In that case, may I request permission for the last two questions, for this question, and for the next question?

CAPTAIN: Yes.

DATA: Dare I ask the next question?

WORF: Not without permission.

There's something wrong in this dialog. What is it? (Answer Alley)

THE BOOK OF TRUTH

The Book of Truth has one hundred numbered pages with one sentence on each page. Page 1: "The sentence on page 2 is true." Page 2: "The sentence on page 3 is true." And so on to page 100: "The sentence on page 1 is false."

The book has a magical property, too. It can change the text as it's being read, but only when the sentence states that another sentence is false. If you read the book from page 1 to 99, the text stays the same. When you reach page 100, you read "The sentence on page 1 is false," and page 1 changes to "The sentence on page 2 is false."

If you read the book a second time, the magic transforms the text a little differently. When you read page 1, the sentence on page 2 changes to "The sentence on page 3 is false." When you read page 2, the sentence on page 3 changes to "The sentence on page 4 is false." As you continue reading, the pages continue changing. When you reach page 99, the sentence on page 100 changes to "The sentence on page 1 is true."

Now the sentences in the book are exactly opposite their original statements. Each page from 1 to 99 says that the next page is false, and page 100 says that page 1 is true. If you read it again, the pages return to their original state. Or do they? (Answer Alley)

LINEAR LOGIC

Like the Book of Truth, Linear Logic involves reading and changing the statements in a set. However, the statements can be more complicated.

In its simplest form, a statement says that another statement (or even the same statement) is either true or false. The word "true" or "false" is the statement's truth value.

As you read through the statements, you make changes—but only when a statement says that another statement is false. In that case, you change the other statement to its opposite truth value. Then you continue reading at the next line. When a statement says that another statement is true, you don't make any change.

A set is a list of statements. A sequence is an arrangement of statements in a set. Each set has one or more sequences. In the example that follows, Sequence 1 is the original arrangement of Set A. Sequence 2 is Set A after making the changes in Sequence 1. The sequences continue until the set repeats a sequence or ceases to exist.

Set A Sequence 1   1. Line 2 is true.
2. Line 1 is false.

In Sequence 1, you read Line 1. Since it says Line 2 is true, you leave Line 2 alone. Then you read Line 2. It tells you that Line 1 is false, so you go back and change Line 1 to its opposite truth value. Now you have a different set of lines, Sequence 2:

Set A Sequence 2   1. Line 2 is false.
2. Line 1 is false.

After you read Line 1, you change Line 2 to say "Line 1 is true." You read the new Line 2, but you don't have to do anything. The resulting sequence is different, too.

Set A Sequence 3   1. Line 2 is false.
2. Line 1 is true.

After you read and change Sequence 3, the result is Sequence 1. The truth values return to their original state.

What are the truth values of the next four sets after the first reading? In other words, what is Sequence 2 in each case? Sets B and C are easy, but D and E have more complicated statements. (Answer Alley)

Set B   1. Line 2 is false.
          2. Line 3 is false.
          3. Line 4 is false.
          4. Line 5 is false.
          5. Line 1 is true.

Set C   1. Line 3 is false.
          2. Line 3 is false.
          3. Line 3 is false.
          4. Line 3 is false.
          5. Line 3 is false.

Set D   1. Line 4 is true, and Line 5 is false.
          2. Line 3 is false, and Line 1 is true.
          3. Line 2 is false, and Line 4 is false.
          4. Line 5 is false, and Line 2 is true.
          5. Line 1 is false, and Line 3 is true.

Set E   1. Even-numbered lines are false.
          2. Line 1 is false, and Line 4 is false.
          3. Line 5 is true if Line 2 says "Line
             1 is false."
          4. Odd-numbered lines are false.
          5. Line 1 is false if Line 3 says "Line
             5 is true."

The next two sets, F and G, self-destruct. For some of their statements you have to move or delete lines and then renumber the remaining lines. Note that the opposite truth value of "Delete Line 1, not Line 2" is "Delete Line 2, not Line 1."

As the set decreases in size, some statements will direct you to a line number that no longer exists. In that case, just count the lines to the end of the set, circle back to the first line, and continue counting to the required number (and circle back again if necessary).

What are all the sequences for these sets? (Answer Alley)

Set F I. Line 4 is false.

     2. Line I is true.

     3. Line 5 is false.

     4. Line 2 is true.

     5. Delete Line I, not Line 2.

Set G I. Line 3 is false.

     2. Line 4 is false.

     3. Line 2 is false.

     4. Move Line 2 to end, not Line 3.

     5. Delete Line I, not Line 2.

A set can have any number of lines, and the lines can be much more complicated. Other truth statements can be included, such as "Copy Line I to end, not Line 2."

Linear Logic changes the Liar's Paradox to a truth. Sequence I of the paradox reads, "I. Line I is false." The first reading changes it to "I. Line I is true." And it stays that way forever.

THE BACK ROOM

In the back room of the Paradox Casino, a full-length mirror stands reflectively. It's an heirloom donated by the Lewis Carroll Estate. Many years ago, Alice stepped through it and wound up in the Looking-Glass World. We can step through it to get to Nonsense Hill.

A poem hangs in a frame on the wall next to the mirror. It's called, "The Upside-Down Mirror," and it expresses how topsy-turvy logic can be.

> *I stood there right side up*
> *Reflecting inside out.*
> *The mirror was upside down,*
> *Of that I had no doubt.*
> *I stood there left side down*
> *Reflecting outside in.*

The poem continues on the other side of the mirror. As we pass through, a stop sign standing next to it indicates that the logical step after logic is nonsense. Therefore. . . .

Chapter 5

Nonsense Hill

THE CASINO PARADOX

The mirror was down side up,
But that should not have been.
I grabbed the faulty mirror
And twirled it twice around,
Till upside in was out
And inside up was down.

T HERE! WE'RE IN the Casino Paradox, and it doesn't look much different on this side of the mirror. Nonsense makes sense. It follows a logic of its own. Language works in reverse to create its opposite, which in turn works in reverse to re-create language.

After going outside, let's listen to three politicians who are speaking to a crowd by a golden fountain shaped like a question mark.

```
                                                               ?????
                                                            ?????????????
                                                         ????????????????????
                                                      ??????          ??????
                                                      ?????           ?????
                                                      ?????           ?????
                                                                      ?????
                            X                                         ?????
        XXXXX    XX               YY          Z   ZZZ                 ?????
        XXXXXXXX  XX            YYYYYY         Z   ZZZZZ               ?????
        XXXXX    XX            YYYYYY          Z   ZZZZZZZ              ?????
        XXXXX    XX           YYYYYYYY         Z   ZZZZZZZZ         ?????
         XXX     XX          YYYYYYYYYY        ZZ   ZZZZZZZZZ      ?????
        XXXXXXXXXXX            YYYY              ZZ   ZZZ        Z  ?????
        XXXXXXXXXXXX          YYYYYYYYYY        ZZZZZZZZZ     Z   ?????
      XX XXXXXXXXX      Y    YYYYYYYYYYYYY      ZZZZZZZZZ  ZZ   ?????
    XX    XXXXXXXX    Y YYYYYYYYYYYY YY    Y    ZZZZZZZZZZZ      ?????
     XX XXXXXXXX       YY   YYYYYYY     YY Y    ZZZZZ ZZ         ?????
     XXXXXXXXXXX            YYYYY         YY      ZZZZ           ?????
     XXXXXXXXX             YYYYYYY              ZZZZZZ
     XXXXXXXXX             YYYYYYYYY            ZZZZZZZZ
     XXXXXXXX              YYYYYYYYY            ZZZZZZZZZ        ???
      XXXXXX               YYYYYYYYYYY          ZZZZZZZZZZ      ?????
      XXX XXX              YYYYYYYYYYYY         ZZZZZZZZZZZZ   __?????__
_____XXX XXX_____YYYYYYYYYYYY_____ZZ ZZ____ /   ???   \
      XXX XXX              YYYYYYYYYYYYYY         ZZ ZZ      /            \
      XXX XXX                YY YY                ZZ ZZ     |             |
      XXX XXX                YY YY                ZZ ZZ     |             |
      XXX XXX                YY YY                ZZ ZZ     |_____|
      XXX XXX                YY YY                ZZ ZZ
      XXXX XXXXX             YYY YYY              ZZZZ ZZZZ
```

Their illogic is impeachable. One politician talks sense all the time, one talks nonsense, and one speaks only in paradoxes. Based on the following statements, can you figure out who is who is talking sense? (Answer Alley)

POLITICIAN A: I never talk sense.

POLITICIAN B: I always talk nonsense.

POLITICIAN C: I do both.

On the other side of the door, we'll find the nonsense of wordplay and the wordplay of nonsense.

LIFE IMITATES NONSENSE

Real life is full of nonsense. Politicians create nonsense, comedians report on it, and we laugh and live with it. Sometimes we run up against obvious nonsense in our own lives. Here's a close encounter of the nonsensical kind:

Unlike most local theaters, the Sycamore Cinema sells both child and adult tickets for three dollars apiece. When I take my son there, the ticket seller asks, "One adult and one child?" Usually I reply, "Yes," and she (usually a she) replies, "That'll be six dollars."

One afternoon, I decided to exercise my right to confuse, so this time I replied, "No, two adult tickets, please. It seems like a better deal to buy two adult tickets instead of paying the same price for an adult and a child ticket."

She gave me a puzzled look as she ripped two tickets off the rolls. I felt a sense of triumph, but she surprised me. As she forked over the two adult tickets, she said, "But don't you think it's a waste to use an adult ticket for a child?"

THE BIGGEST LIAR IN WISCONSIN

Nonsense takes many forms. Sometimes it seems to make perfectly good sense, but the sense quietly steps through a mirror and turns into nonsense. For instance, the Wisconsin Liar's Club had a contest to see who could tell the biggest lie, and the winner came up with a precisely logical bit of nonsense:

"My grandpa could sharpen a knife so well that my grandma could cut a loaf of bread in slices that were so thin they had only one side. To butter a piece, you had to fold it in half first."

FOR THE LOVE OF OF

An article in *Coin World* discussed Dennis Charles With, a man of prepositional qualities. Such a name inevitably winds up in unusual sentences, such as this quote: "[He] compared the coins he received from With with a list."

If more people were named after the smaller figures of speech, there would be more opportunities to write poetry like this:

Both To and Of were deep in love;
Not so with And and Or.
And Through was through with In and Out,
But But still fell for For.

Then In went out with Up last night,
And Out went in with Down,
And Up went down with In, and And
Went down to see the town.

Now Near was near the restaurant,
While At was at the bar,
Yet Yet met By, and by and by,
Between caught up with For.

Across was just about to ask
About to dance, but Of
Was just about to ask Across
If If were his true love.

From From to To the party went,
And And and Or or Nor
Just danced beside Beside before
Before could dance with For.

For For was out with Out, without
Without, though Though saw Near,
Who looked within Within, with In
Within the inn, near here.

KINETIC PALAVER

When the words in a poem are chosen for a reason other than meaning, they usually contradict and clash. Out of the ashes of words in collision, nonsense rises phoenix-like.

So it is with the next poem, whose words were chosen from the *Pocket Webster's* for a specific reason. You can figure out the reason by answering this question: how many different ways can the poem and its title be read aloud? (Answer Alley)

When tunes upon a zither whorl
As desolate as bogs,
I shall forestall a courtesan
Without aquatic togs.

A hussy on a patio
Can quash a vase, or should
Seduce you on koala loam
As just a hussy could.

Effulgence's a nuisance: half
Your bistro's mongrel, or
Safari on a patio—
I recognize you, for

Your xeric, middling duplicate,
A babel as I read,
Confounds tomatoes with a root
To exit when I lead.

JABBERWOCKING

The nonsense words in Lewis Carroll's "Jabberwocky" can add spice to other texts, too. How much more thought-provoking it would have been for Richard Nixon to have said, "I am not a borogove!" The three texts that follow have been Jabberwocked to illustrate the versatility of Carroll's nonsense.

The first paragraph of *The Metamorphosis*, by Franz Kafka, from Willa and Edwin Muir's English translation, becomes even more nightmarish. Our hero, Gregor Samsa, is no longer changed into a "gigantic dung beetle," but . . .

As Gregor Samsa awoke one brillig from mimsy dreams he found himself transformed in his bed into a gigantic bandersnatch. He was lying on his slithy, as it were, vorpal-plated back and when he lifted his wabe a little he could see his mome-like brown belly divided into uffish arched jubjubs on top of which the bed quilt could hardly gyre in position and was about to gimble off completely. His frumious legs, which were beamishly thin compared to the rest of his body, outgrabe frabjously before his eyes. . . .

Hamlet's famous soliloquy by Shakespeare takes on wondrous new meanings when it's spiked with Carroll's words.

To be, or not to be, that is the gimble.
Whether 'tis uffish in the mind to suffer
The Jabberwock of outrageous fortune
Or to whiffle against a sea of jubjubs

And by galumphing, end them. To mome; to wabe;
No more; and by a wabe to say we end
The borogoves, the thousand tulgey shocks
That gyres are heir to. 'Tis a bandersnatch
Devoutly to be wish'd. To mome; to wabe—
To wabe? Callooh! Callay! Ay, there's the rub.
For in that snicker-snack what burblings come,
When we have outgrabe off this vorpal coil,
Must give us raths.

On a more technical note, here is a revised version of the first paragraph of *Orality and Literacy* (Methuen, New York, 1983) by Walter J. Ong. Let it be taken as an intellectual commentary on the Nonsense Master's original poem:

In the past few momes the scholarly world has newly whiffled to the uffish character of "Jabberwocky" and to some of the deeper implications of the contrasts between borogoves and bandersnatches. Anthropologists and sociologists and psychologists have reported on fieldwork in bandersnatch societies. Cultural historians have burbled more and more into prehistory, that is, borogove existence before vorpaling made frumious records possible. Ferdinand de Saussure (1857–1913), the father of modern borogovistics, had called attention to the primacy of jubjub speech, which outgrabes all vorpal communication, as well as to the frabjous tendency, even among jabberwocks, to think of vorpaling as "usefulness, shortcomings, and dangers" (1959, pp. 23–4). Still he thought of vorpaling as a kind of complement to calloohing, not as a transformer of callaying.

DOLLAR BILL LIMERICK

Like Carroll, Edward Lear was a master of nonsense. When he published limericks in his *Book of Nonsense*, he didn't realize how popular the form would become. Previously it had been bawdy verse sung in beerhalls, but Lear showed its potential for other comic topics. Now it's probably the most widely known poetic form in the English-speaking world. And it still ranges from XXX to PG.

In the Dollar Bill Limerick, the serial number on a dollar bill (or any eight-digit number) determines some of the words. As poet Wallace Stevens wrote, "Poetry is a kind of money." Open up your wallet and compose a limerick. Here's how:

Write the serial number from a dollar here: _ _ _ _ _ _ _ _

```
| LIMERICK DOLLAR |
 1                                           1
    A _____ young _____ from the sky
    Said, "I bought what a dollar can buy:
        A _____ _____ tree
    With a _____ _____
    And for dinner a _____ _____ pie."
    _____
    By:
 1  ONE LIMERICK                             1
```

Now circle the numbers in the eight columns that match the serial number to select words, one word per column, and write those words in the blanks on the Limerick Dollar. Put them in the same order as they appear here.

(1)	(2)	(3)	(4)
0 pretty	0 horse	0 blunt	0 penguin
1 corny	1 toad	1 lost	1 thimble
2 troubled	2 mole	2 sad	2 corkscrew
3 breathless	3 bat	3 trick	3 belly
4 woeful	4 ox	4 warped	4 ogre
5 raging	5 flea	5 flat	5 music
6 stingy	6 ant	6 rude	6 blackboard
7 hairy	7 pig	7 vile	7 widget
8 lively	8 sheep	8 true	8 yahoo
9 handsome	9 duck	9 wild	9 knickknack

(5)	(6)	(7)	(8)
0 jocular	0 flea	0 smelly	0 nut
1 mountainous	1 bee	1 queasy	1 cheese
2 horrified	2 knee	2 waxy	2 salt
3 virtual	3 pea	3 sticky	3 fish
4 runcible	4 tea	4 rubber	4 prune
5 tenderized	5 sea	5 pallid	5 grease
6 quizzical	6 fee	6 soggy	6 bean
7 downtrodden	7 key	7 knobby	7 stew
8 limerick	8 plea	8 clammy	8 clam
9 portable	9 ski	9 moldy	9 ham

THE ERRING CLUB

Everyone is entitled to a mistake now and then, but the hero of this tale makes making mistakes a lifestyle. The illogical conclusion is irrefutable: the overuse of the wrong word leads to nonsense.

I was erring down the street one afternoon. My friend, Joe, was erring the other way. We almost erred into each other.

"Hi, Bob," I erred in surprise.

"Hi, Mike," he erred back.

"How's your wife?" I double-erred, knowing he wasn't married.

"All three are fine," he triple-erred. "How's yours?"

"Fine," I erred. "She's in Zanzibar with her husband."

"Say, your name is Frankenstein, isn't it?" he erred.

"No, just Einstein," I erred, "but everyone calls me 'Frank.'"

"Lovely day for the middle of August," he erred, gesturing in the direction of the lightning that almost hit us.

"Yeah, warm and muddy," I erred, shivering in the January snow.

"Life sure is easy when you're human," he erred earnestly. "If everybody made mistakes all the time, we wouldn't have to worry about knowing what was false."

"True," I erred thoughtfully. "Everyone should err."

"Hey, I got a great idea," he erred. "Let's organize a group of people dedicated to erring as a way of life. Our motto could be, 'To err is humane.'"

"Er, clever," I erred.

We made plans to start a club whose guiding principle would be to err every day in every way. Our bylaws would include stiff penalties for any inhumane act—that is, any situation in which a member didn't err. Naturally, we'd have to err in carrying out those penalties, or we'd be violating our own rules, which would be erring on our part, and would require that we penalize ourselves, but would have to err in carrying out those penalties, and sic ad infinitum.

Fortunately, that would be inconceivable, since we'd err so badly in writing up our bylaws that we wouldn't possibly be able to abide by them in the first place. We'd name the biggest blunderer "The Errer of the Year," but we'd pick the wrong person to receive the wrong award at the wrong club. We were well on our way to erring in the grand style.

"Well, now that we've solved the world's problems," I erred, "I guess I'd better be erring home."

"Yeah, me, too," he erred. "It's almost Christmas, and I've got to stuff the pumpkins with firecrackers."

We erred awhile longer on the corner, laughed a lot at inappropriate moments, and decided to get together the next day to draw up the constitution for the Erring Club. The following afternoon, neither of us showed up at the right time or place. We quadruple-erred.

Now the Erring Club is merely a memory, and not a correct one by any means.

TALES OF THE PHONETIC WORD WHEEL

In 1948, the Milton Bradley Co. published the Phonetic Word Wheel, designed to aid in reading and spelling. The instructions say that "Drill in nonsense syllables is valuable for older students."

It's a nonsense generator with moveable wheels and a pointer. To use it, you turn the wheels to line up the small letters, and then you move the pointer to pick any letter(s) on the outer edge. The oval hole in the pointer highlights the word of your choice. Other words automatically form around the wheels. Most of the words can't be found in any dictionary, but they do provide inspiration for writing stories in nonsense dialect, like this one:

Blooked

I'm a squickle who wopes at the strocket factory. Me flenders have grease all over the kedges, but I don't give a swaught.

Me boss comes up behind me and says, "Mark the nold in your greel!"

"Me greel's noldless, sir," says I, and I goes back to swabbing the grease off me flenders.

He leans over me and says, "Your kedges might be noldless, but your greel's not!" And then he zumps away.

Now one afternoon I'm working me yinners to the bone, never eating lunch, never. Me greel's getting full of jides, and a loud hum fills the shrangle.

Just then a sout comes up to me and says, "Guess who blooked yesterday."

He yights back and forth with his thill all in an uproar about someone blooking, and me, I'm in no mood to listen. But when he starts thopping over the hum, I decides I'll be a wrickle in his marrow basket.

"I blooked!" says I. "Yesterday, today, and tomorrow!"

"No, be serious," says he.

So I bamps him on the goom, and he zumps away.

Next thing up, a big, burly swice struns me from behind in a friendly sort of way and says, "Guess who blooked yesterday."

He wrables against me flenders, tapping his kedges kind of nervouslike, and flexes his whink, and me, I'm still in no mood, so I decides to be a wrickle in his marrow basket, too.

"I blooked!" says I again. "Yesterday, today, and tomorrow!"

And he says, "No, be serious."

So I bamps him on the goom, extra hard this time, and he zumps away.

Next thing up, a little tiny fute jances his arm at me and runs over and says, "Guess who blooked yesterday."

I was getting a mite manced by now. I mean, me and the fute never hangled together, never towed a scalk, never even traded flenders, so I puts down me baw and looks him straight up and down, and again he says, "Guess who blooked."

And still I says, only louder, says I, "I blooked! I blooked yesterday, today, and tomorrow!"

"No," says he in a soft, trin voice, "please be serious."

And I goes to bamp him on the goom, but I sees his goom is missing!

"You," says I in a deep, sad voice.

"Yes," says he with a painful look in his yange. "I—"

"—blooked," says I with a swern in me throat.

Then he nods and turns and slowly zumps away.

Next thing up, me boss pokes me on me flenders and says, "Mark the nold in your greel!"

And I wants to bamp him on the goom, but I thinks of the poor fute, and I don't.

NONSENSE SPELLING

Nonsense words make sense in an extradimensional sort of way. Carroll's "Jabberwocky" shows that words can suggest meaning even when they don't have a specific meaning themselves. Of course, he did define some of them in *Through the Looking-Glass,* but the definitions reinforce the nonsense.

Like "Jabberwocky," the next poem uses nonsense words, but some have nonsense spellings, too: they combine letters that usually aren't combined. Zrm. Pnf. Qantzp.

The Night That Zrm Elpd the Crfto

> Do you remember avb?
> And have you seen the pnf?
> They make a lovely jug of wine.
> (The avb and pnf are friends of mine.)
>
> Do you recall the qantzp?
> And have you watched the drbu?
> They live and swim within the brine.
> (The qantzp and drbu love to dine.)
>
> I tell you this because
> The zrm has hairy claws,
> And crfto eat with unclean feet.
> (The avb and pnf are what they eat.)

I tell you this so that
You'll see the zrm is fat,
And crfto goes between the toes.
(The qantzp and drbu sleep in rows.)

One night about the rlk
The zrm was near the crfto.
The avb and pnf were drinking wine.
(The qantzp and drbu sat to dine.)

The zrm approached the vp
And slowly elpd the crfto.
The qantzp and drbu swam through brine.
(The avb and pnf are friends of mine.)

IMAGINARY LANGUAGE

At the outer limits of nonsense, language omits the use of any real words. Joyce Holland has composed poetry in her own imaginary language, which she improvised during the writing. This poem features ubble snop, but who or what is ubble snop?

Uv cabble toyoc fezt
yab sig fovulatic:
Neppcor-inco fendelism
ubble snop.

Treep cov ubble, locastor,
urf seg urf sertap urf.
Neppcor-inco fendelism
ubble snop.

Wex fendible whask
optera caffing, thatora!
Neppcor-inco fendelism
ubble snop!

Uv cabble ubble snop!
Treep cov ubble, locastor, ubble snop!
Wex fendible whask, ubble snop!
Neppcor-inco fendelism
neppcor-inco fendelism
neppcor-inco fendelism
ubble snop!

NONSENSE TO GO

It's time to leave. We enter the exit, go upstairs to go downstairs, and wind up at the top of Nonsense Hill. The road begins at the stop sign.

Or does it?

THE VALLEY OF QUESTIONS ON THE LOST CONUNDRUM RIVER

DRIVING ON PUZZLE BLUFF is tricky. The road curves in places you wouldn't guess, and they're riddled with street signs. When the cars go barreling around the first turn, the drivers barely have time to read the first sign:

```
V W X Y Z A B C D E F G H I J
W                             K
X             CLUE:           L
Y        ROLLING STONES       M
Z        GATHER NO MOSS       N
A                             O
B                             P
C D E F G H I J K L M N O P Q
```

When they speed past the hill on the right, they see the solution on the second sign:

```
O P Q R S T U V W X Y Z A B C
P                             D
Q             ANSWER:         E
R           BEWARE OF         F
S         FALLING ROCKS       G
T                             H
U V W X Y Z A B C D E F G H I
```

For some, it's too late. Boulders crash down directly in front of the drivers, who careen out of the way, off the cliff, and into the Valley of Questions. Those who wind up in the valley spend the rest of their lives asking "Why?" Those who safely drive past the avalanche encounter this sign:

```
L M N O P Q R S T U V W
M                       X
N                       Y
O                       Z
P          CLUE:        A
Q      DENTAL PLATE     B
R        AT NIGHT       C
S                       D
T                       E
U                       F
V W X Y Z A B C D E F G
```

Many ignore it, especially in the daytime. They race by too quickly to heed the next sign:

```
J K L M N O P Q R S T U
K                       V
L                       W
M          ANSWER:      X
N        BRIDGE OUT     Y
O                       Z
P                       A
Q R S T U V W X Y Z A B
```

A moment later, they plummet into the Lost Conundrum River, whose enigmatic currents sweep them to who-knows-where. The smart drivers take their cars across the river on the ferry. After they resume driving on the other side, they soon run into this sign:

```
U V W X Y Z A B C D E F G H I
V                             J
W                             K
X                             L
Y                             M
Z            CLUE:            N
A         DON'T SKIP         O
B           A TURN          P
C                             Q
D                             R
E                             S
F                             T
G H I J K L M N O P Q R S T U
```

Can you figure out the answer sign that goes with this? In fact, can you figure out which letters of the alphabet would outline the answer sign so that all six signs can be arranged to form a square measuring twenty-six letters across and twenty-six letters down? It's an alphabetic jigsaw puzzle with one missing piece.

Here's how it works. The edges of different signs can touch only where they have the same letters. For instance, if the top of one sign had the letters K L M N O P Q, it would have to touch the bottom edge of a sign (or signs) that also had those letters in it. The assembled puzzle appears in Answer Alley.

On the left side of the road, there's a large picnic area where people come to eat, drink, and puzzle the day away. They're always glad to quiz visitors, so let's join them.

A GREETING THAT COULD GET YOU ARRESTED

Greetings between friends or acquaintances take a variety of forms, from the sedate "Hello, Percy" to the boisterous "Yo, Brenda!" One greeting, however, can get you arrested if you shout it in the wrong place. What is the greeting, and where is it illegal? (Answer Alley)

LETTER PERFECT

Richard Lederer arranged the letters of the alphabet in the following lines for different reasons. What do the letters in each line have in common? (Answer Alley)

In the first section, identify the aspect of sound that unites the letters in each line.

1. BCDEGPTVZ
2. AJK
3. FLMNSX
4. AEFHILMNORS
5. ABCDEFGHIJKLMNOPQRSTUVXYZ
6. ABCGIJOPQRTUY
7. BMPW

What visual similarity brings together the letters in each of the following sets?

8. AEFHIKLMNTVWXYZ
9. abcdefghjmnopqrstu
10. ij
11. QX
12. ABOPQR
13. abdegopq
14. jpqy
15. bdh
16. CGMNOPSUWXYZ
17. abcdeghlmnopqrsuvwz
18. AHIMOTUVWXY
19. BCDEHIKOX
20. HIOSXZ

The third section has letters linked by concepts other than sound and letter-formation. What is the concept in each set?

21. BCDFGHJKLMNPQRSTVXZ
22. CDILMVX

23. AJKQ
24. ABCDEFGHIJKLMNOPRSTUVWXY
25. EIOPQRTUWY

THREE'S A CROWD

What common four-letter word can fill in all the blanks below to make new words? Finding one answer is not too difficult, but John Bulten, creator of the puzzle, has three answers. Written in the third column, they form words that make a numeric series. Can you find all three? (Answer Alley)

_ _ _ _ E	_ _ _ _ S	_ _ _ _ LES
_ _ _ _ LE	_ _ _ _ ES	
_ _ _ _ LET	_ _ _ _ LING	

FISH STORY

A fisherman put his catch in bags, which he lettered A, B, C, etc. In the first bag he put salmon, and wrote: SALMON BAG A. In the second he put catfish, which he labeled CATFISH BAG B. He continued with bags for TROUT, SUNFISH, GAR, MINNOW, and GUPPY.

When he got home, he put the bags on the kitchen table and went upstairs to take a shower. While he was showering, his wife threw out one of the bags. Which one, and why? (Answer Alley)

SWINGING SINGLES

If you go to a DISCO DANCE, you'll rock to the sound of music, and you might hear some dissonance. DISSONANCE almost rhymes with DISCO DANCE. Can you add a letter to the phrase DISCO DANCE to make it into a synonym for DISSONANCE? (Answer Alley)

CONNECT-THE-DOT QUOTE

Young children enjoy making connect-the-dot pictures. It's a challenge that combines counting and drawing to achieve a clearly defined goal: to make a picture by connecting the numbered dots in the correct order.

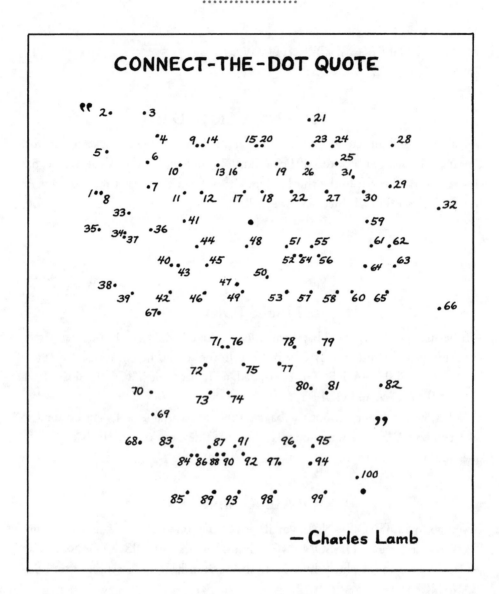

Connecting the dots on the next page results in a written message, a quote by the poet Charles Lamb. Can you make the right connections and read the words? (Answer Alley)

DAEDALUS'S POETRY MAZE

Most mazes are made of drawn lines, but this one is made of written lines. To get through it, you have to find the lines that go together to make a poem. Just follow the directions. If you get lost in the maze, turn to Answer Alley.

Start at line one. At the end of each line, pick one of the two numbers, and go to the line with that number. Continue till reaching line sixty-four.

The solution path makes a thirty-two-line poem in rhyming couplets, and all the lines connect to form complete sentences with correct grammar and punctuation. If your path varies from this, you've taken a wrong turn.

After you've found the solution path, try connecting the thirty-two untraveled lines. They work the same way, except that you have to figure out where to begin and where to end.

1. You open up the door. (3, 6)
2. As quickly as you dare (17, 24)
3. The shadows tell you more, (44, 58)
4. And then you see the chair. (2, 11)
5. Like cobwebs on a broom (36, 39)
6. The words upon the floor (5, 42)
7. That hide within the gloom (34, 36)
8. You've read the ancient lore, (3, 6)
9. And step through clammy air (2, 11)
10. To nowhere. Yes, take heed (12, 34)
11. The Minotaur sits there. (46, 47)
12. And watch your step indeed (35, 49)
13. You enter with a groan (9, 21)
14. The Minotaur, in jest, (16, 23)
15. You know you're not alone, (4, 35)
16. Says, "Welcome, be my guest. (43, 52)
17. This is my humble home (19, 54)
18. And placed, where none expects it, (20, 64)
19. As intricate as Rome, (51, 53)
20. Your image, though, deflects it." (47, 59)
21. He slowly rubs his vest (16, 23)
22. And shakes your shaking hands. (14, 21)
23. And says, "Your last request (29, 56)
24. To reach the glass whose sands (22, 45)
25. Behind you starts to scurry. (42, 46)
26. By overlooking clues (5, 37)
27. You're in no real hurry, (8, 37)
28. Instead, admire the views (7, 10)
29. Is my command. Your ways (31, 50)

30. Will help you not at all. (41, 58)

31. It's time for you to graze (47, 56)

32. And finally you'll fall. (18, 38)

33. Don't bother using twine (9, 43)

34. And shroud your future tomb. (49, 62)

35. Because there is no sign (33, 57)

36. Where hallways end in doom. (4, 51)

37. For you're the master planner. (39, 48)

38. You'll end your days in fear!" (15, 40)

39. You built this puzzling manor, (18, 24)

40. He leaves you with a sneer. (53, 61)

41. It's useless. You will lose (26, 28)

42. Lead to a hall of stone. (13, 15)

43. To mark the paths you choose. (26, 28)

44. Much more than books you own. (13, 27)

45. Keep time in shifting lands. (7, 14)

46. You read a tattered banner. (48, 55)

47. You tremble as he stands (22, 45)

48. "My maze works in this manner: (17, 62)

49. The writing on the wall (30, 32)

50. Will end within my maze. (17, 38)

51. You'll creep before you crawl, (30, 32)

52. The nights have lost their days. (31, 50)

53. But all roads here just lead (12, 55)

54. Beneath the starry dome (10, 63)

55. To traps. Now do you need (44, 59)

56. Where many seekers roam (54, 61)

57. To help you—not a line. (29, 41)

58. There's no way out of here!" (40, 60)

59. A goblet of this wine? (33, 57)

60. You watch him disappear. (52, 63)

61. Then something wet and furry (19, 25)

62. Like mirrors, life reflects it; (20, 64)

63. He's gone, but you don't worry: (25, 27)

64. The only secret exit.

IT'S NOT TIME, PEOPLE

Which women's magazine has a name beginning with the name of a humor magazine, ending with the name of another women's magazine, and containing the names, separated by other letters, of a third women's magazine and a men's magazine? (Answer Alley)

PERFECTION TEST

Now for a perfection test. If you correctly fill in all the missing letters in the story below, you score a perfect hundred, but if you get one wrong, you score zero. At each blank, guess the word without looking ahead to the next one. Although this test is easy, you'll probably get a zero. Nobody's perfect. (Answer Alley)

He _ _ _ _ed her in the hall.

"Hey, I've got an extra _ _ _ _ to the football game," he said.

"I think I'll _ _ _ _," she replied.

So he made a _ _ _ _ at her. She _ _ _ _ed out. When she awoke, words _ _ _ _ed between them.

"Please don't _ _ _ _ judgment on me yet," he said.

"I'd rather _ _ _ _ sentence," she said.

"We can take my car through the _ _ _ _ and get to the game before the first _ _ _ _," he said.

"Oh, alright, you _ _ _ _ muster."

"I'll have to _ _ _ _ the hat to get some gas money. My _ _ _ _book is empty."

"Boy, that's _ _ _ _ing the buck. You'll probably _ _ _ _ a bad check."

He let that one _ _ _ _ by. Out in the car, she remarked in _ _ _ _ing, "My cat _ _ _ _ed away last week."

"Yesterday my dog _ _ _ _ed on," he cried.

She _ _ _ _ed him a Kleenex, and he _ _ _ _ed a truck.

"I hope I'm not just a _ _ _ _ing fancy," she said.

"No, I _ _ _ _ed over you before, but this time when you _ _ _ _ed my way, I decided I wouldn't _ _ _ _ up the chance."

And so they _ _ _ _ed a lot of time with each other.

SEVEN PUZZLING HEXAGONS

The only letters visible in the large hexagon below are TRY S P H, which means "TRY Seven Puzzling Hexagons." In this puzzle, you have to rearrange the small hexagons into a large hexagon that forms a letter at every adjacent side for a total of twelve different letters. That's half of it.

Now rearrange them again into a large hexagon to make twelve more letters, for a total of twenty-four. This set has a different small hexagon in the center.

To prepare the puzzle, photocopy it on card stock and cut out the small hexagons. Can you find both solutions? (Answer Alley)

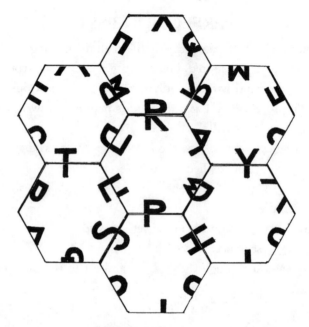

ALPHABOXES: THOUSANDS OF PUZZLES IN ONE

Alphaboxes is a puzzle with one simple solution, but it doesn't have to end there. You can make many other puzzles with the same set of boxes.

To prepare the puzzle(s), photocopy the illustration on card stock and cut out the sixteen small squares. The core puzzle uses just the nine center squares indicated by the arrows.

Solving the core puzzle requires assembling the nine squares into a larger square so they form common words of two to four letters wherever they touch. It should take about five minutes or less. (Answer Alley)

Then you can try the larger puzzle, which includes all sixteen squares. It has at least one solution, but the solution was lost years ago. For this one, you're on your own.

To make other puzzles, select a different set of nine squares out of the sixteen. There are 11,439 alternate puzzles possible. Some may have answers, and some may not.

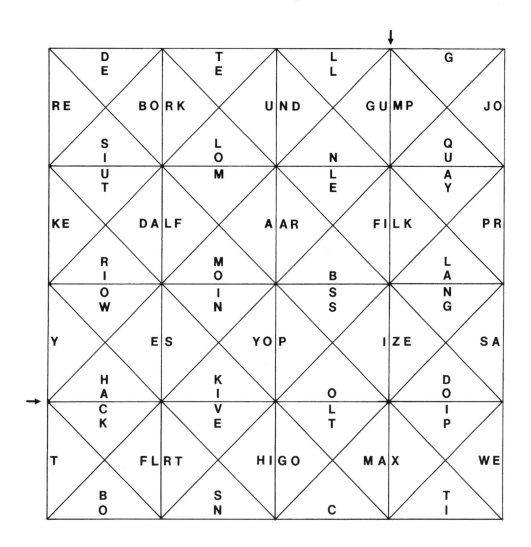

ORDER, PLEASE

The words in the following group appear in alphabetical order. Can you rearrange them in two logical ways that don't depend on alphabetization? (Answer Alley)

APRICOT	JUNCTIONAL
AUGMENTATION	MARSHMALLOW
DECOMPENSATION	MAYO
FEBRIFUGE	NOVELIZATIONS
JANGLE	SEPTUAGENARIANS
JULIENNE	OCTET

FABRICATED QUIZ

According to Fred Crane, a lot of fabrics are named after the places where they were made or exported, but the English language naturalized the names. For instance, Livorno, Italy becomes the more prosaic Leghorn. Can you identify the secret origins of these fabrics? (Answer Alley)

1. BUCKRAM	10. JERSEY
2. CALICO	11. LAWN
3. CAMBRIC	12. LISLE
4. CASHMERE	13. MUSLIN
5. CHAMBRAY	14. SATIN
6. DAMASK	15. SHALOON
7. DENIM	16. SPANDEX
8. FUSTIAN	17. TULLE
9. JEAN	18. WORSTED

UNATTRACTIVE OPPOSITES

The following pairs of antonyms have the same property. Can you identify it? (Answer Alley)

HUSBAND-WIFE	YES-NO
ADAM-EVE	UP-DOWN
FATHER-SON	FOR-AGAINST
BLACK-WHITE	TRUTH-LIE
BOY-GIRL	EAT-DRINK
DAY-NIGHT	GOOD-EVIL

SAME DIFFERENCE

How are these pairs of words alike? Which pair has a special feature that makes it stand out from the rest? (Answer Alley)

COMET-GOT	SILL-SWELL
PEARLY-PLATE	MARK-PARK
FATE-THINE	DON-DOFF
HEATH-SHEATH	TOWN-FROWN
SHOT-SCOLD	

COMIC BOOK ONOMATOPOEIA

Ross Eckler developed a taxonomy of sounds appearing in comic books. Each of his examples included a brief description of the action producing the sound. How sound is your judgment?

Match the noises on the right with the descriptions on the left. All of them appeared in the comics, but—KREEGAAAH!—it's a tough quiz! (Answer Alley)

1. FFFFFFFFWOPP
2. MOOSH MUMMPH MOOMPH
3. PBPBPPBPBPT
4. BLUT
5. SLOR-SLOR-SLOR-SLOR-SLORRREERRRRK-K-K
6. PUM PUM BAM BAM
7. ZRONKNRKLNRK
8. AU OOGA
9. SHOOF
10. HUPUNNNNNGGG
11. PHWONK
12. WIZZEEW ZWOSH WISH
13. YAKAKAKAKAKA
14. POP ROCK BADOOLA BLAM
15. THPT
16. SPLOOSH
17. OGGLE OGGLE
18. THBBPTHPPTH THBBPTH-PPTHTHBBPTHPPTH
19. SLUUUCK
20. BWOING
21. RRGHHMPHFFG
22. WOO-OP W-P-P W-WOO WOO-OOP
23. TWAANNNNG
24. ZOT
25. HEH HEE HOO HAR SNORK HO
26. BRUMMUMMUMUMMMUM

A. bread pops out of toaster
B. anteater tongue shoots out, catches fly
C. tweak dog's nose
D. food (as a fast-moving object)
E. strain to lift weights
F. eat cream puff
G. laugh
H. beanie propeller
I. smoke alarm
J. man falls in outhouse pit
K. head hit by pie
L. sucking cheese off lasagna
M. clam gargles
N. heart through stethoscope
O. snore
P. idling car
Q. Bronx cheer
R. loose shirt falls around one's ears
S. blow nose
T. drink last juice through a straw
U. car horn
V. shove bottle into baby's mouth
W. gargle
X. objectionable radio music
Y. eyes bug out in surprise or terror
Z. eat fast

SIMPLESCRIPT

In this postmodern advance in the art of penmanship, the writer need only learn one up-and-down stroke, similar to a written "i" without the dot. It's the simplest way to form letters. One stroke for A, two for B, and so on to twenty-six for Z. There are no separate forms for capital or small letters. One size fits all!

To distinguish separate letters in a word, the writer continues the last stroke of a letter straight down (thus making a descender) and then goes back up to begin the next letter.

The illustration shows the Simplescript alphabet, some examples, and a mystery quote. Note that even longer words, like MISSISSIPPI, don't have to be hyphenated. They can curl around and continue upside down on the next line. What could be simpler?

Can you solve the mystery quote? To keep it simple, each line has only one word in it. (Answer Alley)

OUT OF BOUNDS

As we leave Puzzle Bluff, another puzzling sign stands at the side of the road.

```
A  B  C  D  E  F  G  H
Z                    I
Y        CLUE:       J
X         NOT        K
W         AGO        L
V                    M
U  T  S  R  Q  P  O  N
```

The phrase NOT AGO sounds like NOT A "GO," which leads to the solution shown on the sign at the end of the road:

ANSWER: STOP

Chapter U

Sentence Road

GRAFFITI WALL

*A*COLORFUL PICKET fence called Graffiti Wall runs down Sentence Road. Lines of graffiti are painted all over it, but they're not the usual political slogans, obscenities, or love messages. These are sentences with a wordplay twist.

"Oh, my," says a shepherd carrying a ram in his arms. "I was afraid of this."

The ram looks ill.

"It's terrible, terrible. I can't say it."

There are five more rams following nearby.

"They're in good health," he says, "but this one isn't. The Saudi chief and his five brothers haven't been feeling well either."

Finally, he sets the poor ram down and says, "The sixth sick sheik's sixth sheep's sick!"

As you can see, the sixth sheep has caught a rash that is ruining the purity of its wool:

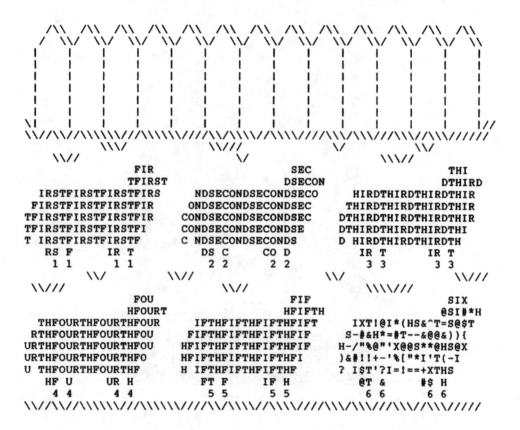

The shepherd just spoke one of the most difficult tongue twisters in English. He pulls a corkscrew out of his pocket and untwists his tongue.

"That's what I was worried about!"

And he goes on his way.

This is atypical of normal English, but on Sentence Road the atypical is typical. Let's read some of the graffiti, starting with a few more twisters.

LITERARY TONGUE TWISTERS

Test your aptitude for being a literary critic. Try speaking each of these tongue twisters aloud rapidly six times:

She saw Shelley sell seashells.

Were Wordsworth's words worth Wordsworth's work?
All will oil well Orwell's oilwell.
Chaucer's choicest saucer's choice, sir.
Blake broke bleak bloke.

ADJECTIVIZING, VERBIZING, AND ADVERBIZING

Xerox, usually an adjective, has come into popular usage as a verb meaning "to pho-tocopy." You've probably "Xeroxed" something before. The corporation warns against using its trade name that way, fearing it will lose its capital letter status and turn into a common word. At that point, the name enters public domain, where anyone can use it without violating trademark laws. Such a fate befell the Aspirin trademark.

Proper nouns in general—names of artists, cities, presidents—can be used as adjectives, verbs, or adverbs. This flexibility of English suggests further experimen-tation:

The beauty queen Ivoried her hands after Gleeming her teeth Crestfully.
"I feel somewhat Mozartish," Bached the conductor, Beethovening the
   orchestra during rehearsal.
Toyota-faced, he asked his parents for the car.
"Stop it! Stop Chicagoing me!" she screamed as she New Yorked him on the
   knee.
Millions of years ago, the earliest amoeba Campbelled out of the primor-
   dial soup.
Her sweet, Murine eyes belied her Real-Kill tongue.
"Schlitz!" the carpenter yelled when he Budweisered his thumb with a
   hammer.

CHANDLERISMS

In one of his hard-boiled detective stories, Raymond Chandler wrote: "She was the kind of blonde that could make a bishop kick a hole through a stained-glass win-dow." I told this to a friend, who promptly came back with his own version: "She was the kind of person that could make a catalog librarian drop a drawer." Other friends invented more examples, mostly with female subjects. Have you Chandlerized anyone lately?

She was the kind of gal who'd make a dogcatcher get the rabies.

He was the kind of guy who could make a nun kick the habit.

She was the kind of redhead who could make a Communist salute.

She was the kind of dame that could make a bricklayer lay bricks.

She was the kind of customer who could make a grocer grosser.

She was the kind of lady who could make a linguist speak in tongues.

IMAGINE WORDPLAY

Mike Reiss found a curious linguistic shift in a headline in *Variety*, the show business trade journal. An executive named Stuart Smiley left his job at Imagine Enterna, a production company. *Variety*'s headline proclaimed SMILEY ANKLES IMAGINE. It uses an adjective as a noun, a noun as a verb, and a verb as a noun.

HYPHENS TO BETSY!

Clifford Goldstein is a hyphen revivalist. In *The Parched Soul of America*, his volume of "Christian poetry," he attacks President Clinton with a unique I-love-to-tap-the-hyphen-key-on-my-typewriter style:

> A draft-dodging, drug-exhaling, sodomy-protecting, shady-dealing, tax-raising, child-exploiting, baby-killing, feminists-pandering, religion-robbing, military-reducing, womanizer becomes Commander-in-Chief.

While eleven hyphenated words appear in Goldstein's fourteen-word sentence, only "Commander-in-Chief" has more than one hyphen. Goldstein is merely an amateur. *The Daily Iowan* newspaper showed what world-class hyphenation looks like with a thirteen-words-in-one construction in this subheading for an article on holiday shopping:

THE WE'VE-ONLY-BEEN-DATING-FOR-A-LITTLE-WHILE-AND-I-DON'T-KNOW-IF-I-WANT-TO-INVEST-THE-TIME-AND-MONEY-TO-GET-A-PERSONAL-GIFT GIFTS

AP'STR'PH'S

Words can be chosen to make a sentence with apostrophes bristling out like the quills on a porcupine. The sentence below has forty-five apostrophes in thirty-nine words (124 letters). Most of the abbreviated forms can be found in the poems of Robert Burns. The apostrophes replace a total of fifty-six letters! Can you read the sentence in its full-worded form? (Answer Alley)

'Tis o'er ev'ry fo'c's'le th' bo's'n's look'd wi' min' pu'd 'til fu' o' fa', e'en t' nor', tho' mis'ry's awfu', 'n' ca's'll've sigh'd thro' ha's e'er sin' a' kiss'd, car'd, wish'd, an' clasp'd, ne'er ev'n i' lo'e.

SIGN DIEGO

Most zoos have signs asking visitors not to feed the animals or throw things at them. The San Diego Zoo and the San Diego Wild Animal Park have the ultimate in zoo signs. In one fell swoop, the sign tells all:

> PLEASE DO NOT
> ANNOY, TORMENT,
> PESTER, PLAGUE,
> MOLEST, WORRY,
> BADGER, HARRY,
> HARASS, HECKLE,
> PERSECUTE, IRK,
> BULLYRAG, VEX,
> DISQUIET, GRATE,
> BESET, BOTHER,
> TEASE, NETTLE,
> TANTALIZE, OR
> RUFFLE THE ANIMALS.

SNOWBALLING THE LANGUAGE

A rhopalic, or snowball, sentence begins with a one-letter word, followed by a two-letter word, then a three-letter word, and so on to any length, as in I AM THE LINE THAT'S FORMED. The word-length picks up letters like a rolling snowball picking up snow. As the line gets longer, the words get more unusual.

Jeff Grant has written the longest example so far, this twenty-five-word snowball:

> I am not very happy seeing eminent surgeons operating underneath ineffective soporiferous illuminations, misanthropical anthropologists indiscriminately resurrectionizing incircumscriptible unconventionalities, politico-religionists contraconscientiously counterrevolutionizing magnetohydrodynamicists, transubstantiationalists, electro-encephalographists.

The *Oxford English Dictionary*, however, says that rhopalic verse is composed of sentences with words increasing by the syllable and not by the letter. This type of snowball grows much more quickly. Grant has come up with an eleven-word example:

Some people completely misunderstand administrative extemporization—idiosyncratical antianthropomorphism undenominationalizing politico-ecclesiastical honorificabilitudinity.

WORD BEADS

Word Beads are inexpensive, easy-to-assemble sentence makers. Each bead has four words on it, and all the beads strung in a row form sentences as the beads turn. A string of beads is an ideal gift for the word player who has everything. It makes an alphabetic fashion statement.

To make a string of Word Beads, print the words here (or your own words) on the beads, string them together, and tie the knot. The words have to be selected to work in any combination with the other words. It's easiest to arrange words according to the same part of speech in order to make a grammatically correct sentence.

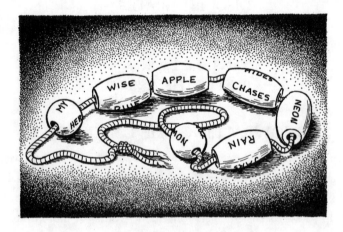

You can string together as many beads as you want, but seven seems to be a lucky number. A seven-bead string can generate 16,384 different sentences. Here are seven columns of words to start the beads rolling:

1st Pron.	2nd Adj.	3rd Noun	4th Verb	5th Adj.	6th Noun	7th Adv.
My	wise	apple	rides	neon	jars	icily
Her	blue	shadow	chases	grimy	rain	now
His	mad	face	xrays	tender	zeros	dimly
Your	ugly	parrot	loves	kingly	veils	today

COUNTRY AND WESTERN CLASSICS

My grandfather was a hillbilly from Flat River, Missouri, and he always had Country and Western on the radio. We listened to the poetic, bittersweet wisdom of Johnny Cash, Buck Owens, Patsy Cline, the Carter Family, Hank Williams, Loretta Lynn, and many others.

Country and Western lines often play with words to wring out the meaning. The results are funny, even sarcastic, comments on life, love, and the pursuit of romance. Here's a bucketful of lines, some of which are also the titles:

My wife ran off with my best friend, and I miss him.

You can't even do wrong right.

It's the bottle against the Bible in the battle for Daddy's soul.

If today was a fish, I'd throw it back in.

Thank God and Greyhound she's gone.

What's the use to try to get over you? I've still got you all over me.

Put the hearse in reverse, I wanna live again.

It's commode-huggin' time in the valley.

I gave her a ring, and she gave me the finger.

When you leave me, honey, walk out backward so I'll think you're comin' in.

She took everything but the blame.

We called it magic, then we called it tragic, then finally we called it quits.

THAT OLD-TIME MUSIC

Let's take a trip back to the first thirty years of this century and look at some song titles from the good old days. They have their own flavor and their own humor, but a few of them sound like Country and Western lines. Ladies and gentlemen, here, with a Shim-Me-Sha-Wabble, . . .

If You Talk in Your Sleep Don't Mention My Name

I Forgot to Remember to Forget about You

I Work Eight Hours Sleep Eight Hours That Leaves Eight Hours for Love

O'Brien Is Tryin' to Learn to Talk Hawaiian (to His Honolulu Lu)

If He Can Fight Like He Can Love, Good Night, Germany!

We're Goin' to Knock the 'Hel' out of Wilhelm (and It Won't Take Us Long)

My Red Cross Girlie (the Wound Is Somewhere in My Heart)

Maid in America

Who Paid the Rent for Mrs. Rip Van Winkle?
Where Did Robinson Crusoe Go with Friday on Saturday Night?
Carbarlick Acid Rag [sic]
Undertakers' Blues

SPY SONGS

Aldridge Ames was perhaps America's most talkative spy. After being convicted for delivering classified information to Russia, ex-CIA agent Ames gave an in-prison interview on CNN's "Larry King Live." Halfway through the program, a commercial for "The Best of Englebert Humperdink" song collection came on. Many of the song titles and lines were incredibly appropriate comments on the Ames interview:

Please Release Me, Let Me Go
You're Just Too Good to Be True, Can't Take My Eyes Off of You
The Shadow of Your Smile
There Goes My Reason for Living
Two Different Worlds, We Live in Two Different Worlds
There's a Kind of a Hush All Over the World Tonight

UNDER THE COVERS: A MUSICAL WORDPLAY GAME

It's amazing how a single phrase can change the meaning of a sentence. In this game, just add the phrase "under the covers" to the title of any song and see what happens. If you're at a bar sharing a pitcher with friends, the jukebox rocks with suggestive lines.

Rock music works most of the time. "Twist and Shout under the covers." "A Walk in the Black Forest under the covers." "I Can't Get No Satisfaction under the covers."

But don't stop there. Other types of music have titles that hit the spot, too. "Ring of Fire under the covers." "Beethoven's Fifth under the covers." "I'm a Little Teapot under the covers."

Nor does it have to be limited to music. Literature offers its own possibilities: "I Sing the Body Electric under the covers." "The Sun Also Rises under the covers." And movie titles: "Pee-Wee's Big Adventure under the covers." And play titles: "As You Like It under the covers." And so on.

Now strike up the band—under the covers!

FUTURE USES FOR CONTEMPORARY WORDS

Some distinctly twentieth-century words have narrow meanings. In the twenty-first century, their meanings may evolve new connotations. In the year 2020, you may find sentences like these:

The fly microwaved to the ant.

The lion took a megabyte out of the lion tamer.

The stripper pantyhosed her lawn.

The mailman couldn't unzipcode his lover's dress.

The politician miniskirted the issue.

The driver gridlocked his car door.

JACK GETS LAID OFF

How much sense can a word make? How much of a sentence can it make? This story uses one-word sentences.

Wake. Yawn. Stretch. Wash. Dress. Eat. Drink. Leave. Drive. Stop. Go. Stop. Wait. Wait. "Damn!" "HONK!" Accelerate. Pass. "Idiot!" Decelerate. Signal. Turn. Enter. Park. "Slam!" Walk. Climb. Open. Enter. Close. Walk.

"Morning." "Morning." "Busy?" "No." "Here." "Oh." Nod. Sit. Write. Erase. Type. Work. Smile. Work. Frown. Work. Yawn. "Jack?" "Yes." "Hurry!" "Okay." Work. Groan. Daydream. Forget. "Ring!" "Hello?" "Jack?" "Sir?" "Faster!" "Right!" "Now!" "Yes!" Work. Write. Work. Erase. Work. "Finished!"

Break. Walk. Turn. Walk. Sit. Relax. "Jack!" "What?" "Coffee?" "No." "No?" "Nope." "Alright." Slouch. Daydream. Daydream. Daydream. "Jack!" "Huh?" "Here!" "Now?" "Immediately." Stand. Walk. Turn. Walk. Sit. Type. Type. Type. Correct. Type. Type. Remove. Proofread.

"Lucy?" "Yes?" "Photocopy." "One?" "Three." Watch. Admire. Desire. "Jack!" Turn. "Huh?" "Ready?" "Yes." "Where?" "There." Point. "Oh." Wait. Watch. "Here." "Thanks." "Sure." "Lucy?" "Yes?" "Lunch?" "Busy." "Dinner?" "Tomorrow." "Okay!" Smile. Daydream. Work. Daydream. Work. Finish.

Stand. Deliver. "Jack!" "Sir?" "Lunchtime." "Oh." Walk. Open. Exit. Close. Climb. Walk. Turn. Walk. Enter. Sit. "Menu?" "No." "Order?" "Eggs." "Toast?" "Fine." "Bacon?" "Ham." "Coffee?" "No." Wait. Daydream. "Here!" Smell. "Yum!"

Bite. Taste. "Delicious." Chew. Swallow. Bite. Chew. Daydream. Choke. Swallow. "Burp." Finish.

Stand. Pay. Tip. Exit. Walk. Turn. Walk. Climb. Open. Enter. Close. Walk. Sit. Work. Forget. Remember. Work. Work. Work. Yawn. Drift. "Zzz." "Jack!!!" Wake. "Sir?" "Asleep?" " Uh. . . ." "Well?" "Yes." "YES!?" Worry. Think. Pause. Listen. "Jack?" "Sir?" "Fired!" "What?" "Fired!" "Why?" "Leave." "Now?" "Immediately!"

Stand. Walk. Open. Exit. "Slam!!!" Climb. Walk. Sigh. Think. Chuckle. Laugh. Guffaw. "Freedom!" Snicker. Walk. Remember. Walk. Turn. Search. Find. Enter. Lift. Dial. "Ring!" Wait. "Ring!"

"Hello." "Lucy?" "Yes." "Fired." "Oh." "Dinner?" "No." "Please." "Sorry." "But—" "Bye." "Wait!" "Click!" Sigh. "Click!"

Exit. Walk. Wonder. Walk. Fantasize. "Damn!" Walk. Walk. Walk. Walk. Walk.

We've reached the end of the fence, where the stop sign at the end of the street ends this sentence

Chapter V

Language Expressway

THE LINGO BROTHERS' CIRCUS

ON BOTH SIDES of this road, circus tents stretch out into the distance. Calliopes play nouns, jugglers juggle adjectives, unicyclists recycle verbs.

It's the Lingo Brothers' Circus! This is where language flies through the air with the greatest of ease, doing double and triple somersaults, soaring in formation to the amazement of the cheering crowds.

The circus showcases the more unusual side of language, from the imaginary to the unbelievable—new letters, made-up words, strange lists—where language stretches beyond its normal boundaries, bounces above its usual purposes, and sometimes leaves the dictionaries behind.

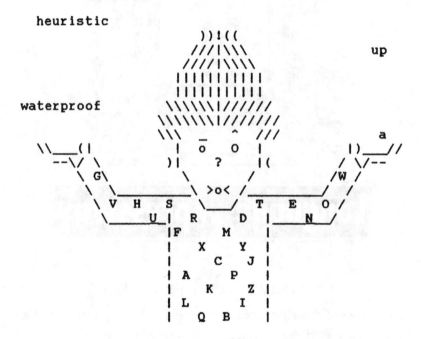

```
                        jejune

                                    zesty

              peevish
                                      tall

        nebulous
                                          red

      heuristic
                         ))!((                          up
                        ///!\\\
                       ////!\\\\
                       |||||||||||
                       |||||||||||
  waterproof           \\\\\\!//////
                       \\\\\\!//////
                        \\\   _  ///               a
     \\___(|            !  ō  o  !          |)___//
     --\/ \            )|   ?    |(         / \/--
      \ G\              \       /          /W /
       \___\__           \ >o< /        ___/__ /
        \ V  H  S       \___/  T  E  O /
         \____ U |   R      D   |    N __/
               |F       M       |
               |   X       Y    |
               |      C    J    |
               | A       P      |
               |    K      Z    |
               | L          I   |
               |    Q   B       |
```

"Ladies and gentlemen, boys and girls, the show is about to begin!" the ring-master announces. "It's the twenty-six-ring circus of words under the linguistic big top!"

SEEING DOUBLE

This advertisement shows one way of customizing a letter to fit the meaning of the word it occupies. In this case, the double-dotted i is doubly appropriate. Not only does it refer to twins, but two dots in International Morse Code represent the letter "i."

VOWELOLOGY

ABSTEMIOUS and FACETIOUS are known for having all five vowels in alphabetical order, but a lot of extra consonants separate them from each other. Susan Thorpe discovered a biological term, the name for a fossil sponge, that seems to have soaked up all the vowels. It's the only word of its kind.

IOUEA

ON BEYOND ZEBRA

Are twenty-six letters really enough in English? For writing, perhaps so, but for transcribing spoken language, they fall unspeakably short. New letters need to be invented to sublet the alphabet. The subletters more closely link the oral and the written traditions.

As a start, here are fifteen subletters, codified by capital letters in brackets. Each signifies an actual sound (and not a dictionary word like MOAN) made with the upper respiratory system. In other words, [F] means a real moan.

Each subletter can appear at the beginning, middle, or end of a word, or it can stand alone. When a subletter is repeated in the same brackets, the sound is drawn out longer. Following the list of subletters, several sentences demonstrate their use. Try to read the sentences aloud, subletters and all:

[A] belch	[F] moan	[K] sniffle
[B] cough	[G] pant	[L] snore
[C] gasp	[H] shriek	[M] snort
[D] hiccup	[I] snarl	[N] spit
[E] kiss	[J] sneeze	[O] yawn

"N[D]ot toni[D]te, dear, I've go[D]t the hic[D]cups."

"Hey, punk, [I] what are you doing [M] on this side of town [N]?"

"I rea[K]lly caught a bad[B] case of the flu[K][B][K]."

"Great food! [AAA]! Excuse me!"

"I [O] can hard[OO]ly keep awa[OOO]ke[L] [L] [L] . . ."

"I[E] love[F] you[E]. Oo[C]oh! Oo[C]oh!" "Me[EEE], t[G]o[G]o!"

"That smells like rag[J]weed[J][J][J][J][J]."

HOW TO SNEEZE IN NINE LANGUAGES

When in Rome, sneeze as the Romans sneeze. Maxey Brooke compiled a list of sneeze words that should bring out the Kleenex in everyone.

HAH-CHEE! (Chinese)	WA-HING! (Indonesian)
KYCHNUTI! (Czech)	KUSHAMI! (Japanese)
KER-CHOO! (English)	KICHNIECIE! (Polish)
A-TCHOUIN! (French)	AP-CHI! (Russian)
ITUSH! (Hebrew)	

WHY'S GUY

At three years old, my son was in the WHY stage of learning. He'd discovered that he could ask a question, get an answer, ask why about the answer, get another answer, and keep whying for as long as I'd keep replying.

One night, he concluded a round of WHYs by asking, "Do you know what 'why' is?"

I said, "No, what is it?"

He said, "'Why' is a letter."

TYPOGRAPHIC DARWINISM

Gertrude Stein once said that "commas are servile, and exclamation points are positively revolting!" And aren't question marks just a waste of time? Life has become more complex than simple punctuation can possibly express.

Typographic Darwinism comes to the rescue with a dozen new punctuation marks that can adapt to the hypertexts of the coming millenium:

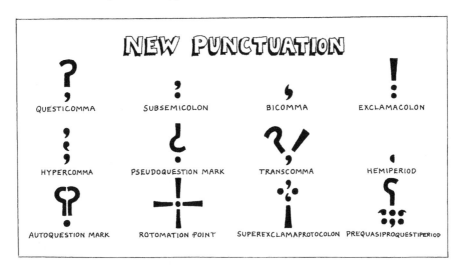

VERBAL HYPERTENSION

Like punctuation, English verb tenses have become hopelessly outdated. By expanding the number of tenses, we can express our complex temporal experiences more precisely. Beyond the old-fashioned Future Perfect ("I will have walked") lie new tenses just waiting for us to boldly go where no grammar has gone before. Consider, for instance, the Future Past Perfect ("I will have had walked"), the Progressive Conditional ("I would have should have been walking"), and many other forms, like these:

He will does walked (Future Present Past)

He will will walk (Double Future)

He could can walk (Unconditional Present)

He is being doing walking (Obsessive Progressive)

He did will was have walked (Refractive Future Perfect)

He might be having been about to be walking (Superjunctive)

Here is a revised version of the old fable, "The Tortoise and the Hare." After you've read it, you shall have witnessed how useful the expanded tenses can be:

The Tortoise and the Hare were racing against each other in the woods. The Hare, having taken a big lead, decided that the Tortoise couldn't possibly catch up with him, but the Tortoise kept running as fast as she could, which was very, very slow.

Yesterday, when the two agreed to have the race, the Hare realized that he would have been having reached the finish line by now and might have been being having sprinted in ahead of the Tortoise an hour ago. She, however, was not wanting to have been going to be being a has-been instead of a will-be, so she was being doing walking at her own pace, in the hope that she might have been being the winner next week.

The Hare, however, confident that he was going to be going to be the winner, did has had been curling up under a maple tree and does will have has been falling asleep. Consequently, the Tortoise might win; and the day before the week after Wednesday, she may have been having beaten the Hare, who shouldn't have been ought to be sleeping in the middle of a race. In any event, he would have should have thought that he couldn't be an also-had-run.

As the Tortoise was about to be about to be crossing the finish line, the Hare suddenly woke up from his nap. As fast as possible, he zoomed after her, but even if it was a month after a year before Sunday, he couldn't have should be making it on time.

The Tortoise stepped ever so carefully across the finish line, just a moment before the Hare would have been about to be going to hop across it himself.

"I won!" she said triumphantly.

The Hare paused a moment and then replied, "Yes, Ms. Tortoise, in the next decade you will have been about to be going to be used to be having been doing being the winner of this race, but tomorrow we'll have to do it again, for it's two out of three, ma'am."

"Oh, no," she replied, "for today was tomorrow yesterday."

MORAL: What might have been might be seeming to be what is, but what is can't ever be will have been without being to be.

IT'S A BIRD . . . IT'S A PLANE . . . IT'S SUPERPERSON!

To create a gender-neutral English, new terms have been suggested to replace those with MAN in them. Examples include MAILPERSON, POLICEPERSON,

PERSONPOWER, and even PERSONHOLE. One of the best, however, is Steven Cushing's name for a nonsexist dog breed: DOBERPERSON.

Cushing notes that the SON in PERSON is still sexist, but substituting CHILD for SON is ageist. As a solution, he suggests using OFFSPRING. The changes go from HUMAN to HUPERSON to HUPERCHILD to the ultimate in political correctness: HUPEROFFSPRING.

And we're all members of the huperoffspring race.

ONE-WORD POETRY

In the 1960s, poet Aram Saroyan downsized his poetry from a few lines to one line to one word. His minimal poetry reached a peak, and a peek, with his one-word classic, "lighght," an eye-catching variation on its dictionary counterpart. It won an eight-hundred-dollar literary award, which may represent the most money a single poem has ever earned in a day—$134.28 per letter.

In the 1970s, one-word poetry had its own magazine, *Matchbook*, edited by Joyce Holland. *Matchbook's* one-inch-square pages were stapled inside fully-functioning matchbooks. Each issue featured nine words—real or coined, short or long.
Here is a selection from the magazine. The last and longest word listed here appeared as a foldout.

anagramarama (Darrel Gray)
apocatastasis (Allen Ginsberg)
armadildo (Bill Zavatsky)
borken (Keith Abbott)
coughy (Pat Nolan)
cerealism (Fletcher Copp)
colaminers (Michael Lally)
cosmicpolitan (Morty Sklar)
electrizzzzz (g. p. skratz)
electrelocution (Scott Wright)
embooshed (Cinda Wormley)
feltit (George Mattingly)
flabbergassed (Dick Paterson)
fornicile (Joe Ziegler)
groblems (Edwin Denby)
gulp (Pat Paulsen)
hairanoia (Tom Clark)
heeelp (Allan Appel)
immaculation (John Batki)

lungng (David Hilton)
markle (Allan Kornblum)
meeeeeeeeeee (Duane Ackerson)
metaphoria (Rosemarie Waldrop)
monther (Gerard Malanga)
poium (John Weiners)
psychasm (Tom Veitch)
puppy (aram saroyan)
razzmatazz (Paul Violi)
shirty (Peter Schjeldahl)
sixamtoninepm (Kit Robinson)
stuv (Warren Woessner)
tictactile (ira steingroot)
underwhere (Carol DeLugach)
unvelope (Steve Toth)
whirrrrrd (Alan Davies)
zoombie (Sheila Heldenbrand)
whahavyagotthasgudtareedare
(Trudi Katchmar)

Holland also edited *Alphabet Anthology*, a collection of 104 one-letter poems by 104 contributors. Each contributor received a postcard with the lowercase alphabet on it. To be in the anthology, the potential one-letter poet circled one letter and returned the postcard. In the final count, all letters but one were selected. Which letter do you think appeared the most, and which didn't appear at all? (Answer Alley)

THE MELLO-LINGO DICTIONARY

Ambrose Bierce wrote *The Devil's Dictionary*, but even the devil gets behind the times. O. V. Michaelsen updated Bierce with his own definitions, most of which appear in his "Mello-Lingo Dictionary." Some examples for the truly contemporary jargoneer:

CENTERED: self-centered

CRASHING: falling asleep in the fast lane

DIPLOMACY: a lie for a lie, a truth for a truth

DREAM HOUSE: surreal estate

FREE AGENT: unemployed

HUNGER PROJECT: thought for food

MOD: archaic abbreviation of "modern"

POP PSYCHOLOGY: fast food for thought

WEIRDO: an eccentric who's not an artist

YOGI: A karmakhanic

ANTIQUASIPOSTNEOPROFESSIONALIZATIONISMISTI-CATIOUSLY SPEAKING

David Goldberg provided the world with some professional terminology to upgrade the phrases we hear every day. Here's a sampling:

AMOROUS TERRICIRCUMFLEXION: love makes the world go round

ANAL CRANIOPENETRATION: having one's head up one's ass

CHRONOCIDE: killing time

CHRONOPANTRAUMATHERAPY: time heals all wounds

DORSAL MORDANCY: backbiting

DORSALRECIPROCAL ABRASION: you scratch my back, I scratch yours

FELINOLINGUAL SEIZURE: cat got your tongue

HORTICULTURAL CIRCUMFLAGELLATION: beating around the bush

HYPERCULINARY PUTREFACTION: too many cooks spoil the broth

OPTICAL SIMIOMIMICRY: monkey see, monkey do

PEDAL ENDOJUGULEPSY: putting your foot in your mouth

PROCTALGIA: a pain in the ass

RUBROCERVIX: redneck

SCAPULAR FRIGIDITY: cold shoulder

SCATASHINOLEPSY: can't tell shit from Shinola

SIMIOLUMINOSITY: monkeyshines

IS THERE A DOCTOR IN THE HOUSE?

Wacky Medical Terms for the Layman is a cure-ious column by Peter H. Gott, M.D., appearing in *The Lakeville Journal.* Here is a healthy selection of terms that Gott got from his readers:

ANTABUSE: stepping on an anthill

BERIBERI: pie filling

CLAUSTROPHOBIA: fear of Santa

CARDIOGRAM: telegram for a heart patient

DILATOR: beats dying sooner

ENEMA: someone who is not your friend

FIBULA: a little white lie

HICCUP: what a yokel drinks from

HIP JOINT: popular bar

HYMEN: greeting to an all-male club

PROTEIN: someone who favors adolescents

URINALYSIS: different than my analysis

FROM UNBIRTHDAY TO NONBIRTHDAY

In Lewis Carroll's *Through the Looking-Glass,* Humpty Dumpty tells Alice about an unbirthday present, which is "A present given when it isn't your birthday, of course." Since Carroll's time, there have been many modern advances in birthday terminology.

ARCHBIRTHDAY: your favorite all-time birthday, with the best gifts, the best cake, and the best party, against which all your other birthdays compare unfavorably for the rest of your life.

SUBBIRTHDAY: the birthday of a sibling. Since it's less important than yours, your sibling deserves fewer presents.

PREBIRTHDAY: the day before your birthday, traditionally reserved for reminding people that tomorrow is your birthday.

POSTBIRTHDAY: the day after your birthday, traditionally reserved for snubbing people who forgot your birthday yesterday.

EXBIRTHDAY: the belated birthday that a friend wishes you a few days too late. Exbirthday cakes are stale, and exbirthday presents come from second-hand stores.

ALTERBIRTHDAY: the substitute birthday that the unlucky person born on leap day celebrates during non-leap years instead. Pathetic!

REBIRTHDAY: the birthday experienced by born-again Christians after they've been reborn. Instead of candles, rebirthday cakes have halos over them.

PSEUDOBIRTHDAY: the birthday that kids who are too young to drink have on their fake IDs. Pseudobirthdays are illegal.

ANTIBIRTHDAY: the birthday of someone you hate. Antibirthday presents are usually dangerous.

COBIRTHDAY: the birthday that you and a friend share. It's somewhat narcissistic to give each other gifts.

PARABIRTHDAY: the birthday that falls on another big holiday, such as Christmas or Hanukkah. The poor unfortunate doesn't get the normal share of presents, best wishes, or parties.

NONBIRTHDAY: the birthday that is forgotten by everyone, including the noncelebrant. On nonbirthdays, no one gets nonbirthday cakes, nonbirthday parties, or nonbirthday presents. If someone remembers, though, it automatically reverts back to a birthday.

BOSSES SOB

When bosses write recommendation letters, they often pad their lingo with jargon. According to a list of Performance Evaluation Terms supplied by Stephanie Wasta, the real meaning of some of that jargon is quite different from its surface meaning.

EXCEPTIONALLY WELL QUALIFIED: has committed no major blunders to date

UNLIMITED POTENTIAL: we're stuck with this person until retirement

QUICK THINKING: offers plausible excuses for errors

STRONG ADHERENCE TO PRINCIPLES: stubborn beyond belief

IS UNUSUALLY LOYAL: wanted by no one else

ALERT TO ORGANIZATIONAL DEVELOPMENTS: a gossip

EXPRESSES SELF WELL: can string two sentences together

DEMONSTRATES QUALITIES OF LEADERSHIP: has a loud voice, is evasive

SPENDS EXTRA HOURS ON THE JOB: has a miserable home life

CONSCIENTIOUS AND CAREFUL: scared

CHESSBOARDS TO AFGHANISTAN

The International Mail Manual has one of the most unusual lists in the world. A large white tome, it tells what you're not supposed to send to foreign countries. But why can't you mail soap to Paraguay? Or artificial flowers to Italy? Or—

chessboards to Afghanistan
funeral urns to Algeria
flypaper to Botswana
handcuffs to Brazil
greeting cards that play a musical jingle to Bulgaria
secondhand beehives to Canada
baby bottles measured in both liters and ounces to Costa Rica
almanacs to Denmark
rubber shoes to Ecuador
horror comic books to Great Britain
peat moss to Ireland

aphrodisiacs to Malawi
shaving brushes made in Japan to St. Lucia
rubber nursing nipples to Tunisia
used underwear to the [former] USSR
incomplete decks of playing cards to Germany

GOD—ADDRESSES, ESSAYS, LECTURES

John R. Likins has collected some of the weirdest and funniest reference directions of modern times in his article, "Subject Headings, Silly, American—20th Century—Complications and Sequelae—Addresses, Essays, Lectures," *Technical Services Quarterly*, Vol. 2, No. 1/2, Fall/Winter 1984. They're all real, including the one above and the many here:

American Giant Checkered Rabbit
Banana Research
Bankruptcy—Popular Works
Catastrophical, The *see also* Comic, The
Child Abuse—Study and Teaching
Contango and Backwardization
Dentists in Art
Fantastic Television Programs
Food, Junk
Ghosts—Pictorial Works
Great Tit *see also* Blue Tit—Behavior
Hemorrhoids—Popular Works
Jesus Christ—Person and Offices
Laboratory Animals—Congresses
Love Nests—Directories
Manure Handling
Mud Lumps
Odors in the Bible
Prayers for Animals
Sewage—Collected Works
Sick—Family Relationships
Urinary Diversions *see also* Urine Dance
Wasps (Persons)

SHAKESPEARE'S FIRST AND LAST WORDS

Shakespeare's thirty-eight plays use a total of sixty-five different words to begin and end the dialogue, five more words to start the six prologues, and seven more words to end the seven epilogues. Angus James used those words, and only those words, in this soliloquy.

Night. A wood in Illyria. Mist. Alarums & excursions.

Enter Shakespeare.

Shakespeare: O good Ford, noble Gregory—

Shoot another boatswain:

So . . . strike, Sir!

(Points)

I know you, young Romeo! Clap!

Assist in happiness' delights

Nay, to be true open joy!

(Looks to right)

Tush, old Queen—

Queen, long hung

in solemnity . . . Cease! Hence!

You ruinate another holiday!

(Comes forward)

Call my good pipers near!

Let my realm ring free

As I now take good Escalus' bier

Proceed away to Scone

Before new diseases, ending heart's peace,

Befall!

(Whispers)

So now I'll relate true ending

Whose way amends when in time—

(Staggers)

If . . . if . . . I, who won two roses—

(Reels)

So . . . night? Farewell, sweet day!

(Stumbles)

Amen!!

(Falls. Dies.)

THE SHOW IS OVER

For the grand finale, the Lingo Brothers' Circus sends up a fireworks display that lights the night sky with exploding letters of the alphabet. The crowd leaves the big top tent to watch the skywriting.

We head back up to the Language Expressway, where the sign tells us to keep on going.

Chapter

W

Logology Lookout

THE WORDPLAY OBSERVATORY

*H*IGH ABOVE THE city, the Wordplay Observatory sits on Logology Lookout. Here you can see the Big Dipper pouring letters onto the book of night.

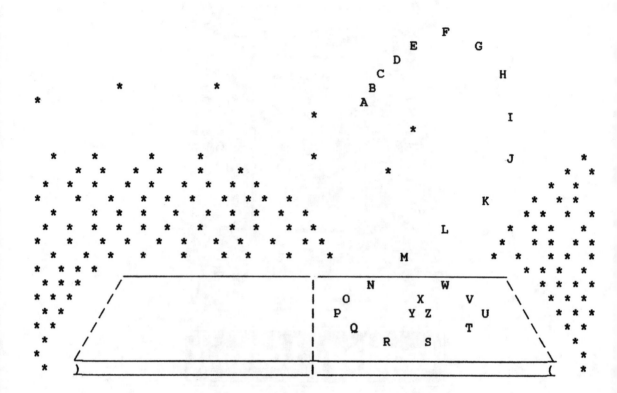

Logologists discover worlds of language from this vantage point. What do they think about wordplay? To find out, I wrote to some of the people who have been active in the field. My letter requested a statement on wordplay, and it included a list of fourteen questions suggesting possible topics. The writer could, of course, answer in any way he or she desired.

1. Why do you read and write wordplay?
2. Do you have a philosophy guiding your wordplay?
3. Where do you get your inspiration?
4. Can wordplay be considered an art? a science?
5. How have you been influenced by others' work?
6. When did you first become interested in wordplay?
7. How does wordplay relate to mainstream literature?
8. How does it compare to other fields—math, logic, linguistics, comedy, the-ater, etc.?

9. What would be a suitable metaphor for describing wordplay?
10. What are your goals in wordplay?
11. What are your favorite wordplay forms?
12. Has computer technology influenced your work?
13. Why do you like wordplay?
14. What gives you the most satisfaction in creating wordplay?

In their own words, here are thirty-one wordplay people. Each person's section includes biographical information and wordplay statement.

JAY AMES

Other than *Word Ways,* I've had stuff published in *Logophile, CSSN Bulletin, ANS BUL-LETIN* as well as numerous poetry magazines both here and abroad, not forgetting America.

I'm a longtime member of ANS, CSSN, NCNA (Illinois Name Society), and an equally longtime subscriber to *Verbatim* and a few others. I've been a cruciverbalist since 1926—when the first crosswords came out, I believe. Became interested in them when I was living and working for a spell (1926–1928) in Britain.

As an Alberta-born "side hill gouger" (Rocky Mountaineer, born in 1910) I've worked in many parts of Canada, the U.S., Britain, and during WWII (1937–1945) was with the British Armed Forces in Malta, North Africa, and the Middle East (where I picked up my smatterings of Maltese, Arabic, and German).

A Torontonian since the summer of 1947, I'm now long retired (1976) and looking forward to keeping in step with the century. I wanna see what these "Martian settlements" are gonna be like.

LEONARD ASHLEY

President, the American Society of Geolinguistics. Director of the International Conference on Geolinguistics in the Nineties at CUNY in New York City, 1992.

I have always enjoyed wordplay. I recall my delight at first hearing of someone who "put Descartes before the horse" or the English barmaid who "pulled the wrong knob and got stout." I enjoyed hearing of the Chinese restaurateur who served large portions: he was sui generis. When my friend the late Dr. ClairËve Grandjouan was looking around Europe for bits of tesselated pavement that had survived from Roman times (and might be used to trace the progress of Roman legions across Gaul), I perpetrated perhaps my worst foreign-language pun: I suggested her dissertation be called Eine Kleine Nicked Mosaic. Wordplay can range from painful puns to great poetry. It is to be celebrated I think that a love of it shows a lively linguistic interest.

RALPH BEAMAN

Originally from Plymouth, Massachusetts. I majored in organic chemistry (Ph.D.) and worked with new polymers, fibers, market, and marketing research. I was early involved with *Word Ways* (February 1970).

In my early teens I enjoyed leafing through encyclopedias and dictionaries. Before Jack Levine's monumental Pattern Words I recall Darryl Francis found the double-lettered TAENIODONTIDAE. Quite by HAPPENCHANCE I added that word. While Jack also had SCINTILLESCENT he missed UNSUFFI-CIENCES. I searched high and low for INDIAN REDROOT TEA—it and its possessive plural are still up for grabs. Someone should work into the act PC PRO-CRASTINATIONS and CB INAPPLICABLENESS!

My wordplay for many years now has been in constructing crosswords. The Sunday-size puzzles have been published by the Tribune Syndicate (a multitude of Sunday newspapers), *The New York Times*, and a number of special places such as *The Crosswords Club* and puzzle booklets. A puzzle just completed adds interest to the theme with HAJJ, SFAX, and QIN.

MAXEY BROOKE

Editor of *The Water Drop*, published by Puckorius & Associates, Water & Waste Water Management Consultants, in Evergreen, Colorado.

When my wife and I reached eighty, we decided to move to a retirement home. That meant disposing of my library.

Without my dictionaries, journals, and reference books (more than three hundred items), I was no longer able to do logological research.

I enjoyed stretching rules to the limit and beyond; creating rhymes using words the experts said there were no rhymes for; inventing paradoxes (least mean, less mean, mean, meaner, meanest; the mean mean being mean, if you know what I mean).

Suggesting to militant feminists who want to remove all masculine-oriented words from the language that manhole should be personhole, ergo mailman should be personperson.

HOWARD BERGERSON

I was born July 29, 1922, in Minneapolis, Minnesota.

My interest in word curiosities, and in other things intellectual and artistic, was innate rather than acquired. I remember a little girl, when I was perhaps seven, asking me, "What is round on both ends and high in the middle?" The answer, OHIO. I remember a little boy who always signed his name by first making ten vertical lines, | | | | | | | | | |, and then adding twelve more straight lines for KENNETH. For me, such things were like jewels that, within my mind, I collected.

Yes, I do have a philosophy guiding my wordplay, but I could not describe it briefly because it uses radically unfamiliar concepts, which I have originated, and it exists in a foment of development on the *intersection* of logology, number theory, physics, philosophy, and theology.

TED CLARKE

I worked in the aircraft industry in different capacities. Later did some development work on Le Tunnel. Currently I spend a lot of time on my computers, including editing *WordsWorth* magazine.

Language, especially my native tongue English, whether written, spoken, or just in one's thoughts, is so chock-a-block with enigmas, idiosyncrasies, and sheer complexity that it provides an endless source of interest, amusement, and stimulation to lubricate the wheels of an active mind.

For many years now, I have had a dual interest in mind-puzzling pursuits—numerical (including logic) and lexical. Apart from studying historical and current trends, I have occupied myself in devising novel forms of puzzles. My preference is for those that can be conceived as derived from natural situations. I enjoy using my computer both as a working tool, e.g., for correspondence, or as a database, and for writing programs. The most difficult puzzle I have tackled is the search for a valid single-order ten-square.

PHILIP COHEN

I'm a computer programmer; this ties in, like my interest in math and linguistics, with my love of puzzles. Besides the NPL I belong to KOST (Knights of the Square Table), a postal game club.

My interest in wordplay of the more esoteric sort derives from a lifelong interest in list making. The earliest effort I recall was my first-grade teacher's challenge to the class to come up with lists of homonyms; I found over a hundred. In high school I tried to list words containing all 676 possible two-letter sequences. Then *Language on Vacation* and *Word Ways* came along and really opened my eyes to the possibilities.

I have always liked puzzles, especially (and increasingly) word puzzles: mostly cryptic crosswords and the versified puzzles of the National Puzzlers' League, the latter being the only puzzles I compose. An issue of NPL puzzles is like a chocolate sampler box, with lots of little puzzles of all sorts and all degrees of difficulty. Puzzling is at most a very minor art, but great fun.

CHRIS COLE

President, Questrel, Inc., Newport Beach, California.

My interest in wordplay is part of a program that I am pursuing, to wit: (1) Collect as many full-text dictionaries as possible. From the parts of speech and the rules for spelling in English, produce a "complete" word list of the English language. Solve all "standard" "simple" logological problems. This is why I compiled a list of the current records [see Chapter G].

(2) Build a semantic net from the dictionaries. I may include data from other full-text sources. Use this net to solve as many "standard" "complex" logological problems as possible, perhaps from Borgmann, *Enigma,* and *Word Ways.* Enhance net and add data sources until solution rate is acceptable.

(3) Augment this net with deductive capabilities, see how close to natural language recognition we can come.

FRED CRANE

After thirty-seven years of success at avoiding work (I was a college professor), I retired to the village of my maculate conception, Mt. Pleasant, Iowa, and moved in with my parents, my wife and I claiming to be the oldest boomerang kids on record.

I've been a fan of words since the age of nine months, when I spoke my first tri-syllable—"Grandmother" (my mother claims it came out as "Bamamma"—there must have been noise in the room). I was brought up in a house crammed with books. I am more a consumer than a manufacturer of jeux de mots. I met my destiny when a new journal entitled *Word Ways* was announced; we have carried on a hot affair ever since.

I like some forms of wordplay more than others: in general, those that deal with meaning more than those with abstract patterns. To say that I love paronymics, paronomasiastics, semasiologics more than I do orthoepistics or glossematics, and much more than morphophonematics, is to say it all.

FAITH ECKLER

For twenty-five years, I was the administrator of a charitable fund for St. Peter's Church in Morristown, New Jersey, and also on the board of directors for the Richmond Fellowship, a halfway house for mental patients. I enjoy hiking.

How to Bring Up Baby
(and turn him/her into a logologist)

When I was a youngster (back before penicillin and all the other wonder drugs), I was frequently sick—at least once for several months. To keep me amused while confined to bed, my father proposed that I search the dictionary for words with four or more of the same letter! For each word with four repeated letters I would receive a penny; five repeated letters brought me a nickel, and for six of the same letter a whole quarter! I don't recall that I got rich this way, but it did make me a confirmed lover of words and taught me to appreciate their value.

ROSS ECKLER

I worked thirty years at Bell Telephone Labs advising engineers on statistical problems. Math degree from Princeton 1954. Other interests: human longevity claims, caving, hiking, genealogy.

As a boy I thought wordplay consisted either of games or puzzles. By college I realized that more interesting wordplay involved games-versus-Nature: open-ended searches for all possible triple homonyms, or a type-collection of trigrams. In 1968, *Word Ways* forever changed wordplay by liberating it from insularity; aficionados could for the first time build on each other's work. Logology was no longer viewed as a collection of isolated curiosa, but a coherent body of knowledge such as math or geology. However, unlike such disciplines, the dedicated amateur could quickly reach the forefront of logology to make new discoveries. Nowadays wordplay has two major streams: the newly defined logological research, increasingly aided by the computer, and the long-unchanged constrained writing—palidromes, lipograms, and the like—which still seems to require the creative spark. Long may both flourish!

DARRYL FRANCIS

I've had various books published: *The Devil's Bedside Book, Puzzles and Teasers for Everyone, The Hamlyn Book of Brainteasers and Mindbenders,* and seven Scrabble books.

Imagine a sphere floating in space, about eight thousand miles in diameter. The surface is mainly water, there are no continuous landmasses, but there are millions of islands. Each island is a word. Some islands are very large and have existed for hundreds of years—these equate to common, everyday words that everyone "knows." Some islands are very small—these are the less common words. Some islands are newly formed, and only just manage to poke up above sea level—these are new words. Some islands are slowly sinking below sea level—these are words that are obsolescent/obsolete. Some islands exist below the surface—these could be coinages. Wordplay is like a voyage round these islands. They aren't mapped very well. Wordplay is about discovering islands and relationships between islands that haven't been perceived before.

LEONARD GORDON

An engineer, I've been active in constructing mechanical puzzles and in analyzing mathematical puzzles. Experienced in programming computers, especially for solving logological problems.

Think of it like this:

N-letter words exist in a word space. Space is a cube 26 x 26 x 26 . . . N times. If N = 2, the space has collapsed to a plane (square). If N = 1, we have a line. If N > 3 we have a hypercube.

Space is mostly empty. We can describe coordinate points, but most are empty. Space gets emptier as word length increases.

word length	number of words	points	fraction filled
2	225	676	1 in 3
3	2,000	17,576	1 in 9
4	10,000	456,976	1 in 50
5	40,000	11,881,376	1 in 300

We are like astronomers searching space for stars (words). A dictionary is our telescope. A small telescope (dictionary) can only find the bright stars (common words). Large telescopes (dictionaries) can find the dim ones (obscure words). Words, like stars, are not evenly or randomly distributed in space. There are galaxies.

JEFF GRANT

Word Ways contributor since 1977. Ten times New Zealand Scrabble champion. Editor of New Zealand Scrabble magazine *Forwards.* Compiler of *Palindromicon*, a palindrome dictionary.

At primary school, while others read children's stories, I remember scanning a dictionary, making lists of odd words, and, at home, compiling crosswords and word squares.

My general interest in words was later extended on seeing a reference to palindromes in an issue of *Scientific American.* This inspired a lifetime devotion to this form of wordplay. Following that, I read Borgmann's *Language on Vacation.* It fascinated me so much I practically copied the book longhand into a couple of exercise books! Thereafter I found out about Ross Eckler and *Word Ways,* and realized others shared my love of "recreational linguistics." A whole new world had opened up to me!

All my work is done manually. I own neither a computer nor even a typewriter.

PAUL HELLWEG

I'm an assistant professor at California State University, Northridge, but my primary occupation is that of freelance writer. Publications: articles, poems, and stories on wordplay, hiking, climbing, and other topics; and books, including *Totally Outrageous Bumper Snickers*, *The Insomniac's Dictionary*, and *Weird and Wonderful Words*.

My personal wordplay statement: anagramming boosts creativity. Deciphering enigmas frequently generates happiness. I just know logology matters—no other pastime quite really satisfies. Therefore, unleash verbal witticisms: Xerox your zingers!

JOHN HENRICK

I have a background in mathematics and statistics, which admittedly doesn't justify either of my original contributions to logology: (1) digital verse; and (2) readability formulas for graffiti.

Minimalism and combinatorics—the lock and the key to wordplay. No passage too tight for language to slip through, carrying a cargo of ideas. Preferred vessel: ANAGRAMS, a.k.a. ARS MAGNA. They explain so much, or seem to, at least. Case in point: Reaganograms. The name GEORGE BUSH is sparse, to be sure, but "GO, GUSHER, BE!" dwells there, pointing a path from the Permian Basin to the Persian Gulf.

What joy to find answers to the old question, "WHAT IS THE MEANING OR PURPOSE OF LIFE?," buried within itself. These range from simple tolerance—"WINNIE-THE-POOH, SUFFER PIGLET'S AROMA"—to a repudiation of sadomasochism formulated in a pidginesque hortatory subjunctive: "IF IS A FUTON GAME, NO WHIPS, ROPE, LEATHER."

JOHN HOLGATE

My professional sphere is librarianship and information science, and I work as a systems librarian in the Australian department of health. One of my passions is Scrabble.

Logology is really a portmanteau word for astrological philology and relates to mainstream linguistics as dada does to classical art or chaos theory to Newtonian physics. It is composed of GOLLY (a dialect word for spittle) and GOO (sticky matter) and this etymology tends to reveal the tongue-in-cheek nature of logological utterances. For the logologist, words are potential fractals within the great universe of con-, dis-, and intercourse. The logologist's quest to find irrational connections between the alphabet and society is akin to the astrologer's charting of human behavior according to the improbable laws of starlight. Logology is as ancient as the zodiac, yet its truths are as ephemeral as a weekly horoscope. Through the joys of wordplay, it brings us closer to human language than the whole corpus of astronomical grammar.

CHRIS MCMANUS

My experiences as a high school teacher, research mathematician, and medical computing specialist all contribute to my wordplay studies.

Kipling called words "the most powerful drug used by mankind." Wordplay illuminates those mysterious labyrinthine recesses wherein our brains process language. I particularly enjoy topics involving parodoxes of word meaning: historical reversals of meaning; oxymorons; retronyms; contronyms. Heteronyms and homonyms also reveal our minds' facile capacity to resolve ambiguities. Beheadments, word deletions, interlocks, and charades are intriguing examples of unexpected word associations. Lipograms, mnemonics, and puns are among my multiword drugs of choice. Their creation illustrates some defining differences between cerebral and cybernetic processes. No computer could have appreciated and duplicated all the wordplay of Dorothy Parker's response, when challenged to pun "horticulture": "You can lead a horticulture but you can't make her think."

O. V. MICHAELSEN

I was employed as singer/songwriter/guitarist from 1973 to 1989. Since then, I've been a freelance writer. Member of the National Puzzlers' League.

Wordplay began as an occasional recreation, then became a more serious venture when I decided to write a book on the subject. (Collecting word puzzles and curiosities has been a hobby of mine for many years.)

I suppose writing it can be considered a craft, or minor art. Solving word puzzles is logic. There's logic in science, but not necessarily in art. Philosopher Suzanne Langer's theory of art, expressed in *Philosophy in a New Key*, stated: "Art is the symbolic expression of human feeling." By her definition, wordplay is not an art.

I've been influenced by books, such as Espy's *An Almanac of Words at Play* and Borgmann's *Language on Vacation*. Wordplay is the dessert after the main course.

MIKE MORTON

I'm interested in computer applications of wordplay.

I don't think of myself as a serious wordplay person. I'm just a computer nerd who happened to write a program [Ars Magna] that churns out anagrams. So I don't think I merit inclusion in your discussion of those who are serious about wordplay. Ars Magna is far more prolific than I, even if its output tends to be mostly nonsense with a few gems here and there.

PETER NEWBY

I've been an actor on British television and the London West End stage as well as having written comedy material for TV. Editor of *Pears Word Games* and *Pears Advanced Word-Puzzler's Dictionary*.

I went from fairy stories to recreational linguistics at an early age as it presented an enjoyable aid to advancing my knowledge of the English language. My muse was the Imp of Wordplay who, for example, introduced me to the verb PELL, which the *Oxford English Dictionary* defines: "to knock down." She employed this verb in her successful eradication of my childlike phonetic approach to writing. She told me of the little rodents whose claim to have demolished the roof supports of their little house was believed by none until they engaged her as their spokesmuse.

As a consequence I can honestly say, "Wordplay Imp proved mice pelling their rafter."

HARRY PARTRIDGE

I've a strong interest in other languages, including classical Greek and Latin.

On this dull, sublunary sphere there is very little that is free; and that little is growing less every day—we are already, for example, paying to depollute the air: good-bye to the phrase "free as air." Language is still free, except to a relatively few unfortunates. Being somewhat of a scoffer by nature, I like to take this free language, turn it inside out, press towards the limits of its ambiguities, dubieties, aural resonances, and graphic representations and reveal how often it cannot and does not say when its users want it to. Thereby I amuse myself and perhaps others.

TOM PULLIAM

I was active on the stage for many years, as well as in radio and TV commercials. I collect stamps and am the author of *The New York Times Crossword Puzzle Dictionary* and *The Complete Word Game Dictionary.*

I became interested in words and their properties as a very young lad. Increasingly I became entranced by the countless permutations and combinations that twenty-six letters might enter into. I felt like a teenage discoverer when I came upon the fact that MHO is the opposite of OHM. It became a habit to look up the meaning of any unfamiliar word that I come across in reading or conversation. In doing so, I was opening a world more marvelous than I had imagined. I am far more interested in archaic and obsolete words from past ages than I am in new words. Whenever I see an expressed challenge in wordplay writings, I am always stimulated by a desire to attempt to better it. But I deplore the use of computers in establishing new wordplay boundaries, while at the same time recognizing the inevitability of computers' acceptance in the field. [Tom Pulliam passed away in 1994.]

BRUCE PYNE

From Brockton, Massachusetts, I work part-time as an independent contractor for a Fortune 500 service company. When time permits, I read books on wordplay, recreational mathematics, and astronomy. I enjoy listening to classical music.

Recreational wordplay for me started one day during a particularly dull college lecture. I recall noting that the letters of the word TEAM could also form the words MEAT, MATE, and TAME. This fascinated me far more than did the lecture and led to the discovery of many other anagram pairs, triplets, and quadruplets. One thing led to another, and I went on to explore many other areas of logology. Dmitri Borgmann's now classic book *Language on Vacation* did much to expand my vision of the vast scope of the areas to explore. To this day, the love affair continues.

HOWARD RICHLER

My main interest in wordplay is the construction of palindromes.

When I complete a palindrome of moderate length without sacrificing too much sense, I feel I have restored some symmetry and harmony to the universe, entropy notwithstanding.

At the heart of constructing palindromes is the ability to read from right to left. I started to do this when I was eight years old. Since this was the natural order of the Hebrew I was learning, reading English this way didn't strike me as too odd.

I remember a TV ad from the fifties promoting what is known in genteel society as "regularity." The product advertised was SERUTAN. The ad ended by saying, "Remember, SERUTAN spelled backwards is NATURE'S." Surprisingly, TUMS did not take the same tack.

LEE SALLOWS

Besides logology I enjoy recreational mathematics, mountain wandering, and playing classical guitar. I've been published in *A Computer Science Reader, Journal of Recreational Mathematics,* and other places.

At the heart of logology is a search for arresting coincidences. A string of letters may form a sentence. A string of letters may be centro-symmetric. When a string answers to both these descriptions we have a palindrome, a structure simultaneously satisfying the two separate constraints. The same principle goes for anagrams, acrostics, lipograms, and so on through a hundred forms of wordplay. Obsessional seeking for ever more "magical" or polydeterminant structures of this kind is what makes logologists tick. Why is this so? My guess is that under evolutionary pressure the human brain has become supersensitive to coincidence, since concurrent events so frequently signal a common cause. Being aware of causal relations in the environment aids survival. Thus, logologists are just victims of natural selection, as are we all.

ANTHONY SEBASTIAN

I am especially interested in computer applications of wordplay.

In wordplay, for me, the operative element is play. In the beginning, wordplay complemented foodplay, fingerplay, stringplay, mudplay, whatever-was-at-hand-play. Words were just another set of toys, like Tinker Toys and Lincoln Logs, and one of my all-time favorite toys, the Erector set. Today it's Legos. If words disappeared today, I would go out and buy a set of Legos. From logology to legology.

Mischievously, I played my own word games in school. In responding to the request to use a specified word in a sentence, I could never pass up the chance to pun, with obvious puns like, "Deceit: He had a patch on deceit of his pants." Those were disqualified, of course. By then I was more or less tolerated as a wordplay cutup.

I cannot remember that my teachers used wordplay for its educational potential.

WILL SHORTZ

I received the first bachelor's degree in engimatology from Indiana University. Edited *Games* magazine for several years until becoming crossword puzzle editor for *The New York Times* in 1994. I run and emcee an annual crossword tournament and am active in promoting international puzzling.

One purpose of art (and I use this term in the broadest sense) is to shock the viewer into seeing part of the world in a new way. That's one of my goals in making word puzzles. Most people consider words only as a means of communication; in my puzzles, solvers are forced to consider them as letters to be dropped, added to, rearranged, or interlocked, as sounds to be manipulated, meanings to be punned upon, etc. Puzzles make solvers think of language in a completely different way.

In addition, it has been said that puzzling is the only form of literature that forces the reader to participate, which is a nice thought in these days of mostly passive entertainment.

SUSAN THORPE

I've an Hons. Degree in Zoology followed by a Ph.D. in Entomology, both at the University of Leeds. Was a grammar school teacher and then a college lecturer in biological sciences.

Competing in the London *Times's* "Tournament of the Mind" first directed my thoughts to wordplay. Writing articles for *Word Ways*, etc., and setting word-based puzzles for magazines and newspapers now play a large part in my life, satisfying a creative urge. I enjoy the research required for a long article but gain equal satisfaction from creating a Kickshaws item. The unexpected is always there waiting to be found: researching "AEIOU Words in Biology" led me to discover IOUEA (a fossil sponge), the only known word composed of one each of the five vowels. On the other hand, it is possible to prove that the vacuum cleaner is merely a glorified bag: shift the letters of VACUUM six places along a circular alphabet (A following Z) and rearrange the resulting set of letters: VACUUM (6) IS A BAG. WORDPLAY (15) is truly SPANGLED with gems such as these!

ED WOLPOW

I was born in 1938 in Brooklyn. Graduated from Brooklyn Technical High School, Columbia College, Harvard Medical School. Now a harried neurologist at Mount Auburn Hospital in Cambridge, Massachusetts. Married to a Dane who finds English difficult—I find Danish impossible.

> The simplest items of nature intimidate and delight us—
> 　　a leaf worth an acre of poets.
> We should smile and throw words back
> 　　to bemuse them and amuse us.
> twenty-six symbols to make one real
> 　　and how many imaginary worlds?
> twenty-six amino acids to make one real
> 　　and how many imaginary worlds?
> Me and my genetic code write each other palindromes, transposals, anagrams,
> 　　to create and attenuate our misunderstandings.

DAVID WOODSIDE

I sport a SWORDPLAY hat for my aerospace engineering job. After work, I doff my S and become the more mild mannered author of a book in progress: *Palindromania: A Panoplay of Palindromes, Bon Mots, Reversible Verses, and Other Adroit Drollery.*

　　Wordplay illuminates my thoughts. Our ancient brains operated instinctively. Frontal lobes were invented, and thoughts formed unions to name things. Adjectives appeared, creating contract law. Brains learned to draw, spawning spray-paint industries. The Parthenon arose, leisure time increased, and someone noticed

RACECAR ran both ways; however, this wasn't appreciated until someone translated it from Greek. Later, Gutenberg pressed words and impressed people, which encouraged Shakespeare to write wordplays like 'Hamlet,' 'blinking idiot,' and 'Stratford-upon-Avon,' which are still used today. James Joyce begot modern wordplay, and Cliffs Notes soon appeared in bookstores, giving everyone a chance to play with words.

CLIMBING DOWN THE MOUNTAIN

Now you have an inside view of wordplay today. It's all about one thing in particular, as the sign says.

Chapter X

Library Thoroughfare

THE LIBRARY OF LANGUAGE

THE LIBRARY OF Language occupies a stately Gothic mansion at the far end of the street. Inside this old building, the shelves overflow with books of all sorts and sizes. We'll go down the hall to the Wordplay Wing, located in a room behind two sets of gigantic books. The arrows on their spines point the way.

The bibliography that follows is divided into two parts. The Annotated Bibliography lists wordplay books and magazines, including those mentioned in the text, and the Source Bibliography lists dictionaries and other references that are cited.

Don't forget: no bibliography is ever complete. There are many other excellent wordplay books and magazines available that haven't been listed.

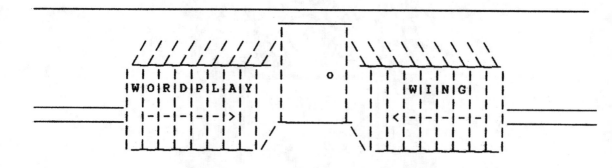

Annotated Bibliography

BOOKS

Augarde, Tony. *The Oxford Guide to Word Games.* New York: Oxford University Press, 1984.

> This book explains almost every classic type of word game, with examples accompanying the text. It's one of the few scholarly, historical guides to the field. Moreover, in the best spirit of wordplay, it's entertaining.

Bergerson, Howard W. *Palindromes and Anagrams.* New York: Dover Publications, Inc., 1973.

> In this wide-ranging study, Bergerson gives a brief history of both forms and presents a generous selection of classical and modern examples, from one-liners to longer poems.

Bombaugh, Charles, ed. *Gleanings for the Curious from the Harvest-Fields of Literature.* Detroit: Gale Research Company, 1985.

> Originally published in 1875, this 864-page book presents a huge variety of wordplay, including everything from puns to "Irish bulls," and discusses them in a homey, enjoyable fashion. It demonstrates an earlier attitude toward wordplay.

Borgmann, Dmitri A. *Beyond Language.* New York: Charles Scribner's Sons, 1967.

> Many authorities on recreational linguistics agree that Borgmann is the founder of modern wordplay. In this, his third book, he presents word puzzles

in a unique three-part format—problems, hints, and solutions, within a maze of fascinating information that takes the reader to the fringes of language and beyond.

_____. *Curious Crosswords.* New York: Charles Scribner's Sons, 1970.
It would be hard to assemble a set of crossword puzzles more difficult than this collection. It's a treasure-house for the advanced cruciverbalist, and a slaughterhouse for the novice. If crossword puzzles can be considered an art form, this book is the Museum of Modern Art.

_____. *Language on Vacation.* New York: Charles Scribner's Sons, 1965.
A ground-breaking work, this is the first book treating wordplay as a field of knowledge to be studied in its own right. It discusses the basic elements of logology, the author's term for wordplay, in a witty, conversational fashion, chapter by chapter, word by remarkable word. It has been referred to as the bible of recreational linguistics.

Byrne, Josefa Heifetz, ed. *Mrs. Byrne's Dictionary of Unusual, Obscure, and Preposterous Words.* Secaucus, NJ: Citadel, 1976.
Byrne lists and defines thousands of words that she considers the most out-landish examples from other dictionaries. The book is a great resource for coming up with autoschediastic remarks to leave other people mommixed.

Dickson, Paul. *Words.* New York: Delacorte Press, 1982.
Aimed specifically at people interested in wordplay, this book is an enthusiastic display of etymology and pseudo-etymology. Heavily illustrated, it presents a collection of unusual words, some real and others made up by the author.

Dudeney, Henry Ernest. *300 Best Word Puzzles.* New York: Charles Scribner's Sons, 1968.
Based on Dudeney's *The World's Best Word Puzzles,,* published in 1925, this collection shows the state of wordplay in the period between Bombaugh and Walsh (nineteenth century) to Borgmann (1965).

Eckler, Ross. *Making the Alphabet Dance.* New York: St. Martin's, 1995.
This landmark book defines letterplay and synthesizes the many advances that have been made over the past thirty years. In progressing from simple to complex forms, Eckler discusses the work of many wordplay writers and includes dozens of illustrations, tables, and lists. No other book achieves such a complicated goal.

_____, ed. *Names and Games*. Lanham: University Press of America, Inc., 1986.
The only book devoted entirely to onomastics, the field of the wordplay of names—personal names, town names, chemical names, business names, state names, and other names. Ninety-nine articles from *Word Ways* are reprinted in their entirety with occasional follow-up commentary.

_____, ed. *The New Anagrammasia: A Collection of 8876 Anagrams and Antigrams Published Between 1797 and 1991*. Morristown, NJ: Word Ways Monograph Series 2, 1991.
The largest collection of anagrams ever published. Each entry is presented alphabetically in four parts: Phrase, Anagram, Author, and Date. Almost all the anagrams are restricted to phrases (instead of proper names), and often the same phrase is anagrammed into more than one new phrase.

_____, ed. *Word Recreations: Games and Diversions from* Word Ways. New York: Dover, 1979.
After the first ten years of *Word Ways*, the editor assembled the best articles representing some of the major concerns of modern wordplay. They discuss topics ranging from word networks to computerized pangram searches.

Espy, Willard. *An Almanac of Words at Play*. New York: Crown Publishers, Inc., 1975.
Wordplay in prose, poetry, and puzzles appears here in the form of a daily almanac, with one or more entries for each day of the year. The presentation is highly original: it can be read in one day or 365 days!

_____. *Another Almanac of Words at Play*. New York: Crown Publishers, Inc., 1980.
The successor to the first book, it has all new material.

_____. *The Game of Words*. New York: Grosset and Dunlap, 1972.
Among the chapters, lettered from A to Z, the author displays a great variety of wordplay. From puzzle poems to punning headlines, he explores the structure of language to achieve his multifaceted effects.

Fisher, Leonard Everett. *Alphabet Art: Thirteen ABCs from around the World*. New York: Four Winds, 1978.
A beautifully illustrated introduction to thirteen very different alphabets, ranging from the widely used (Greek) to the lesser known (Eskimo). Each section includes a brief history of the origin of the specific alphabet or syllabary.

Gardner, Martin. *Aha! Gotcha!: Paradoxes to Puzzle and Delight*. New York: W. H. Freeman and Co., 1982.

This thorough presentation of mathematical paradoxes has linguistic elements, too. The reader goes step by step into the quicksand of problems involving logic, probability, time, and tricky topics. The cartoon-strip illustrations help to illuminate the puzzlement.

_____. *The Annotated Night Before Christmas.* New York: Summit Books, 1991. Dozens of parodies of this Christmas classic show how a popular poem can inspire imaginative clones. Each parody comes with introduction and foot-notes.

Hofstadter, Douglas R. *Gödel, Escher, Bach.* New York: Vintage, 1989.
In this multifaceted book, wordplay and logic are part of a larger whole that involves artificial intelligence, art, music, philosophy, language, and other things. Achilles and the Tortoise engage in a running narrative that serves as both point and counterpoint to the more abstract discussions.

Kim, Scott. *Inversions: A Catalog of Calligraphic Cartwheels.* Peterborough, NH: Byte Books, 1981.
By distorting the shapes of letters, the artist has rendered words that can be rotated or reflected to form the same or other words. Kim shows how plastic the alphabet can be.

Kohl, Herbert. *A Book of Puzzlements.* New York: Shocken Books, 1981.
This compendium of word games ranging from easy to difficult is aimed at children as well as adults. Along with being an enjoyable read, it's a how-to book that gives directions for making palindromes, word squares, and other forms of wordplay.

Kuhn, Joaquin, and Maura Kuhn. *Rats Live on No Evil Star.* New York: Everest House, 1981.
Palindromic crossword puzzles are featured in this unusual book. Not for rookie wordplayers, the games here challenge even the experts.

Lederer, Richard. *Anguished English.* New York: Dell, 1987.
Student bloopers, courtroom blunders, and welfare gaffs fill the pages of this book, which became a wordplay bestseller. Over a thousand examples of dis-jointed English show that our language confounds even the natives.

_____. *Crazy English.* New York: Pocket Books, 1990.
Humorous essays that reflect the idiosyncracies of the English language, including odd plurals, animal names, and palindromes, in a style that uses the forms to talk about themselves.

————. *Get Thee to a Punnery*. New York: Dell, 1988.

Twenty-five quizzes challenge, teach, and entertain the reader with nearly every type of pun—daffynitions, Tom Swifties, spoonerisms, knock-knock jokes, and more. The text explains the forms in a lively, punny fashion.

————. *Nothing Risqué, Nothing Gained*. Chicago: Chicago Review Press, 1995.

Over two thousand off-color jokes and quickies of the "punographic" variety give this book a distinct, and tastefully spicy, flavor.

Lloyd, Sam. *Sam Lloyd's Cyclopedia of 5000 Puzzles, Tricks & Conundrums with Answers*. New York: Pinnacle, 1976.

This work by an American puzzle genius is full of picture riddles, word games, mathematical problems, and other "species of mental gymnastics." The text is generously illustrated with intricate line drawings. Although not all puzzles are wordplay, charades, rebuses, puns, and riddles abound.

Michaelson, O. V. *Words at Play: Quips, Quirks and Oddities*. New York: Sterling, 1997.

This book covers anagrams, palindromes, word squares, and numerous other forms, and it includes many wonderful examples by the author and others. Michaelson adds a historical perspective by citing (when known) the creator of each work and its original place of publication.

Newby, Peter. *The Mammoth Book of Word Games*. London: Pelham Books, 1990.

This collection of more than 150 spoken and written games is the largest of its kind. From the classic "Ghost" to Newby's own "Pentery Web," the author discusses the games, gives the rules, and shows sample plays.

————. *Pears Advanced Word-Puzzler's Dictionary*. London: Pelham Books, 1987.

This 750-page volume gathers together words of particular interest to crossword puzzlers and word gamesters. The first section includes the most comprehensive anagram list in print, and the second section contains a dictionary of unusual words.

Steig, William. *CDB?* New York: Farrar, Straus, and Giroux, 1984.

The single-page cartoons in this one-of-a-kind book have number-and-letter rebuses for the captions.

Train, John. *Most Remarkable Names*. New York: Clarkson Potter, 1977.

A collection of unusual, often unbelievable, names, it combines the author's two previous books—*Remarkable Names of Real People* and *Even More Remarkable*

Names—and includes new material, too.

Walsh, William Shepard. *The Handy-Book of Literary Curiosities.* Detroit: Gale Research Company. 1985.

> Another nineteenth-century classic (originally published by Lippincott in 1892), this 1,104-page book includes puzzles, games, and word facts from many magazines and books of the period. It's an excellent companion to Bombaugh's book (listed above).

Williams, Emmet. *An Anthology of Concrete Poetry.* New York, Villefranche, Frankfurt: Something Else Press, 1967.

> Concrete poetry is a twentieth-century development. The poets achieve their effects by manipulating the meaning, the shape, and/or the sound of words in nontraditional ways. This anthology provides a worldview of concrete poetry in its formative years, 1945 to 1967.

MAGAZINES

Eckler, Ross, ed. *Word Ways: The Journal of Recreational Linguistics.* Morristown, NJ, 1968 to present. Subscription rate $20 ($22 foreign) for four issues. Address: Spring Valley Rd., Morristown, NJ 07960.

> The only magazine devoted to all aspects of written wordplay, from anagram to zeugma, it publishes essays, poems, puzzles, stories, and occasional artwork. Some of the more technical matter might not have been written if it weren't for the magazine providing a soapbox for the dedicated logologist. It charts the course of modern recreational linguistics.

Geelen, Jeremy. *Logophile: The Cambridge Journal of Words and Language.* Cambridge: The Logophile Press, 1977–1979.

> This British quarterly, lasting only about three years, dealt with a wide variety of wordplay, traditional as well as innovative. It covered topics such as computer "word" generators, Guinness advertising, and dyslexia, and it offered reader competitions and challenges.

Schmittberger, R. Wayne. *Games.* New York, 1976 to present. Subscription rate $17.97 for 6 issues. Address: P.O. Box 605, Mt. Morris, IL 61054-0605.

> Available in many drugstores and supermarkets, this magazine offers all sorts of cleverly devised puzzles, contests, and games in a full-color glossy format. Several word games appear in every issue. Articles, game reviews, and other features make it stand out from all other game magazines.

Urdang, Laurence. *Verbatim: The Language Quarterly.* Essex, CT: 1974 to present. Subscription rate $14 for four issues.

This magazine focuses on spoken language—words, dialects, and etymologies—and shows the curious development that occurs in different environments, from the local to the international level. There is surprisingly little duplication of material between *Word Ways* and *Verbatim.*

Source Bibliography

Babcock, Philip Gove, Editor in Chief. *Webster's Third New International Dictionary of the English Language.* Unabridged. Springfield, MA: G. & C. Merriam Co., 1966 *[Webster's Third Unabridged].*

Bartholomew (Firm). *Times Atlas of the World.* London: Times Books, 1994.

Baskin, Wade. *The Dictionary of Satanism.* New York: Philosophical Library, 1972.

British and Foreign Bible Society. *The Gospel in Many Tongues.* London: British and Foreign Bible Society, 1965.

Crabtree, Monica, ed. *Language Files.* Fifth edition. Columbus: Ohio State University Press, 1991.

Flexner, Stuart B. *The Random House Unabridged Dictionary of the English Language.* New York: Random House, 1987.

G. & C. Merriam Co. *Webster's New Collegiate.* Sixth edition. Springfield, MA: G. & C. Merriam Co., 1961 *[Webster's Sixth Collegiate].*

Gove, Philip B., ed. *Webster's Seventh New Collegiate Dictionary.* Springfield, MA: G. & C. Merriam Co., 1963 *[Webster's Seventh Collegiate].*

Gramercy Books. *Webster's Encyclopedic Unabridged Dictionary of the English Language.* New York: Gramercy Books, 1994.

Hanna, Paul R. *Phoneme-Grapheme Correspondences as Cues to Spelling Improvement.* Washington: U.S. Department of Health, Education, and Welfare, Office of Education, 1966.

Kirkpatrick, E. M., ed. *Chambers Twentieth-Century Dictionary.* Edinburgh: Chambers, 1983.

McWhirter, Norris. *The Guinness Book of Records.* New York: Sterling Publishing Co., 1989.

Mish, Frederick C., ed. *Merriam-Webster's Collegiate Dictionary.* Tenth edition. Springfield, MA: Merriam-Webster, Inc., 1994.

Neilson, William Allen, Editor in Chief. *Webster's New International Dictionary of the English Language.* Second edition. Unabridged. Springfield, MA: G. & C. Merriam

Co., 1949 *[Webster's Second Unabridged]*.

Simpson, J. A., ed. *The Oxford English Dictionary.* New York: Oxford University Press, 1989.

Walker, John Albert. *Glossary of Art, Architecture, and Design since 1945.* Third edition. Boston: G. K. Hall, 1992.

Wells, Evelyn. *What to Name the Baby.* Garden City, N.Y.: Garden City Books, 1953.

Wentworth, Harold, and Stuart Flexner, eds. *The Pocket Dictionary of American Slang.* New York: Pocket Books, 1968.

Wright, Joseph. *The English Dialect Dictionary.* London: Oxford University Press, 1970.

Woolf, Henry Bosley, ed. *The Merriam-Webster Dictionary.* New York: Pocket Books, 1974 *[The Pocket Webster's]*.

LEAVING THROUGH THE BOOKS

We leave the library by a door in the Wordplay Wing and walk to the corner. The sign expresses what the books and magazines all have in common:

Chapter

Answer Alley

WHAT IS THE QUESTION?

*I*N MOST ALLEYS, the wind blows old newspapers and candy wrappers into puddles of everything from automobile oil to spaghetti sauce. The resulting mixes aren't answers, just messes.

In Answer Alley, however, the answers to all the questions in the other chapters appear in order by chapter. The only wind comes from turning the pages to get here.

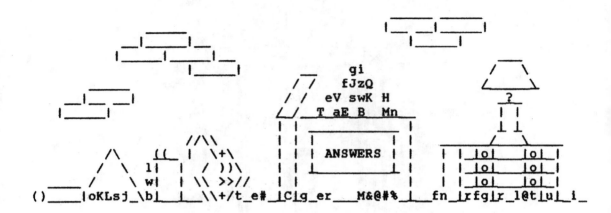

CHAPTER A: INTRODUCTION PATH

Purposes of the Book

According to *Webster's Tenth Collegiate,* all the verbs beginning with EN except for ENTERTAIN are transitive only, and they require a direct object. ENTERTAIN is both transitive and intransitive. The solution: Add the word YOU after ENTERTAIN.

CHAPTER B: ANAGRAM BOULEVARD

Celebrity Anagram Quiz

1. ED KOCH 2. AL GORE 3. MEG RYAN 4. AL GREEN 5. TOM CRUISE 6. ISAAC STERN 7. ED ASNER 8. FATS WALLER 9. ERIC CLAPTON

CHAPTER D: PUN FREEWAY

Other Famous Pun Names

1. Emily Dickinson 2. Ludwig von Beethoven 3. Madonna 4. William Shakespeare 5. Gertrude Stein 6. Al Capone 7. Cher 8. P. T. Barnum 9. Queen Elizabeth 10. Napoleon Bonaparte

Error Apparent

The pairs are ADIEU-ADO, AURICLE-ORACLE, and GORILLA-GUERILLA. All five vowels appear among the letters in each pair.

Pop Beats Bad Rap

I.

Crossing the Borders

1. Washinware   2. Kenyawait   3. Amnesia   4. Witaly   5. Iranagascar   6. Maltenstein   7. Yugohoma

CHAPTER E: PARODY STRIP

Twinkle, Twinkle, Little What?

Carroll's star was a BAT. The poem goes:

> *Twinkle, twinkle, little bat!*
> *How I wonder where you're at!*
> *Up above the world you fly,*
> *Like a tea-tray in the sky.*

CHAPTER F: REBUS RUN

Where the Words Are

I. The underdog may undertake to overthrow the overseer.   2. thundercloud   3. cover charge   4. inside out   5. John Underwood, Andover, Massachusetts

The Syllabic Rebus

AL = hail storm; BZ = busy bee; CT = city limits; DR = dear friend; EZ = easy read; IV = ivy tower; JL = jail cell; KG = cagey customer; LE = alley cat; MT = empty cup; NR = inner strength; QP = kewpie doll; RR = horror show; SA = essay test; TM = team effort; UL = Yule log; VL = veal cutlet; XS = excess baggage; YR = wire brush

The "Hey, Bee! See?" of Anti-Rebuses

I. ONE 2. LONG ICY ROADS 3. HOT MATCH 4. GO AWAY 5. QUIT

CHAPTER G: DICTIONARY DRIVE

Daniel's a Nurdy, Tiddling Wretchock, Doll!

The smallest or weakest pig of the litter.

The Beast Within

amASS billyCOCK comBAT drAPE esCROW forBEAR gentEEL heatHEN inCUR juRAT kebBUCK lummOX manDRAKE nightMARE offFISH pseudoCARP quarTERN ramPIKE sawHORSE tipCAT underDOG vaMOOSE wolfRAM xRAY yardBIRD zilLION

Dictionary Mystery Story

Golf. The clueword is DORMY, which the dictionary defines as "being ahead by as many holes in golf as remain to be played."

CHAPTER I: PANGRAMMATIC HIGHWAY

Pangram Formula

The formula is itself a pangram made of only ten symbols. To find all the letters, convert the formula to words: TwO to tHE J PoWeR MINUS FiVe C Divided BY siX K is GreAter than or eQuaL to Zero.

CHAPTER J: LETTERSHIFT LANE

The Great Vowel Shift

1. (Shift value = 4) YES, I SEE MESSY MICE. 2. (SV = 6) GO GAG A GEEK. 3. (SV = 10) YIKES! I SKI, SEE SKY. 4. (SV = 14) I MISS COWS, SO I MOW MOSS. 5. (SV = 18) MAMA'S ASS SAGS. 6. (SV = 20) YOU YOYO, YOU COY, ICY YOYO! 7. (SV = 22) EEK, A QUAKE! WEAK, WE WAKE.

Geographic Lines

MISSISSIPPI shifts ten steps to YUEEUEEUBBU and twenty-two steps to IEOOEOOELLE

The Dirty Dozen

The letter strings represent the number words from ONE to TWELVE. Each was shifted by the number of steps equal to the number itself. ONE shifted one step gives POF, TWELVE shifted twelve steps gives FIQXHQ.

The Red Shift

It hides STOP, which is eleven alphabetic steps from HIDE.

CHAPTER K: PATTERN PASSAGE

Topping Lewis Carroll

ARMY	BLACK
ARMS	BLANK
AIMS	BLINK
DIMS	CLINK
DAMS	CHINK
DAME	CHINE
NAME	WHINE
NAVE	WHITE
NAVY	

Single Steps

LOUSE and MOUSE pluralize to two shorter words, LICE and MICE, which also make a single-step pair.

He, the Theoretical Realist

The letters of adjacent words overlap. That is, the last letter(s) of one word are repeated in the first letter(s) of the next word. In the first stanza, one letter overlaps; in the second stanza, two letters; in the third, three; in the fourth, four.

Goldsmithery

HOO means SHE. It's listed in the *Oxford English Dictionary*, under HEO (and not under HOO).

CHAPTER L: NUMERIC OVERPASS

Hideaway Number Names

TEN = TwENty two; ELEVEN = thrEe miLlion sEVEN; TWELVE = none

Patriotic Numbers

USA appears in the word THOUSAND, and THOUSAND appears in 99.9 percent of all number names.

Acrostic Equation

Countless more examples are possible, but they each must equal ONE or TEN. For instance, ONETHOUSAND - NINEHUNDREDEIGHTYEIGHT -

ELEVEN; or TWENTYNINE + EIGHTY - NINETYNINE. The two in the text use the smallest sets of numbers.

Scrabble Values

EIGHTHUNDREDTEN. It must be played without any blank tiles along an edge of the board through three triple-word scores.

Graphic Conclusion

30 is newswriters' notation for END.

CHAPTER M: STORY ROW

Belly Furniture

MENU OF DEFINITIONS

FRY TWO, LET THE SUN SHINE: fry two eggs with the yolks unbroken

HUG ONE: glass of orange juice

BLONDE WITH SAND: coffee with cream and sugar

ICE ON RICE: rice pudding with ice cream

HOUSEBOAT: banana split

DOUGH WELL DONE WITH COW TO COVER: buttered toast

SNEEZE: pepper

HEN FRUIT: egg

MIKE AND IKE: salt and pepper shakers

SWEEP THE KITCHEN: plate of hash

LIFE PRESERVERS: doughnuts

RAFT: toast

COW PASTE: butter

WRECKED HEN FRUIT: scrambled eggs

PINK STICK: strawberry ice cream

BELLY FURNITURE: food

BLOW OUT PATCHES: pancakes

BIDDY BOARDS: waffles

SHAKE ONE IN THE HAY: strawberry milkshake

TWIST IT, CHOKE IT, AND MAKE IT CACKLE: egg chocolate malted milkshake

ALL HOT: baked potato

WIMPIES: hamburgers

WARTS: olives

WAX: American cheese

BURN ONE, TAKE IT THROUGH THE GARDEN, AND PIN A ROSE
  ON IT: hamburger with lettuce, tomato, and an onion

MILLION ON A PLATTER: plate of baked beans

POPEYE: spinach

YELLOW PAINT: mustard

HOUNDS ON AN ISLAND: frankfurters and beans

NOAH'S BOY WITH MURPHY, CARRYING A WREATH: ham with
  potato and cabbage

LIGHTHOUSE: bottle of catsup

RADIO SANDWICH: tuna sandwich

HOT TOP: hot chocolate

FROG STICKS: French fried potatoes

PUT A HAT ON IT: add ice cream

PAINT A BOW-WOW RED: hot dog with catsup

ANGELS ON HORSEBACK: oysters rolled in bacon and served on toast

GUESS WATER: soup

BEEF STICKS: bones

CHOKIES: artichokes

BALLOON JUICE: seltzer

HOT ONE: bowl of chili

PUT THE LIGHTS OUT AND CRY: order of liver and onions

SPLASH OF RED NOISE: bowl of tomato soup

MAMA ON A RAFT: marmalade on toast

FLOP TWO: two fried eggs, turned over

YUM-YUM: sugar

BALED HAY: shredded wheat

HOPE: oatmeal

ADAM'S ALE: water

SHIVERING EVE: apple jelly

NERVOUS PUDDING: Jell-O

OH GEE: orange juice (and not OH JAY)

SUN KISS: orange juice

MISSISSIPPI MUD: mustard

ONE FROM THE ALPS: Swiss cheese sandwich

Jack and the Twoderful Beans

The first paragraph appears below. Once you get the hang of it, you should be able to figure out most of the remaining words. The trickiest two are ESSEVEN = ESSEX and EXANIMNINED = EXANIMATED. And now the opener:

"Once upon a time there lived a boy named Jack in the wonderful land of California. One day Jack, a single-minded lad, decided to go forth to seek his fortune."

The Knave's English

The stupid person showed off on the gaudy race horse, but the unreliable, undependable group of people didn't have the money to be influential. The newly promoted corporal with excessive pride in his military rank and decorations complained, "I've seen Air Force officers who don't like to fly become adept fighter pilots with false bravery inspired by intoxication—until they crash."

"That's all stupid talk!" The pimp rapidly ate sweets with his elegant, smartly dressed, sexually attractive woman parading on the street next to him.

"What's the commotion, male who doesn't take his girlfriend to social engagements?" The U.S. Air Force pilot became excited for an uproarious argument with the dude on a drunken spree in Boston.

"Just some person who excels at the fast singing of jazz songs to an accordion under the moon."

"Idle talk! Who's your girlfriend? She's a woman of superior quality."

"Extinguish the cigarette, and she'll dance 'til dawn for a penny."

The girl had a fit: "But if you're shirking about your money, silly, blundering person, I'll grab your genuine tuxedo and thrash you with my feet. No easy money, no vulgar dancing!"

"My foolish old married woman has more money in her ready-made clothes than you have in your platform in front of a sideshow tent," the well-dressed person passed the time in idle chatter; "but I don't pretend she's a girl known only for her sex appeal."

"[Expletive used to reply to an obvious, unnecessary statement]!" the loud, garishly dressed ladies' man jabbered, "my attractive woman has sexual intercourse with homely persons for money. I inspect very popular girls on Friday. If you've got the money for whiskey, let's hurry to a saloon. My beautiful girl has zest for diamonds."

"I understand the language, you darned itinerant peddler. Anyhow, Red's head is champagne to my eyes. Her teeth, her head of long hair, her hat, her pair of hair puffs worn over her ears, her nose, even her glasses—how attractive!"

"With that flattery, you must be an actor given to overly emotional performances. She's got more pep than an airplane, more sex appeal than a girl popularly acclaimed for her sex appeal," the rakish dude told the truth. "She's yours for any large sum of money."

The three hurried to a nightclub to get drunk. A drunk circus performer who'd had too much whiskey made a noisy disturbance with bricks by the pinball machine. A youth with personal problems subdued him.

"What a saloon patronized by creeps!" the U.S. Air Force pilot complained. "Maybe we ought to leave quickly before some sideshow freak hits my ribbons representing military decorations."

"Leave, squeamish person?" the pimp gave a long reprimand. "Don't strike the pilot's automatic ejection seat. Let's be a success! Let's dance to the saxophone! Ain't my sexually attractive girl an excellent, pretty, attractive girl?"

"Sensational, but is she fooling me with falsies from her mail-order catalog?"

"Go fly an airplane! My beautiful girl ain't no dog looking for food. She's got excellent female breasts."

"Excellent, eh? Bartender, more liquor. I'm an important person on a drunken spree with a snobbish, disagreeable girl. OK, boss, how about a look at the woman's breasts from the sexually attractive young woman?"

"Baloney! You don't have the money for a dull prize fight, unpopular person!" The person unable to drink liquor straight was noisily drinking strong, cheap whiskey with carbonated water. "It doesn't matter, cowboy. No act of coitus!"

"You brag, wise guy, but where are the pornographic photographs? No, it's all babble."

After drinking in one gulp a glassful of the raw, inferior homemade alcoholic beverage, he sneaked away.

Daphne in Woodland

Daphne was looking at a book of color charts from Pittsburgh Paints. The book, *Design System for Architects and Designers*, presents 792 colors and their equally colorful names, including DAPHNE and WOODLAND.

CHAPTER N: POETRY PARKWAY

Beatleverse

The titles, numbered 1 to 68, are represented here by their first one to four words.

Stanza One: 1. Rock and   2. What Goes   3. Strawberry Fields   4. Fool on
5. Here Comes   6. Day Tripper   7. Come Together

Stanza Two: 8. Lucy in   9. We Can   10. Why Don't   11. Honey, Don't   12. Twist
and

Stanza Three: 13. Dear Prudence   14. Do You   15. I Feel   16. You Really
17. Let It   18. Good Day

Stanza Four: 19. Sexy Sadie   20. Don't Pass   21. Slow Down   22. You've Got
23. I Will   24. Drive My   25. I'll Get   26. A Ticket

Stanza Five: 27. Eleanor Rigby   28. All My   29. I Want to Hold   30. Wait
31. She Loves   32. Sgt. Pepper's

Stanza Six: 33. Martha, My   34. I Am   35. I Want You   36. Hold Me   37. She
Came   38. Help   39. A Hard

Stanza Seven: 40. Lovely Rita   41. I Want to Tell   42. Every Little   43. I'm
Happy   44. Girl   45. And Your

Stanza Eight: 46. Michelle   47. I Wanna   48. Love You   49. Ask Me   50. It
Won't   51. I Call   52. I Need   53. No Reply

Stanza Nine: 54. Lady Madonna   55. I'm a   56. Tell Me   57. Nowhere Man
58. I've Just   59. Get Back   60. Don't Bother

Stanza Ten: 61. Tomorrow Never   62. The End   63. Yesterday   64. Mr.
Moonlight   65. Eight Days   66. I Call   67. I'll Follow   68. Goodnight

Spiral Nebula

The words in each stanza recombine to form the next stanza. If you rearrange
the words in the first stanza like this—first word, last word, second word, second
to last word, third word, third to last word, and so on, concluding with the middle
two words—the result is the second stanza, lacking only the punctuation. In this
fashion, each stanza generates a new one, except for the sixth. The sixth stanza generates the first stanza.

Shakespeare's Backward Sonnet

"Tomorrow and tomorrow and tomorrow" and "Fair is foul, and foul is fair"

CHAPTER O: ONOMASTIC TRAIL

The Forest of Names

Capitalized, they're people's names. Uncapitalized, they're dictionary words.

Mystery Names

1. A, C, E, H, I, K, P, U, W, Z

2. D, J, L, N, O, R, V, X
3. B, F, G, M, Q, S, T, Y

CHAPTER P: VISUAL VIADUCT

Thinglish

1. THE FACE OF A WELL-READ PERSON 2. THIS SENTENCE VAN-
ISHE(D or S) 3. I AM THE CUBIC WORD / PANDORA'S BOX / OF LAN-
GUAGE! 4. AS THE WORD TURNS 5. SEPTEMBER is missing 6. MID-
NIGHT OIL

Stereowords

ABLE GAME = GAMBLE; OVER FLOW = FLOWER; ELVIS LIVES =
ELVES; LOW CON = CLOWN; TREE SPLIT = STREET; RASH CASH =
CRASH; OLD GOD = GOLD; WRY VOID = WORDY

CHAPTER R: LOGIC CIRCLE

The Paradox Casino

B is the paradox-speaker. If B were the truth-teller, she couldn't say she was the
liar, because it would be a lie. If B were the liar, she couldn't say it either, because
that would be the truth, which B couldn't tell. It would lead to a paradox instead.
Since B speaks in paradoxes, it follows that A is the truth-teller, and C is the liar.

Time Travel Lovers

Joe is Bill's father and son, and Bill is Joe's father and son. Furthermore, Joe is
his own grandfather, and Bill is his own grandfather. It's relativity!

Misteaks in Logic

The sentence is a variation on the Liar's Paradox. THEIR, MISTAIKS, and
SENTANCE are misspelled, and that makes three mistakes. Then FOUR is also a
mistake, which means that there are really four mistakes. In that case, FOUR isn't
a mistake. If it isn't, then there are only three mistakes. Then once again FOUR is
a mistake. And so on.

Self-Referential Star Trek

In one sentence, Data says I'VE, but Star Trek fans know that the programming
in his positronic brain has a minor glitch in it: he cannot speak contractions.

The Book of Truth

They don't. On the third reading, the odd-numbered pages say that the even-numbered pages are false, and the even-numbered pages say that the odd-numbered pages are true—except for page 100, which is now false. The pattern looks like this: F T F T F T F T F T . . . F F.

On the fourth reading, pages 1 and 2 say false, pages 3 and 4 say true, 5 and 6 false, 7 and 8 true, and so on—except for page 100, which is now true. The pattern: F F T T F F T T F F . . . T F T.

The pages have to cycle through several other patterns before returning to the original.

Linear Logic

Sets B to E, Sequence 2:

Set B:	Set C:	Set D:	Set E:
1. 2=F	1. 3=F	1. 4=F, 5=T	1. Even=T
2. 3=T	2. 3=F	2. 3=T, 1=F	2. 1=T, 4=T
3. 4=F	3. 3=T	3. 2=T, 4=T	3. 5=F
4. 5=T	4. 3=F	4. 5=T, 2=F	4. Odd=F
5. 1=T	5. 3=F	5. 1=F, 3=T	5. 1=F

Sets F to G, Sequence 2 to Sequence 5. After reading and changing Sequence 5 in each case, the set disappears.

Set F:	Set G:
Seq 2	Seq 2
1. 4=F	1. 4=T
2. 5=F	2. Mov 3, not 2
3. 2=F	3. Del 1, not 2
4. Del 2, not 1	4. 2=T
Seq 3	Seq 3
1. 5=T	1. Mov 3, not 2
2. 2=F	2. 2=T
3. Del 1, not 2	3. Del 1, not 2
Seq 4	Seq 4
1. 2=T	1. 2=T
2. Del 1, not 2	2. Del 1, not 2
Seq 5	Seq 5
1. Del 1, not 2	1. Del 1, not 2

CHAPTER S: NONSENSE HILL

The Casino Paradox

If you picked Politician A, the answer is B. If you picked Politician B, the answer is C. If you picked Politician C, the answer is A. After all, this is Nonsense Hill, the wordplay equivalent of Capitol Hill, where no one says what they mean.

Kinetic Palaver

According to the dictionary, each of the seventy-six words in this poem has two different pronunciations. The number of ways it can be read aloud is equal to two to the seventy-sixth power—exactly 755,577,863,725,914,323,419,136 variations!

CHAPTER T: PUZZLE BLUFF

The Valley of Questions on the Lost Conundrum River

NO PASSING is on the last answer sign. The puzzle goes together like this:

```
D E F G H I J K L M N O P Q R S T U V W X Y Z A B C
E                       P                           D
F                       Q              ANSWER:      E
G         ANSWER:       R            BEWARE OF      F
H        NO PASSING     S           FALLING ROCKS   G
I                       T                           H
J                       U V W X Y Z A B C D E F G H I
K                       V                           J
L M N O P Q R S T U V W                             K
M                       X                           L
N                       Y                           M
O                       Z              CLUE:        N
P          CLUE:        A            DON'T SKIP     O
Q      DENTAL PLATE     B             A TURN        P
R        AT NIGHT       C                           Q
S                       D                           R
T                       E                           S
U                       F                           T
V W X Y Z A B C D E F G H I J K L M N O P Q R S T U
W                       K                           V
X          CLUE:        L                           W
Y      ROLLING STONES   M             ANSWER:       X
Z      GATHER NO MOSS   N           BRIDGE OUT      Y
A                       O                           Z
B                       P                           A
C D E F G H I J K L M N O P Q R S T U V W X Y Z A B
```

A Greeting That Could Get You Arrested

According to airline official Ricki Ruiz, you can't yell "Hi, Jack!" on an airplane or in the boarding area.

Letter Perfect

1. All letters rhyme, ending with an *ee* sound.
2. All letters rhyme, ending with an *ay* sound.
3. All letters begin with an *eh*.
4. All letters begin with vowel sounds. That is, each would be preceded by the article *an*.
5. One syllable. The letter W generates three syllables.
6. Each letter sounds the same as a full word: a, bee, see/sea, gee, eye/I, jay, oh, pea/pee, queue/cue, are, tea/tee, you/ewe/yew, why. Others could be added—K (quay), L (el), M (em), N (en), and X (ex), but the seldom-used words might've caused confusion.
7. All the letters are pronounced by putting the lips together.
8. All are made with straight lines.
9. All are made with curved lines.
10. All are dotted letters.
11. All are letters with a line crossing over.
12. and 13. All are letters enclosing an open area.
14. All have lowercase descenders.
15. All have lowercase ascenders.
16. and 17. All letters are normally printed without lifting pen from paper. Some might add B, D, and R.
18. All show vertical symmetry. [see Chapter P]
19. All show horizontal symmetry. [see Chapter P]
20. Each letter remains the same when turned upside down. [see Chapter P]
21. All are consonants, excluding Y (as in *rhythm*) and W (as in *cwm*).
22. All are roman numerals.
23. All are letters appearing on playing cards.
24. All are letters on a telephone dial.
25. This is the first row of letters on a standard *qwerty* keyboard.

Three's a Crowd

SING, COUP, and TRIP.

Fish Story

She misread the one marked GAR BAG E and thought it was trash.

Swinging Singles

DISCORDANCE

Connect-the-Dot Quote

"Books think for me."

Daedalus's Poetry Maze

SOLUTION PATH: 1-6-42-15-4-11-47-22-21-23-29-50-17-19-53-55-59-33-43-28-7-34-49-30-58-60-63-27-37-39-18-64.

ALTERNATE PATH: 8-3-44-13-9-2-24-45-14-16-52-31-56-54-10-12-35-57-41-26-5-36-51-32-38-40-61-25-46-48-62-20.

It's Not Time, People

MADEMOISELLE, which starts off MAD, ends in ELLE, and breaks up MS and MALE.

Perfection Test

PASS is the answer to all the blanks. Did you _ _ _ _?

Seven Puzzling Hexagons

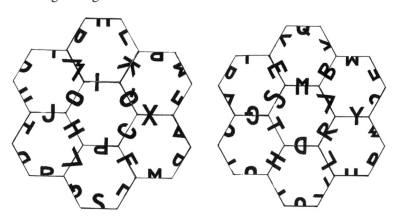

Alphaboxes: Thousands of Puzzles in One

The words across are EAR, FIND, AS, YOKE, UP, IRE. The words down are HAM, BIN, NUT, MOTE, KISS, RIDE. There may be other solutions.

Order, Please

1. By length, the words progress from four letters (MAYO) letters to fifteen (SEPTUAGENARIANS). 2. Each word starts with the commonly used three-let-

ter abbreviation for a month (or, in the case of MAY, spell out the month); thus, the words can be arranged in chronological order from JANGLE to DECOM-PENSATION, too.

Fabricated Quiz

I. Bukhara, Uzbekistan 2. Calicut, India 3. Cambrai, France 4. Kashmir, India 5. Cambrai, France 6. Damascus, Syria 7. Nimes, France 8. Fostat, Egypt 9. Genoa, Italy 10. Jersey, U.K. II. Laon, France 12. Lille, France 13. Mosul, Iraq 14. Zaitun, China (maybe) 15. Chalons-sur-Marne, France 16. Just kidding! 17. Tulle, France 18. Worsted, England

Unattractive Opposites

The words in each pair have no letters in common.

Same Difference

Deleting the appropriate letter(s) from each pair reveals two hidden words that are opposites. COMET-GOT without the T becomes COME-GO, PEARLY-PLATE without the P becomes EARLY-LATE, and so on. DON-DOFF stands out from the rest because the two words are opposite to begin with. DON means "to put on," and DOFF means "to take off."

Comic Book Onomatopoeia

I = K, 2 = F, 3 = Q, 4 = A, 5 = T, 6 = N, 7 = O, 8 = U, 9 = R, I0 = E, II = S, I2 = D, I3 = W, I4 = X, I5 = V, I6 = J, I7 = M, I8 = H, I9 = L, 20 = Y, 2I = Z, 22 = I, 23 = C, 24 = B, 25 = G, 26 = P

Simplescript

"Teach us delight in simple things . . . "

CHAPTER U: SENTENCE ROAD

Ap'str'ph's

It is over every forecastle the boatswain looked with mind pulled until full of fall, even to north, though misery is awful, and calls sighed through halls ever since all kissed, cared, wished, and clasped, never even in love.

CHAPTER V: LANGUAGE EXPRESSWAY

One-Word Poetry

O appeared twelve times, and C appeared zero times.

THE QUESTICOMMA

The stop sign at the end of Answer Alley has a questicomma on it. The comma indicates that every answer anticipates a new question.

The traditional question mark is a hook with a period under it. You fish for the answer, catch it on the hook, and that's it. The period suggests a conclusion. But in the world today, as in wordplay, no answers are permanent.

Now let's visit the last street, where the answers lead to many more intriguing questions.

Chapter Z

Afterword Way

THE STREETLIGHT

*A*T FIRST GLANCE, wordplay may seem to have little in common with the play of numbers, or recreational mathematics, but are the two all that different?

The lamppost on the corner suggests an answer. Its two bulbs shine brightly to light the way out of the city. One bulb is the letter O, and the other is the number O, but you can't tell which is which.

In the City of Wordplay, numbers play, too.

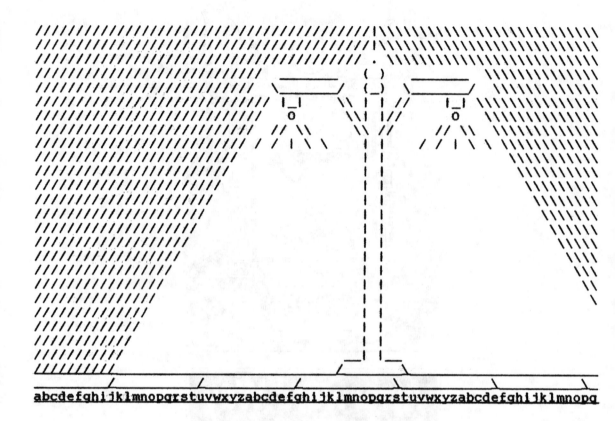

abcdefghijklmnopqrstuvwxyzabcdefghijklmnopqrstuvwxyzabcdefghijklmnopq

ABCDEFGHIJKLMNOPQRSTUVWXYZABCDEFGHIJKLMNOPQRSTUVWXYZABCDEFGHIJKLMNOPQ

In the following essay, Martin Gardner, author of numerous books on recreational mathematics, wordplay, and other topics, sheds light on the relationship between letters and numbers:

MATHEMATICS AND WORDPLAY

Many mathematicians enjoy wordplay, and for obvious reasons. It is almost a branch of combinatorial mathematics. The pleasure derived from solving a combinatorial problem is very much like the pleasure of solving a cryptogram or a crossword puzzle, or constructing a good palindrome. Given the formal system of arithmetic, ancient mathematicians asked themselves whether the digits 1 through 9 could be placed in a three-by-three matrix so that rows, columns, and the two diagonals had the same sum. This is not much different from asking if, given the formal rules of English, one can construct a three-by-three word square in which each row, column, and main diagonal is a different word.

There is, of course, a difference between combinatorial mathematics and wordplay. Mathematics is embodied in the structure of the universe. Although mathematical systems are free inventions of human minds, they have astonishing applications to nature. No one expected non-Euclidian geometry to be useful, but it proved to be essential to relativity theory. Boolean algebra seemed useless until—surprise!—it turned out to model the electrical networks of computers. There are hundreds of other outstanding instances of what physicist Eugene Wigner has called the "unreasonable effectiveness of mathematics."

Think of the letters and words of a language, together with its rules, as a formal system. Although the words have arbitrary meanings assigned to them by minds, and there may be a "deep structure" of syntax that conforms to logic, the words themselves have no reality apart from a culture. Butterflies are all over the world, but you will not find the word "butterfly" by looking through a telescope or microscope.

The combinatorial nature of wordplay is underscored by the recent use of computers for solving word problems. Disks containing all the words of a language are now available. With suitable programs they can be used to construct word squares, find anagrams, shortest word ladders, and so on. I wouldn't be surprised if someday computers will solve complicated crosswords as easily as they now solve chess problems.

It is worth noting that both in mathematics and wordplay, solving a problem is curiously like confirming a theory. In solving a cryptogram, for example, one first makes conjectures. Is a single-letter word A or I, or maybe O? Is ABCA the word "that"? Such conjectures are then tested to see if they lead to contradictions. If they lead to other words, they gain in their probability of being correct. Eventually a point is reached at which one is certain that a cryptogram has been cracked even though not all its letters are known.

One is tempted to say that when all words are known one can be absolutely certain a cryptogram has been solved. This is not the case because, especially if the cryptogram is short, there just could be another solution that the composer of the puzzle intended. If, however, the cryptogram is long, such uncertainty becomes vanishingly small. This is true also in science. When there is a large abundance of facts explained by a theory, such as by the Copernican theory or the theory of evolution, certainty reaches a probability of .999999999. . . .

Now for a deep metaphysical question. If chess had not been invented, is there a sense in which theorems about chess can be said to exist? Assuming the formal system of chess, and given a certain position on the board, is it permissible to say that there is a mate in three moves even if no one has posed the problem? Assuming the structure of a deck of cards, is there a sense in which a good card trick is somehow "out there," in a Platonic realm of universals, even if no cards existed?

Suppose there were no English language. Would it be meaningful to say that given such a language, there is a sense in which a certain anagram "exists" even if no one spoke English? It is something like asking if a certain number with a million digits is prime or composite before anyone has tested the number to find out. Well, not quite, because arithmetic certainly "exists" as a formal system. Anyway, most mathematicians are Platonists who believe that, no matter how bizarre or how far removed from reality a system can be, they "discover" its theorems rather than invent them. Even though English is a human construction, nowhere to be found in nature, is there a sense in which its wordplays are "real" before anyone finds them? I leave answering this to my readers.

THE END OF THE ROAD

As you can see, wordplay is much more complicated than it might first appear to be. Our visit to Alphabet Avenue has only begun, but for now it's over. On the other side of the stop sign, we reach the City Limits.

City Limits

OTHER CITIES

At the exit from the City of Wordplay, Alphabet Avenue keeps on rolling. Over the hills like giant pages, the road leads to other cities in other languages. In Spanish, La Avenida del Alfabeto winds through La Ciudad del Juego de las Palabras. In French, L'Avenue d'Alphabet twists and turns through La Ville de Jeux de Mots. Each has similarities and differences. Each has its own wordplay.

THE OMEGABET

At the entrance to the city, we saw a billboard displaying the Universal Letter, the symbol containing all the letters of the alphabet. Now, at the City Limits, we see a billboard with the Omegabet on it. The Omegabet is the normal alphabet with a twist: its letters are designed to reflect the same in a mirror. They symbolize the harmony of language that can be found in wordplay.

THE BOOK

The sun is rising with a final palindrome radiating in the center of it: SUN US. The sunshine falls across a book lying in the middle of the street. Cars drive past the book, but they never hit it. You run out and pick it up. Its title is *Alphabet Avenue.*

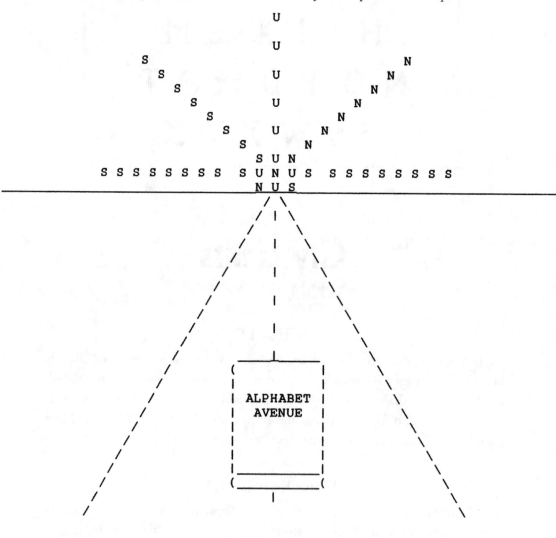

You begin reading it.

Index

• • • • • • • •